TABLE OF CONTENTS

TABLE OF CONTENTS ..	1
"My Life On The Ocean W	5
Copyright © 2012, Dougla	5
DEDICATION	5
INTRODUCTION...............	6
PRE NAVY YEARS	7
H.M.S. RALEIGH	10
LEAVE - 1 MY FIRST LEAVE HOME	13
BACK TO H.M.S. RALEIGH	15
H.M.S. DRYAD	18
LEAVE - 2...	20
WHAT IS A MATELOT ?...	20
PORTSMOUTH - 1..	23
H.M.S. ZULU..	25
THE MED - 1	28
NICE...	29
MALTA - 1	31
GREECE - 1	32
IZMIR - TURKEY	33
RETURN TO THE UK -1	34
ROSYTH - 1	35
JOKE - 1	35
DUNFERMLINE	35
JOURNEY TO THE FAR EAST	37
CROSSING THE EQUATOR	38
DURBAN - 1 SOUTH AFRICA	39
THE BIRA PATROL AND MOMBASSA	40
THE PERSIAN GULF	43
THE SULTAN SAID TO ALADDIN	45
KARACHI - PAKISTAN...	46
COLOMBO - CEYLON	48
THE FAR EAST - SINGAPORE	48

HONG KONG	52
YOKOHAMA - JAPAN	54
DURBAN - 2	56
NOTICE OF RETURN	60
JOKE - 2	62
LEAVE - 3	63
ROSYTH - 2	64
PORTSMOUTH - 2	65
CARDIFF	65
LIVERPOOL	66
THE MED - 2	67
NAPLES	67
MALTA - 2	70
FISHING IN THE MED	71
GLASGOW RECRUITING OFFICE	71
H.M.S. COLLINGWOOD - 1	77
FAREHAM - 1	80
JOKE - 3	82
PORTSMOUTH - 3	83
GOSPORT - 1	86
H.M.S. EXCELLENT	86
JOKE - 4	91
H.M.S. BELTON	91
LERWICK - SHETLANDS	94
OBAN - 1	96
DOUGLAS - ISLE OF MAN	97
DOOGAL - THE DOG	99
THE SHETLAND - FISHING BOAT	102
CRAPPERS THE RAT	103
CEDRIC THE BUDGIE	104
THE HORSES CLUB	104
ANTWERP - BELGIUM	105
WILLEMSHAVEN - THE NETHERLANDS	107
INTER-MESS COMPETITIONS	108
THE THAMES ESTUARY	109

RUNNING AGROUND - LOCH MADDAY	110
H.M.S. CHAWTON	113
RAF PITREAVIE - THE PIT	115
BILLY CONNOLLY	116
HELENSBURGH - SCOTLAND	117
MY FATHER DIED	118
H.M.S. GLAMORGAN	118
THE MED - 3	120
THE GIBRALTAR NATIONAL ANTHEM	120
THE MAG DRAIN ARMS	122
MALTA - 3	123
JOKE - 5	124
THE MALTESE HILTON	124
GREECE - 2 KAVALLA	125
GREECE - 3 THE FIGHT	126
ISTANBUL -TURKEY	127
RETURN TO THE UK - 2	128
H.M.S. COLLINGWOOD - 2	129
LEAVE - 4	131
H.M.S. NUBIAN	133
BERMUDA	133
FORT LAUDERDALE - AMERICA	135
GUATEMALA AND BELIZE - WEST INDIES	137
TRINIDAD - PORT OF SPAIN	140
RAT	141
SHEBA	142
LUNCH TIME - ON THE SHIP	143
ST. VINCENT - WEST INDIES	144
ROBINSON CRUSO ISLAND	145
JOKE - 6	146
ST. PETERSBURG / ORLANDO - AMERICA	147
CARACAS - VENEZUELA - SOUTH AMERICA	148
FORT LAUDERDALE - 2 AMERICA	149
BERMUDA - 2	150
RETURN TO THE UK - 3	151

ALDERSHOT - ENGLAND 152
THE ADMIRAL'S HOUSE - PORTSMOUTH 153
LEAVING THE NAVY 154
RAM IT I'M R.D.P. 156
HOME FOR GOOD - TO ABERDEEN 158
Notes 159
Thanks 159

My Life On The Ocean Waves – Douglas Freeman

"My Life On The Ocean Waves"

Comical Memoirs Of My Time In The Royal Navy

From 1966 - 1976

By Douglas Freeman

Copyright © 2012, Douglas Freeman

ALL RIGHTS RESERVED. This book contains material protected under International and Federal Copyright Laws and Treaties. Any unauthorized reprint or use of this material is prohibited. No part of this book may be reproduced or transmitted in any form or by any means, electronic or mechanical, including photocopying, recording, or by any information storage and retrieval system without express written permission from the author / publisher.

DEDICATION

I would like to dedicate this book to my wife Elaine, my daughter Penny, my Mother and Father and all the rest of my family, especially my brother Bill who was in the Royal Navy at the same time as myself, and also to all my friends in the Royal Navy with whom I share a lot of fond memories

My Life On The Ocean Waves – Douglas Freeman

INTRODUCTION

I used to tell stories about my time in the Royal Navy to my friends and relations, about the places I'd been to, and the things I'd seen and done. One day I decided to write my stories down and put them all together to see how they would come out. This was done mainly for my own benefit, but as the stories unfolded it looked like I had the makings of a good book, so I just continued writing.

I would like point out that all of my recollections in this book are from memory only, and not from a diary, so obviously I have not recalled everything. I have always regretted not having kept a diary. I also regret not having taken enough photographs, especially with all the beautiful and interesting pubs, "I mean places", that I went to all over the world.

I enjoyed all of my years in the navy. I would like to reminisce now and pass on some of my stories. Some of them serious, some of them amusing or even funny, but all of them true. It is my intention to make this book light hearted as well as informative, and in so doing, help to give you an insight what it was like to be in the royal navy between 1966 and 1976.

Those were good years for me. The navy had many ships at this time, and there were a lot of countries around the world where they were allowed to visit. So when I say I joined the navy to see the world, that's exactly what I did, with no regrets and a lot of fond memories.

My Life On The Ocean Waves – Douglas Freeman

Anyway, here are my recollections starting with a brief introduction of my life leading up to the day I joined the Royal Navy.

PRE NAVY YEARS

My name is Douglas Freeman. I am the youngest of a family of seven, with three brothers and three sisters. I was born on October 1949 in an old tenement building called the Hard-up Mansions, on Great Northern Road, Woodside, Aberdeen, Scotland. The reason they were called the hard-up mansions was because the company who were building them ran out of money before they were completed, and they only built about half the length of the tenement. Anyway, that's the story my father told me.

I first got the urge to travel when I was at Woodside Primary School. I was about eight years old, and I remember being in an office at the top of the school building, looking at the horizon out of the window and thinking to myself, I wonder what is over there? I imagined going up to that horizon, and when I got there, there would be another horizon to go to. When I was about ten years old, I satisfied my curiosity by going up to that horizon to see what was over there, but by then the wanderlust was burning within me, and I knew I was destined to travel the world and pass over many horizons.

I left Woodside Primary School at the age of twelve, and went to Powis Secondary School. My older brother Bill, who was just over three years older than me, had left Powis by then and joined the Royal Navy. I remember my mother getting letters from him from far off places all over the world, telling stories of exciting places. It was then that I decide I would like to join the Royal Navy and see the world just like my brother.

My brother in law Sandy Watt taught me a bit of the guitar when I was about twelve. I didn't have a guitar of my own, so he used to let me borrow his guitar to learn on. I didn't learn a lot initially because I just didn't know what kind of music to play. One day, Sandy gave me a song to learn called Putting On The Style by Lonni Donigan. It consisted of three chords, D G and A7. Within a few hours I was playing and singing that song like I'd known it for years. I picked things up on the guitar a lot better after that and I enjoyed it a lot better too, and as time went by I learned more of the songs that Sandy gave me.

I have a lot to thank Sandy for, because the guitar stood me in good stead during my naval career. I ended up singing and playing my guitar in pubs, clubs and at parties all over the world.

I left Powis School at the age of fifteen, and got a job as a van boy with the Co-op baker in Berryden Road, delivering bread and cakes and rowies to the customer's doors. I got to know most of the customer's by their co-op number rather than their name. I remember one day my van driver Dod Swift came up to me and said, 45814 died yesterday, I knew exactly who it was. I stayed at this job for about eighteen months, but during that time I was planning to join the royal navy, just like my brother. It took a while before I got around to telling my mother of my intentions, as I knew she wanted me to stay at home. Because I was the youngest of a family of seven, she didn't want her youngest child to go away and leave her. I remember seeing the hurt and sadness in her eyes when I told her I wanted to join the royal navy, but she reluctantly agreed and gave me her full backing. My father just left it up to me to decide what I wanted to do with my life, and went along with my decision to join the royal navy.

I went down to the Royal Navy Recruiting Office in Guild Street, Aberdeen, where I took a small entry examination to see if I was suitable for the navy. I wanted to go in to electronics as I was interested in that subject and it was also a hobby of mine, but they said that there were no vacancies for that subject, and they offered me a place as a seaman. I knew my brother Bill was a seaman and also a Radar Operator, so I decided to accept their offer with the intentions of changing branches to an Electronics Technician at a later date. They arranged for me to go down to H.M.S. Condor near Montrose for my medical examination. A week or so later I got a letter through saying I had passed my medical and had been accepted for the Royal Navy. In the letter they gave me a date to join H.M.S. Raleigh in Plymouth, I then realised that my life was about to change forever.

My Mother and Father came down to the Railway Station with me to see me off on the train. I went and got my navy rail warrant changed into a rail ticket, then my father took some photos of me on my own and I asked a passer-by to take a photo of the three of us together for a keep sake. I then got settled on to the train for my long journey to Plymouth. It was a very long journey. I had to change trains twice, and it's a wonder I didn't get lost. I was only sixteen and I had never been far outside of Aberdeen in my whole life, never mind travel all the way to the South West Coast of England on my own.

H.M.S. RALEIGH

I eventually arrived at H.M.S. Raleigh the next day, after a long journey lasting almost 24 hours. I was tired and shattered after only managing to grab a few hours' sleep on the way. After I got settled in, I was introduced to the other new recruits, everybody was wondering what they had let themselves in for. We were issued with our bedding and a few other things, then we were given an introduction and welcome to the Royal Navy speech. That evening I went to bed in the long cold mess with about twenty other people feeling lost and homesick, and wondering what the next few days, weeks and years would bring for me, and I fell asleep dreaming of what lay ahead.

We were woken up at 05:30 hrs. What an unearthly time of the morning to wake somebody up. I hate getting up early in the morning. After we had breakfast, we went to a Nissan hut to be told what was in store for us during the coming days and weeks. We were told we were to be here for six weeks of square bashing, which means teaching us discipline, marching and rifle drill etc. I got a bit of a shock with that news, as the recruiting officer in Aberdeen told me I should not be away from home for more than two weeks to start with. I thought great, that would break things up a bit for me, not having been away from home before. Well so much for the easy start I was expecting!

My Life On The Ocean Waves – Douglas Freeman

I signed on the dotted line and joined the Royal Navy on May 24th 1966. Junior Seaman First Class (J/S1). We then got issued with our uniforms and all the rest of the kit that you get when you first join the navy. e.g. A little piece of wood with your initials and name on it for stamping all your clothes with. A knife, boots, boot polish, No.8s, "that is your day to day working shirt and trousers you will be marching around in", and a whole lot of other stuff, including a kit bag to put it all into when you have to travel. We had to wear a blue long sleeve jumper under our No.8 shirt. I'm sure it must have been made out of coconut matting, you used to itch like hell all day, and we were never so glad to get anything off at the end of the day as that horrible jumper. Our blue No.2 uniform, which we had to wear in the evenings, was also made of a very rough material, I used to hate wearing it. I remember getting my first photograph taken with my naval uniform on, I was standing next to a maroon car, and when I sent the photo on to my mother, she wrote me a letter back saying, my, you are getting on well in the navy!

We had quite a tough time of it during that first six weeks, we went through assault courses where they threw smoke bombs and detonators at us on the way round, but it all added to the fun and made it feel like a real war zone. We did a lot of rifle drill and marching drill. If you did anything slightly wrong, the G.I. would send you round the parade ground at the double with your rifle at the shoulder arms position, or even held over your head, it was murder, so you tried not to do anything wrong. We also had to learn to strip our rifle down to all it's different parts, I thought to myself, if I wanted to do this sort of thing I'd have joined the bloody army.

We were not allowed to go ashore very often during this period, it was like being in jail at one of those hard labour camps. But I heard one day that my brother's ship had come in to Plymouth harbour, so I arranged to go and visit him on one of my rare days off. I made my way to the Royal Naval Dockyard, and I had to use my new I.D. card for the very first time to get in to the dockyard. I eventually arrived at my brother's ship H.M.S. Lincoln. I stood at the bottom of the gangway feeling a bit concerned, as we were told we had to salute the quarter-deck when we boarded a ship, and I was not too sure which part of the quarter-deck I had to salute. I must have been so green at that time. It still makes me laugh to this day thinking about it. Anyway I went up to the top of the gangway, saluted, and went over to the Quarter Master and asked for Able Seaman Freeman, and the QM put out a tannoy for him "able seaman Freeman report to the brow". I'm sure he looked a bit concerned when he arrived, because it turned out he was under punishment, and he was probably wandering what they wanted him for this time. He came up to the gangway, and he got a surprise to see me there, he asked me down to the RP's (radar plotter's) mess where within one minute he said, "would you like a can of beer." I said yes, that would be fine, so he pulled out his boot locker from under his feet, and there was a crate of beer in it, no boots, just beer. He introduced his baby brother to all the other sailors in the mess. One of Bill's pals got a great surprise when he looked at the badge on my arm, it was a Boom Defence badge. It consisted of a shackle with a spike through it, and he was one of the last Boom Defence sailors in the whole navy, maybe even the whole world! He went out with a loud shout, oh, look! "A Baby Boomer!" And he's "all mine!" The whole mess collapsed in laughter, and Bill said, you can't have him, so sit down, shut up and have a beer, so we all sat around telling jokes and stories till Tot time. The rum was issued at 11:30, and the rum boson, "who was Bill," had to go and collect the rum rations from the Master at Arms in the mess Fanny, "which is a small stainless steel bucket," for the whole mess. The rum boson always gets sippers from everyone in the mess, and so did I, because I was a visitor to the mess. So you can imagine, by this time I was merrily pissed out of my tiny little skull, and being only sixteen, I couldn't handle it like the rest of the sailors, but as years went by I gladly corrected that anomaly. After a great day out, I eventually made it back to H.M.S. Raleigh, I can't remember how but I did, and of course, I awoke the next day with a great big hangover, the first of many that was to come in the future.

LEAVE - 1 MY FIRST LEAVE HOME

After I passed my first six weeks training, we were told that we could go home on leave for two weeks, we were not allowed to wear civvies, so I had to wear my uniform, but for some reason I was proud to wear my uniform. I remember passing through Stonehaven, which is fifteen miles from Aberdeen, and that last few miles to Aberdeen were always special to me. I used to make my way up to the very first carriage and stand all the way with my head stuck out of the window, letting the wind blow through my hair and in my face, and taking deep breaths of the familiar Aberdeen sea air, feeling glad to be home again. This turned out to be part of my routine whenever I returned home on leave in the future.

I knew I was home in Aberdeen when I got in to a taxi at the station, and the driver said to me in an Aberdonian accent, "fit like min, far kan I tak yi". My mother was delighted to see me, and she gave me a great big hug as soon as I came round the door. She was so proud of me and said how smart I looked in my uniform. I spent the rest of the day telling her how I was getting on and what my training was like.

The next day I went for a casual walk down Woodside with my uniform on. I found myself marching down the street with my head held high and my arms swinging straight out in front of me, parallel to the ground, fingers clenched first and second knuckle, just like I was taught to do during my six weeks square bashing. I must have been brain washed more than I thought, because I found it hard to walk any other way. I suppose it looks very smart on a parade ground, but I must have looked a right prat marching along the pavement on my own. I even found myself doing it when I was in my civvies, which must have looked even more ridiculous. I had to make a conscious decision to try and walk normally. I just hope not too many people noticed me!

I enjoyed my first leave home, but I was soon on my way again, back to H.M.S. Raleigh to complete the rest of my fifteen weeks training. I found myself being a little home sick as I left Aberdeen on the train after my leave at home. My mother and father waving goodbye to me as the train slowly made its way along the platform. My mother always kissed me goodbye with a tear in her eye before I got on the train. She once told me a story about when she was a young girl during the war. Her older brother Tommy was a sailor in the Royal Navy, and she went down to the station to see him off on the train, he asked her for a kiss, but she was too shy to give him one. That was the last time she saw him alive, as his ship was blown up at sea and he was killed, she always cried whenever she told me that story, because of that she never failed to kiss me before I went away on the train.

BACK TO H.M.S. RALEIGH

I learned a lot about seamanship at H.M.S. Raleigh, which included how to splice rope and wire rope, how to tie all the different kinds of knots, all about boats, ships and anchors, all the points of the compass etc. We even had to learn the Morse code, but I knew it already along with a lot of other things, which I learned in the Sea Cadets. We also had to learn a lot of bullshit, we had mess rounds every evening at 19:30 hrs, and it had to be immaculate. At the weekends we had our divisional officer's rounds where we had to lay out our kit on our bunk with everything clean, ironed and folded in a certain way, which was called a "kit muster". I remember putting spit and polish on to my boots and shoes till you could see your face in them. I used to be able to do spit and polish better than most of the other lads, so I ended up having to do theirs as well, for a small fee of course. We were in competition with all the other messes to see who could win the weekly cake.

Each mess was named after an Admiral, we were called Anson, and there were also Benbow, Collingwood and Drake. We won the cake most weeks but I'm sure they had to let the other lot win some time just to keep up their moral.

1966 had a brilliant summer. I remember one weekend, after having won the cake, we went outside the mess to lie in the sun. I'll always remember the song on the transistor radio next to me as I lay on the grass with my eyes closed, it was called "Lazing on a sunny afternoon", and that's exactly what I was doing.

I did manage to go down to the beach front at Plymouth Hoe a few times, the weather was great, and the Hoe is a beautiful well-kept place. I just wandered around freely. It was just good to get away from the demanding routine of the navy and relax for a while.

During my time at Raleigh I was taught to shoot a wide range of firearms. Because of the high scores I always got with the .303 and SLR rifles during my training, they chose me to shoot for the navy against the army and the RAF. A competition was held at the shooting range at Raleigh, and we had to shoot at those German type targets at three different distances, lying down and standing up. My shoulder was quite sore and covered with bruises at the end of it all, but I did win a Bronze Medal, and it was set in a small silver plate that looks like an ash tray. It was about nine months before I eventually received my medal, and when I did, they had forgotten to inscribe my name on the back of it for me, saying where and when I had won it.

My Life On The Ocean Waves – Douglas Freeman

The Petty Officer who was in charge of us and who took us through our whole fifteen weeks training was P.O. Pontin. We decided to present him with a pewter drinking mug at the end of our training, because he was a good guy and he did a good job teaching us. We were his first class, and it took him by surprise because he had to wipe away the tears from his eyes when we gave it to him. He did us proud and we did him proud, as we won the top award for the best class of that entry period.

Now that we were all qualified seamen, we had options of another three branches that we could follow.

1. Radar Plotter (RP).
2. Torpedo and Anti-Submarine (TAS).
3. Gunnery (G).

I had already made up my mind a long time ago what I wanted to go in to, and that was the Radar branch the same as my brother. It would also stand me in good stead if I was to be accepted for the Electronics branch. To start with they tried to persuade me to go in to one of the other two branches, but I would have none of it, I stuck to my guns till I got what I wanted. I told them I wouldn't be happy in any other branch and if I didn't get what I wanted I would apply to leave the navy. I'm glad to say they saw it my way and a few days later they told me I was to go to H.M.S. Dryad to train to be a Radar Plotter, I was absolutely delighted.

H.M.S. DRYAD

I arrived at H.M.S. Dryad laden down with all my kit, it was a bit much to carry my full kit bag, a large suitcase and a small suitcase, all the way from Plymouth to Portsmouth. Dryad is situated about eight miles outside Portsmouth near a small village called Wickham. It has a couple of pubs, I can only remember the one called the Red Lion, but for some strange reason I hardly ever went in to them. I think maybe it was because they were too close to base, or maybe the fact I was under age as well had something to do with it. When you went ashore you tried to get as far away from your base as possible, so I usually caught the bus in to Portsmouth whenever I went ashore, at least we wouldn't be recognised there.

I enjoyed my radar training. We had to learn how to operate all the different kinds of radar's that the navy had on their ships. Long range air, medium range air and sea, and navigation radar's. One of the main duties of a radar operator was to be in the ship's Operations Room. We had to learn to plot the course and speed of ships and aircraft on the Radar Plotting Tables. We stood behind the plotting tables, and we were taught to write upside down and from right to left, so that the Captain or the officer of the watch could see everything the right way up from their side of the table. All this was done in simulated control rooms so that it appeared like the real thing. We used to play war games all the time to teach us how to react properly in all situations.

Apart from our Radar training, we had our usual divisions on the parade ground every morning, but it was not like the divisions at H.M.S. Raleigh, this was just to muster in the morning to check everyone was present before we marched away to our various classes. We also had Wrens there, they had better accommodation than us, and they lived in a multi-story building that we called Tampax Tower. We lived in old Nissan huts until they eventually got around to building some new accommodation blocks for us.

One day, a guy that I knew in the next mess to me was given a kit muster because he was always scruffily dressed. His personal kit was in a terrible state, "crabby" as we would call it, so he persuaded me to lend him some of my clothes for his kit muster. I loaned him pyjamas and socks etc, he also borrowed £5 off me to buy some toothpaste and things he required. He said he would give it back to me next pay-day. When I got back to my mess in the evening he was gone, he had been drafted, and he must have known all this before I loaned him the money. He didn't even leave a message to let me know where he went, and he didn't leave my things behind either. I was furious, as he went away with all my gear and he owed me a fiver as well, that was a lot of money to me in those days. I never did see him again during all my time in the navy, lucky him! Thinking about it again, maybe he got kicked out of the navy for uncleanliness.

Occasionally we went to Fort Southwick to practice on the 965 long range and 993 medium range radar's. Fort Southwick was a big brick built fort at the top of Portsmouth hill where we trained on real radar's that overlooked the whole of Portsmouth and the surrounding area. We saw all along the coast line and the

Isle of Wight, and we plotted the ships coming in and out of Portsmouth Harbour. The locals used to complain to the navy when we were using our long range air radar, because we blasted out their T.V. reception, I couldn't really blame them for complaining, so we were only allowed to use it for short periods and at certain times of the day.

LEAVE - 2

I was only back at Dryad for about three weeks when I was due another three weeks leave. I was getting accustomed to the navy routine by this time and feeling more like a real sailor, so I was a lot happier within myself when I went home this time. I remember somebody in Aberdeen calling me a matelot, I hadn't a clue what a matelot was, I hadn't heard that name before. I felt so ignorant when I found out it was another name for a sailor, so I'd like to introduce you to this version of "what is a matelot" that I acquired somewhere during my travels.

WHAT IS A MATELOT ?

Between the security of infancy and the insecurity of adultery, we find a fascinating group of humanity (?) called sailors. They come in assorted sizes, shapes, weights and states of sobriety. They can be found anywhere, on ships at sea, in shore bases, in bars, always in debt, and usually where there is no work. Girls sometimes love them, wives and parents tolerate them, and the government almost supports them.

A sailor is laziness with a pack of cards, bravery with a tattooed arm, and the protector of the seas with the latest copy of

Playboy. He has the energy of a tortoise, the slyness of a fox, the stories of a sea captain, the aspirations of a Casanova, the brains of an idiot and the sincerity of a habitual liar. When he really does work, he usually wants something connected with a B13 and a Request Form (S1318, a magic piece of paper that holds the navy together).

Some of his interests are women, dames, girls, females, and of course, members of the opposite sex. He dislikes answering letters, wearing his uniform properly, the "Jimmy", pusser's scran, and Call The Hands. (Nobody can write you so seldom yet think of you so much).

No one else can get into one jumper pocket a pencil, a sharp piece of string, a dogged cigarette, a crushed crushproof packet of cigarettes, a crumpled picture of his girlfriend or wife, a comb, and old dog-eared station card, half an identity card and what is left of his pay. He spends some of his pay on girls, some on beer, some on cigarettes, some on playing cards. The rest is squandered foolishly.

Yet the sailor is a magic creature. You can lock him out of your house, but not your heart. You can scratch him from your mailing list, but not from your mind. A sailor is your one and only bleary-eyed, good-for-nothing bundle of worries; all your shattered dreams become insignificant when your sailor docks, looks at you with weary bloodshot eyes, smiles happily and says, "hello darling, I'm home".

-- : --

My Life On The Ocean Waves – Douglas Freeman

When I got back to H.M.S. Dryad from my leave, I continued my studies and passed with flying colours. I was now an RP "Radar Plotter", and I was given my new badges to sew on to all my clothes, my uniforms, white fronts and work shirtsleeves. The RP's badge looked a bit like a spider's web.

Now that we had completed all our studies they had to find other things for us to do till they found us a ship to go to. During this period I did quite a few different things.

I became part of "Control" for a while, which made you feel important. Part of our training included working in real mock-ups of ship's operation control rooms, I was now one of the mysterious people hidden away in the simulator control rooms which controlled the operations for all the other classes that were going through their courses. Officers learning how to control a ship's operations control room had to go through these simulations. We even had captains from other NATO countries doing these courses, and here I was controlling them. I had a great time.

Whilst I was waiting on my draft, I did a spell of cutting down trees in the nearby forests like a lumberjack. I used to get up in the morning, go and collect my axe and saw along with the other lads that were going with me, get a packed lunch and head away in to the forest for the whole day 'till it was time to come home in the evening. It was great fun, it was just like being on holiday.

We even went down to H.M.S. St. Vincent over at Gosport for a few weeks. That was the establishment my brother joined up at when he was only fifteen. I remember by brother telling me a few stories about when he was at St. Vincent. One of the stories was when he had to climb up to the top of the mast on one of those ceremonial occasions and play the Bugle from the top. Although nobody joins up at St. Vincent any more, the same mast was still standing there at the bottom of the parade ground, and it was very high. I imagined what it must have been like for him climbing to the top of the mast and looking over Gosport, and seeing the hundreds of people down below on the parade ground looking up at him.

One day I sailed over to Cowes on the Isle of Wight in a cutter from the back of St. Vincent. The next day I was a steward at an officer's function, we were dressed up like the sailors of old, with white bellbottom trousers and striped shirts. We had quite a few drinks on the sly when no one was looking, so we had a good evening as well.

PORTSMOUTH - 1

I remember once going down to Portsmouth for a run ashore with a few of my mates; we went into a pub called the Yorkshire Grey. We had a few pints of bitter; we were only about seventeen at the time so we were trying to keep a low profile. An older gentleman came in to the pub, ordered a double gin and tonic and sat down next to us. We started speaking to him, and he was asking us how we enjoyed the navy. I told him how old we all were and that we had not long joined up, and we thought it was great. I went up and bought a round of drinks and one for the gentleman as well, he seemed to be enjoying himself, and he even bought us all a round of drinks as well. I asked him what he did for a living, and he said he was in the army, and he hadn't long left to do, and he was down here in Portsmouth doing a promotional video for the army. I asked him if he liked the army, and he said, oh, yes. Then I asked him what rank he was in the army, and he said, "I'm only a Brigadier". I almost collapsed, that is the equivalent rank of a Royal Navy Admiral, and here we were, the lowest of the lowest in the navy, having under age drinks with an army Brigadier. He knew how we'd react, that is why he didn't tell us earlier, he told us not to worry and bought us all another round of drinks. Just then the whole pub lit up with illuminations from the outside; we wondered what it was. He said, that must be the TV crew's lights, they are expecting me to come out of the pub and give my speech, so I'd better get going. With that, he polished off his gin and tonic, said goodbye to us and left. We watched out the window for a while till they all went away, then we carried on drinking.

When I was back at Dryad I went to the New Forest for a weekend with a pal of mine, he lived there, so we stayed at his parent's house for the duration. We went up there on the Friday, and in the evening we went to the Mecca Ballroom at Southampton. It was a great dance hall, it had palm trees all around with a lot of greenery everywhere, and every table had a parasol. The dance halls in Aberdeen just didn't compare to this one.

My Life On The Ocean Waves – Douglas Freeman

On the Saturday we went pony trekking in the New Forest, I think that was the first and last time I ever went pony trekking, it was good fun while it lasted, even though I was sore the next day. The only kind of horse I'd been on before was a Clydesdale horse, the one that used to pull the coal delivery carts in my home town.

I remember some of the songs that help me to recall my time at Dryad. They are Matthew and Son, Winchester Cathedral, and England Swings. 1966 and 67 were good years for music, in fact the whole 60s are still remembered as some of the greatest years for music ever, it was great fun living through those years.

Eventually my draft to a ship came through. It was to H.M.S. Zulu, which was a tribal class frigate based at Rosyth, Scotland. That was good for me, because that meant I could get home for weekends to Aberdeen quite easily from there. So I said goodbye to Dryad and Portsmouth and made my way up to Rosyth to join my first ship.

H.M.S. ZULU

I arrived on-board my first ship H.M.S. Zulu and quickly got settled in. It was in Rosyth Dockyard for a refit so I got the opportunity to get to know her quite well. She was moved in to the inner basin, which was controlled by a lock so the ship wasn't affected by the rise and fall of the tide.

We were accommodated on the original ship H.M.S. Cochrane that was alongside the dockyard wall, and was converted for accommodation purposes. A shore establishment was built years later just outside the dockyard gate and was called H.M.S. Cochrane after this ship. There was another ship moored alongside, I think it was called the Duncan's B. Head, I can't remember much about it, but it was scrapped soon afterwards anyway.

The three departments of the seaman's branch had a different part of the ship to look after. The "Gunners" had the Forecastle and the Quarterdeck. The "TAS" had the Mid-ships, and me being an "RP" had the Fore Top, which was situated just aft of the Bridge. That was to be my part of ship to keep clean for the next two and a half years on the Zulu. Over the years we put many layers of paint on to the bulkheads and deck, and must have scrubbed them down hundreds of times.

My usual places for a run ashore were Inverkeithing and Dunfermline, so I got to know them quite well over the years. When a ship is designated to a particular port it always returns to that port after any of its trips, and it always uses that port for its refits, so like I said earlier, I got home for weekends when I was not on duty.

During my two and a half years on the Zulu, I went round the British Isles, the Mediterranean about three or four times for about two or three months at a time. I also went on a trip to the Far East for about nine months, so it is hard for me to remember the exact dates I was at a particular place, but as long as I can recall the occasions that I am referring to, that is the main thing.

My Life On The Ocean Waves – Douglas Freeman

After the refit was finished, the ship set sail from Rosyth Dockyard, under the two Forth Bridges, and headed down to Portland on the south coast of England. With most of the ship's crew being new, all the ship's company had to go through rigorous training at Portland. The ship it's self had to go through all kinds of operational trials including ship speed trials, where the ship had to go at full speed over a measured mile, the speed of the ship was then worked out from the time it took to travel between the two points.

All the time we were at Portland, the ship was at a full state of readiness, as if we were at war. During the week, aircraft and submarines attacked us, and we had to go to our Action Stations when we were being attacked. All the ship's weapons were also tested. We fired our 4.5 inch guns at targets pulled by a slow moving aircraft and fired our Sea Cat missiles at remote controlled aircraft. We fired dummy Anti-Submarine mortar Mk10 depth charges and followed submarines around under the water with our sonar. One evening in the cover of darkness we were attacked by Royal Marine Commando's while the ship was alongside the harbour wall, so we had to defend ourselves against attack from them. I also did riot squad training alongside the jetty. We were haggled by the Royal Marines dressed up in civvies whilst we marched along with SLR rifles, keeping our eyes open for snipers on the rooftops and windows.

At the end of the week we had what was called the Friday War. We went out to sea and we were attacked by everything they could throw at us in a full scale war, aircraft, fast patrol boats, submarines the lot, at the end of the exercises we were assessed and told how well we had done.

We were glad to get that training period over and done with. We passed everything with flying colours, but the best news was that we were now heading for the Mediterranean for three months in the sun.

THE MED - 1

We left Portland harbour, sailed down the English Channel and across the Bay of Biscay, arriving at Gibraltar a few days later. Our ship always stayed in port for at least a week wherever we went, often longer, so there was no shortage of runs ashore for the lads. Gibraltar was quite a good place to go ashore and have a few drinks. It was also a good place for Duty Free shopping on the way back home.

On some of our days off we used to go sunbathing and swimming on the other side of the Rock. Most of the time we went through a long tunnel that took us from the dockyard side through to the beach side. It was always cool inside the tunnel even though the sun was scorching outside. I think I only went up the Rock once during my time in the navy. From the top of the Rock you could see the airport and Southern Spain. North Africa could also be seen quite easily from up there. I remember being pestered by the apes half way up, they were quite a tourist attraction.

Walking down the high street we always passed the Commissioner's residence, and there was always an armed guardsman standing at attention outside the house. I don't know what the guard must have thought of all those drunken sailors taking the Mickey out of him every time they passed, but he never ever blinked an eye lid or smiled, it was although we didn't exist.

A lot of the time we used to catch a taxi back to the ship from a rank in the town centre, especially after all the pubs were closed. The unusual thing about these taxi's in Gib was that they were all Mercedes cars. It always puzzled me how they could afford expensive cars like that, especially since the hire to our ship was about one mile, and only came to a few pounds.

NICE

We left Gibraltar and sailed for Nice in the South of France. I don't even know why we went there, but I think the ship had some official engagements to go to. I remember going ashore and going round to the other side of the harbour to take some photos of the ship, as she was illuminated from stem to stern and it really looked impressive in the dark, with the reflections of the ship's lights on the calm harbour waters.

We went for a wander round the town in the evening, but we found the French not very friendly. We couldn't speak French and the French couldn't or wouldn't speak English, so all we could ask for was a coffee or a beer, but then again, that was all we wanted anyway. Apart from being quite a good-looking beachfront with all those Millionaires Yachts, I can't say there was anything special there for me. A few of the lads did go along the coast to Monte Carlo, maybe I should have gone there instead.

My Life On The Ocean Waves – Douglas Freeman

One evening I was ashore with my mates, and a fight started outside this cafe bar, as we were passing, about six of the local thugs saw me and came running towards me, I realised I was greatly outnumbered so I ran in the opposite direction. I remember taking off my hat and throwing it at the guy in the front, and hitting him right on the forehead, just like Odd Job in the James Bond movie, and it floored him, but the rest still came after me. I ran into this ten story derelict building and ran all the way up to the top trying all the doors to try and escape, but they were all locked. When I came to the top landing there were two empty wooden boxes there, so I piled them up and climbed out through the skylight on to the roof. I thought I would be safe up there, but they still came after me, chasing me along the "A" shaped roof. I came to the end of the roof and there was nowhere else to go. I knew they would throw me off the roof if they caught up with me, so I decided to jump across the alleyway to the next building. I was about one hundred feet up, and I had to jump about ten feet across the alleyway, and it was very dark. I remembered the story of Rob Roy McGregor, hundreds of years ago, he was being chased by the English in a place called Peter Culter, just outside Aberdeen, he supposedly jumped across a wide stream to get away from his pursuers and managed to get away. I thought to myself, If he could do it so could I, and it was my memory of that story that saved my life that night in Nice. "Thanks Rob". So I took a long run and jumped right across the alleyway to the other roof, where I clambered through another skylight, and ran down the stairs to freedom and safety. They chasing mob were obviously too scared to jump across that distance in the dark, so I got away, and lived to tell the tale, and all the rest of the tales in this book!

My Life On The Ocean Waves – Douglas Freeman

MALTA - 1

Our next port of call was Malta, it was my first time there, but I went back to Malta many times in the years to come. We always berthed near the naval base H.M.S. St Elmo, just inside the harbour on the left by Kalkara Creek.

To get from one side of the harbour to the other we had to go by Dghajsa or Dyso as we used to call it. A Dghajsa was a long narrow multi-coloured boat with a long single oar at the stern where the boatman stood. He grabbed the oar with two hands and pulled it up and down in a funny kind of circular motion that managed to propel the boat forward. In later years the owners of the Dghajsa's fitted small outboard motors to the stern and they just sat down and steered with the oar as the boat slowly putted its way across the harbour to Valletta. When we got to the other side of the harbour, we had to make our way up to the top of the cliff either by the steps that wound their way up the cliff face, or by an old lift that never seemed safe. There we made our way to the many pubs that Valletta had to offer and to the notorious Gut, the real name being Straight Street, where we normally had a good laugh 'till the early hours of the morning.

Every ship in the navy had a Chinese laundry on board, and the man in charge of the laundry was always called No1.

One night a fight broke out in a club we were in with some local thugs, the police were called, and when they arrived they just started hitting only the sailors over the head with their batons. No1 was with us when the police came in brandishing their batons, and when he saw what they were doing, he came to our rescue and flattened the four policemen with his Kung Fu. We didn't realise we had our own local Bruce Lee on board our ship. He was a really great guy and he saved us from being arrested and beat up by that biased police force.

We had this Leading RP on board, and his nickname was Cat Weasel, due to the long scruffy beard he had. He classed himself as a wine connoisseur, and would only drink the best of wines. Myself and a few of my friends were half way down the Gut knocking back some cheap bottles of wine called Marsovin, Cat Weasel happened to be passing by and saw us from the open door, he came in to the pub to joined us at our table. We hid the labels of the bottles from his view and persuaded him to sample some of our expensive wine. He quite enjoyed it, so we gave him quite a lot more. Eventually we all laughed and turned round our bottles of wine and showed him the Marsovin label, he was so upset he got up and stormed out of the pub in a huff, he obviously didn't see the funny side of our joke. We never let him forget that he praised the wine he said he would never drink.

GREECE - 1

After we left Malta we headed for the Aegean Sea to do some exercises with Nato and the American 6th Fleet. We had quite a good time simulating a real war and testing out all the training we had done. I was in the Ops Room dressed for action stations with my white anti-flash hood and gloves on and my gas mask slung over my shoulder. I was standing behind the Plotting Table tracking all the ships in the area, marking the friendly ships and the enemy ships on to the Plot. There were other people in the Ops Room tracking all the aircraft in the area. Through in the next compartment were the TAS people tracking and searching for submarines, so we were well prepared for any situation.

I remember the enemy was supposed to have fast patrol boats hidden around the small islands of the Aegean ready to attack us as we passed by, so we sent out our Wasp helicopter to scout round the far side of the islands. The helicopter found them, and dropped smoke bombs nearby to let them know they had been blown up. Although we did many exercises around the Med, I am glad to say I was never involved in any real conflicts.

When the exercises were complete we went to a place near Athens. Although I didn't go round Athens Itself, I did manage to go on a day trip to the Acropolis. I really enjoyed my sightseeing round the Parthenon and all those ancient Greek ruins, and trying to imagine what it was like to be alive in those days. We saw all of the original temples and statues named after all those famous Greek Gods, it was very interesting for me.

IZMIR - TURKEY

We then went to Izmir in Turkey. We didn't do much there except look round the stalls in the markets. I bought a pair of those women's slippers that curls up at the front, they were decorated in different coloured glass gems and were quite nice to look at, but more of an ornament than real slippers for wearing. I don't really know why I bought them, I just did. A few years ago I found them up my loft in a box, I thought if I have not done anything with them by now I never would, so threw them out.

I did notice that all the young women were quite beautiful, even though you could not see them properly with their veils over their faces. But that was all you could do was just look, as they never spoke to people who were not of their own kind.

RETURN TO THE UK -1

By this time we had been in the Med for almost three Months and it was time to head home to the UK. We sailed West along the Mediterranean till we got to Gibraltar. We stopped there for a few days to get some "rabbits", that's the navy name for presents, then sailed back across the Bay of Biscay for Portsmouth. As the ship entered the Western approaches of the English Channel most of the ship's crew were getting agitated, and excited about coming home again to the UK. This is where the term "you have got the channels" comes from.

We arrived in Portsmouth where there were lots families and friends to meet the ship coming in. We stayed in Portsmouth a few days, then left for Rosyth our home port. When we arrived at Rosyth, most of our families and girlfriends were waiting on the jetty to welcome us home. We were all sunburned and it was obvious we had just come back from the sunny Med. It was good to be home again, and a few days later I was off home on leave again to Aberdeen to see my family and tell them of my first trip abroad.

ROSYTH - 1

My ship must have been in Rosyth Dockyard for about six weeks, because each leave period was at least two weeks, and the ships company leave is split up into Port and Starboard watches, and when one watch is on leave the other stays behind working. You would always hear somebody say to the leave party that was just returning, "Had a good leave Jack? Well forget the b*****d, you're back"!

While the ships company was on leave there were always dozens of dockyard workers on board doing modifications to various pieces of equipment, there were hoses and pipes running everywhere, and the sound of windy hammers drumming in your ears, the ship was usually in a right mess and upheaval. The dockyard workers had a bit of a reputation for being a bit slow, so here is a joke I remember from that period.

JOKE - 1

I was walking through the dockyard one day, and I came across this dockyard worker strolling slowly along the jetty, as I was passing him he turned around and crushed this small snail with his boot. I said, why did you do that to the poor little snail, and he said, it was beginning to annoy me, because it's been following me around all day.

DUNFERMLINE

We used to catch a bus outside the dockyard gate to Dunfermline for a run ashore; it was usually just a pub-crawl. One of our first stops off the bus was to a pub called St. Margaret's, or Maggie's as we used to call it, before we went anywhere else.

We had a permanent compliment of Royal Marines on the Zulu, and we bumped in to a bunch of them in Maggie's celebrating one of their lad's birthdays. He was quite drunk when we saw him, but the rest of the idiots who were supposed to be looking after him, filled a long thin pint glass with every spirit they could think of out of the optics. He then stood on a table and drank the lot down in one. Five minutes later he stood up on the table again and proceeded to eat the pint glass, his mouth was all cut and covered with blood, he ate half of it before we could get the glass off him, he thought he was being a big Marine. His mates carried him back to the ship absolutely blootered, but luckily no harm came to him from the broken glass in his stomach.

I used to go to a place on Mondays called the Kinema Ballroom, as they had a folk club in the lounge bar. I saw Billy Connolly there when he was in the Humble Bums. I saw Mat McGinn perform there, "before he got drunk". I met Hamish Imlach there for the first time. Gallagher and Lyle had to book the larger hall for their performance, they were good, but it was not the same homely atmosphere as the lounge bar.

I sometimes did a turn up on stage before the main acts came on, and occasionally I made up the numbers when a member of a group never turned up. I had a great time whilst I was there, meeting all the great folk singers of the day.

At the weekends we used to go dancing at the Kinema. I remember one night I was dancing in the middle of the dance floor, and a bouncer came up to me and said, the manager wants to see you in his office right away! I went to the office with the bouncer feeling worried and wondering what I had done. The manager told me to sit down, and then I asked him what this was all about. He said you are a lucky man tonight, you have just been picked at random, and you have won a Gallon bottle of Bells Whisky, but you will have to collect it on the way out. What a great surprise, I could hardly believe it; I took that bottle home with me on my next leave to Aberdeen.

After the ship was ready for sea, and all the crew back from leave, the ship sailed for more exercises again, but this time we were sailed up to the far North of Scotland. Russian ships, submarines and aircraft always shadowed us during the whole of our exercises, and it still happens to this day. We came to expect them after a while. When the exercises were finished we continued heading up North until we were beyond the Arctic Circle; we all got presented with a Blue Nose Certificate having crossed the Arctic Circle.

JOURNEY TO THE FAR EAST

Our nine-Month trip to the Far East was due soon, so the ship went back to Rosyth for a few days for the families to come and see us away. We then went to Portsmouth for a few days for the families of the people who live farther South to come and see their loved ones off.

My Life On The Ocean Waves – Douglas Freeman

We sailed out of Portsmouth harbour waving to the families on the jetty as we went, knowing that we wouldn't see them again for almost a year. The ship sailed round the Isle of Wight and headed West down along the English Channel.

Our first Port of call was Lisbon in Portugal. We went ashore and ventured into a Cafe type bar. A few nights before I was in a Chinese restaurant in Portsmouth with a few of my friends drinking Mateus Rosé wine. It was quite expensive there, and here we were a few days later in Lisbon where they make Mateus Rosé, and they were selling it very cheap. I ordered a round of Mateus Rosé, and the waiter arrived with six glasses and a bottle of Mateus Rosé. I said, No, No, No, I'd like six glasses and six bottles of Mateus Rosé. The waiter could hardly believe his ears, anyway, when we finished them, somebody else got the same round again, and that kept on going till we left the cafe, needless to say, I can't remember getting back to the ship that day.

CROSSING THE EQUATOR

We spent a few days in Lisbon and then went to Gibraltar for another few days. After we re-stored the ship with some fresh supplies we were finally on our way again heading for South Africa. We were at sea a few days when we crossed the equator. The Royal Navy has a tradition of always having a party when a ship crosses the equator going south, the party is called a "Sods Opera", and everybody dresses up in some stupid fancy dress just for a laugh. We had a Bar-B-Q on the quarterdeck with cans of beer all round, and music as well. There were small shows put on by each mess, each with their own theme. I wrote a comedy song about one member of our mess, and sang that along with a few other songs for my part of the act. There were even some sailors dressed up in women's underwear; we can only guess where they got them from. The stokers dressed up as bears and sat in a great big tub of water throwing mud of some kind at each other. All the officers were there as well; even the captain dressed up a little bit for the occasion. But I must say it was a good laugh and a great party, I remember the ship sailing South as the sun was setting over the horizon with all the colours rippling on the mirror flat sea, and saying to myself, I'll always remember this day. Well I suppose I did!

DURBAN - 1 SOUTH AFRICA

All the ship's company was lined up on both sides of the ship as we entered Durban harbour. I was on the Fore Top on the Starboard side, and I saw this very old lady on the entrance of the harbour all dressed in white, and singing through a megaphone all the old time songs that were popular during the war. I found out later that she had been doing that since the war to every royal navy ship that ever came to Durban, and she never missed one for as long as she lived, they called her "The Lady in White".

We were getting ready to go ashore and the Captain mustered us all on the Quarter-deck. He said whilst we were in South Africa, we had to abide by their rules. Which meant we weren't allowed to socialise with black people. Which also meant we were not allowed to go ashore with our mate Sam who was black. We were furious, but there was nothing we could about it.

When Sam went ashore he was told to keep away from us and drink in the black only bars, what a system!

We managed to have a few drinks in some bars whilst we were ashore, and then we went back to the ship. Being permanently in a watch keeping system, we don't always get ashore when we would like to. We were only there for a few days and we had to go again, and sure enough, the Lady in White was there again singing to us as we left the harbour.

THE BIRA PATROL AND MOMBASSA

We sailed up the East Coast of Africa to Kenya, to a place called Mombassa. Our main purpose in that area was to patrol the sea just off Mombassa to stop any ships bringing in supplies destined for Rhodesia, as Britain was enforcing sanctions against Rhodesia at the time. We patrolled up and down the coast for about six weeks, and it was called the Bira Patrol.

Before we relieved the ship already on patrol, we went into Mombassa for a few days and had a few runs ashore. We all got drunk the first night ashore and I lost my mates at the end of the night. I decided to walk back to the ship on my own. I was feeling a bit tired after walking quite a long way, so I sat down on a bench at the side of the road right under the two great big tusks on the main drag. I must have fallen asleep on the bench, because I woke a few hours later wondering where I was. When I realised what had happened, I was absolutely amazed that I hadn't been mugged or rolled, I looked for my ID Card, my wallet, and my watch, and I was amazed they were all still there, especially because of the rough area I was in. Anyway, I eventually made my way back to the ship safely.

When we got back out to sea we took the place of the ship that was on patrol and let it go on its way. You can imagine how boring it could be just sailing up and down for six weeks not going anywhere in particular, so we had inter-mess competitions, we even had inter-ship competitions, and the prize was the "Bira Bucket." The bucket was just an old battered buckled and bent bucket, but everybody was so proud to win it. If you won it, the name of your ship was painted on to the bucket. I heard in later years that the Bira Bucket is now in one of the museums inside Portsmouth Dockyard.

We had inter-mess tug of war competitions. The rope went up the Port side of the ship, through a running block, across to the starboard side, through another running block and down the Starboard side. We never saw the other team when we were pulling, we just heard the loud grunts and groans, the RP's mess won the tug of war competition, even against the Royal Marines team!

We also had fishing competitions. I remember one day we were fishing for sharks off the stern. One guy went and got a big piece of meat and a big meat hook from the chef, he tied it to a heaving line and paid it out over the stern round a capstan. About half an hour later he caught a great big fish, it looked a bit like a salmon but it was about ten feet long. It was leaping about as we reeled it in, it was about twenty feet from the stern of the ship when a massive shark about thirty feet long appeared from below and ate it with one huge bite, and left us with only a head to reel in. The head of the fish was so big it covered the top of the capstan when we placed it there for a photograph.

We did catch some smaller sharks though, about four feet long, we kept their razor sharp teeth as souvenirs, the teeth were so sharp we used to shave the hairs off our forearms to show how sharp they were.

We completed our stretch on the Bira Patrol and handed over the Bira Bucket to the ship that was taking our place then we went back in to Mombassa to get stored up with fresh food and to have another few runs ashore. I went to a beach nearby called Silver Sands for the day, to do some swimming and sun bathing. The sand there looks so white and fine it looks like salt, it is a beautiful beach with its palm trees all along the shore, there were even small huts that you could rent if you wanted to stay there for a while.

The next afternoon we went back into the town centre to buy some souvenirs, I bought two beautiful hand-carved elephants and two hand-carved antelopes for my mother. We went to quite a few bars in the afternoon, and everywhere we went this young black woman followed us around. She was about eight months pregnant at the time, and she wanted one of us to marry her and take her back to England. She was genuine, because she kept buying us drinks, it was embarrassing, we just couldn't get rid of her. in the end we had a whip round between the lads, and asked her to keep the money for her baby. We then quickly flagged down a taxi to take us back to the ship.

THE PERSIAN GULF

We left Mombassa and headed for the Persian Gulf. Our next port of call was Bahrain, although we anchored off a few other places, Bahrain was the only place in the Gulf that we actually went alongside the jetty.

One night I was making my way back to the ship alone, and I had made it as far as half way along the long jetty to where the ship was berthed at the end. I was having a rest, leaning with my elbow's on the small wall which runs along the length of the jetty, when I heard a sound behind me, and the next thing I knew I was in the water. An Arab had crept up behind me and toppled me over the wall and in to the sea. I was very lucky, as at certain times of the day and night, the place where I landed was just soft mud when the tide was out, and I would have just sank right into the mud and died. After I surfaced, I looked around and it was as far to the shore as it was to the ship, so I decided to swim to ship. I suppose it must have been quite funny for the quartermaster on the ship's gangway when he heard shouts of help coming from the seaward side of the ship. When he saw me, he threw a rope ladder over the side and I climbed up with my white uniform clinging to my skin, I looked like a "drookit rat", I was fortunate that I could swim or I may have drowned. I got my leg pulled from my mates about the way I made it back to the ship.

There was a Naval establishment at Bahrain called H.M.S. Sharjah, and that is where we normally went for a few drinks, I must admit though, the weather was so hot in the Gulf, that we mostly drank soft drinks, like Pepsi or 7-UP. There was a swimming pool there so it was quite good fun, just like being on holiday. In the evenings at the weekends there was a disco, there were quite a few wrens there, so at least there were some girls to dance with. Apart from that there was nothing much else to do.

One day we were patrolling out at sea, and I was feeling a bit hot this particular day, so I went up to the Bridge to look at the thermometer to read the temperature. The thermometer was outside, but was in the shade under the tarpaulins on the Bridge wings, and it was reading 130 degrees Fahrenheit, in the shade, that is 54.44 degrees Celsius. No wonder I was feeling hot!

Later that day I was sunbathing on the quarterdeck with my friends, we were accustomed to this extreme heat and we were all as black as the Ace of Spades. A new chef arrived on board that day, and we got the shock of our lives when he appeared on the quarter-deck looking as white as milk, it was a long time since we had seen anybody that white. We told him he shouldn't be out here in this heat, but he wouldn't listen to us, he laid out his blanket and set up his brand new portable record player next to him, then lay down to sunbathe listening to an LP of his favourite group. About a minute later we heard this funny sound the group was making, when we looked round, we noticed his LP had melted right over his record player, we couldn't stop ourselves laughing. About ten minutes later the chef said he was going back inside as he wasn't feeling too well. It turned out he had severe sun stroke and he also had severe sunburn with blisters all down the front of his body, most people would feel sorry for him, but not the navy, he was put on a charge with causing self-inflicted injuries and spent quite some in the sick bay.

The metal decks were so hot, you couldn't stand on them without your sandals on, to prove the saying "it's so hot you could fry an egg on it", we did just that. I went to the galley for an egg, and cracked it on to a bollard, and it fried instantly, "I ate it of course".

One day we went to anchor at a small hiding place near Muscat, it was behind a small island; the space between the island and the coast was only about 50m wide. I never knew why we went there, but painted on the rocky face of the cliffs were the names of every royal navy ship that had ever been in the Gulf. Some of the names were even made up of individual white stones. I suppose some of the ships that went there decided to paint the ship's side, judging by the height of the names from the water and the ship's grey paint along the rock face, but it was a mystery to me why they were even there at all.

Since I'm speaking about the Arab countries, here is a song we used to sing quite often.

THE SULTAN SAID TO ALADDIN

Oh, the Sultan said to Aladdin
My palace you will paint
Aladdin like a big o.d.
Said no I f---ing ain't
He went up to the paint shop
For a pot of black enamel

And he rammed it up the asshole of
The sultan's favourite camel

cho
Singing fa-la-la-la, fa-la-la-lee
Sixteen Anna's one rupee
Feed of ass up a sycamore tree
Poor bugger janner
You may farce, kiss my arse
Make fast the dinghy
You may farce, kiss my arse
Make fast the dinghy
And we'll all go back to oggie land
To oggie land, to oggie land
And we'll all go back to oggie land
Where you can't tell sugar from
Tissue paper, tissue paper
Marmalade or jam
Oggie, oggie, oggie, oi, oi, oi
Oggie, oi, oggie, oi
Oggie, oggie, oggie, oi, oi, oi

There are probably more verses to the song but I can't remember them.

KARACHI - PAKISTAN

After quite a long spell in the terrible dry heat of the Gulf, we made our way to Karachi. The thing that sticks out in my mind about Karachi is the extremes between the rich and poor, but living so close to each other. The city centre was full of high street banks from all over the world; I have never seen so many banks all within walking distance of each other. And at the edges of the city were all the extremely poor people living in cardboard boxes and little shelters with corrugated iron roofs.

The ship's company was given the use of some rich person's private beach, so I went there with a few of my friends to do a spot of sun bathing. We couldn't go into the water for a swim because of the jelly fish, they were the Portuguese Men of War type, and they were everywhere, we were told not to go too close to the water's edge in case we stood on any as their stings were extremely poisonous.

In the evening we went to a party hosted by another rich person, we had a newly formed ship's pop group on board, so they provided the entertainment for the whole evening, I suppose they were quite good really. There were no women there, but the party provided an opportunity for most of the ship's company to have a drink all together.

After the ship left Karachi, I remember this junior seaman coming running and shouting down the centre passage way of the ship called the Burma Way, he was being chased by a huge black cockroach, we call them Bombay Runners, it was really funny to see. It must have come on whilst we were alongside at Karachi. We do have to try and keep them off our ship, the small ones are bad enough, but these ones were monsters.

My Life On The Ocean Waves – Douglas Freeman

COLOMBO - CEYLON

Our next port of call was Colombo, Ceylon, which is now called Sri Lanka, where the weather is more humid and everything was so fresh and green. We were only there for about four days and I didn't go out in the City of Colombo itself, but I did manage to go on a sightseeing trip right in to the heart of Ceylon to a City called Kandy. On the way there we stopped by the botanical gardens which has a superb collection of orchids, I had a ride on the back of this huge working elephant for a while, but I just had my photo taken and came down again soon afterwards. There was some kind of annual religious festival going on in Kandy. It was night time by the time we got there, and there were elephants all dressed up for the parade and floats with people dancing all around them, there were all the usual fireworks lighting up the night sky, it was quite a spectacular sight.

We went to the Dalada Maligava (the Temple of the Tooth), there is said to be a tooth of the Buddha in there, we tried to get in to see it but the temple was closed for the celebrations.

So that was all I saw of Ceylon, but I did buy a huge bag of locally produced tea to take home to my mother, and I remember tasting it when I got home, and it made a really good cup of tea, probably the best I've ever tasted.

THE FAR EAST - SINGAPORE

We then made out way to the Far East to a place near Singapore. The Naval establishment there was called H.M.S. Terror, and the local village was called Sambewang. Nearly every night or day we went ashore, and it was normally to Sambewang, as there was everything there for us, Pubs with music, shopping etc, and it was within a short taxi ride's distance.

There was a Pub in Sambewang called the Melbourne Bar; we used to go there quite often as it was a good bar and they had live music in the evenings. I used to go up on the stage there quite often to sing, so that was another reason that I enjoyed it. The pub had a lot of trophy's and photos of racing behind the bar, and I was told the bar belonged to a famous Far East racing driver who was as famous as Stirling Moss was at home.

There was a girl who worked behind the counter at the Melbourne bar, and one day I asked her if she wanted to go in to Singapore for an evening out with me. She said yes, so I met her at the pub in the evening. We had a few drinks, then we made our way to the local taxi rank in the centre of Sambewang, we jumped in to the back seat and I told the taxi driver to take us to some club in Singapore where she wanted to go to. When we arrived I offered to pay the taxi driver, but he wouldn't take any money from me, then he drove away. I couldn't understand why. We then went in to the night-club and the bouncer just waved us through, and we didn't have to pay to get in there either. I asked her if she knew the taxi driver and the bouncer, and she said, not really, but they all know my father, he is the owner of the Melbourne bar, and that famous racing driver you were asking me about. I had a good laugh to myself about that. I had a good night out, and all the drinks were free. I also didn't have to pay for the return taxi to Sambewang.

My Life On The Ocean Waves – Douglas Freeman

The ship stayed in the Singapore area for quite some time, and we even had a two-week refit there. When the ship was in refit, the ship's company had to stay in Terror Barracks, and we went down to the ship every day to work.

I remember this amazing man called "Peanuts." He was everywhere and did everything. He used to come round all the messes in the early morning and gave us all a shake, you heard him coming from miles away, as he used to shout Peanuts, F****n' a Peanuts! As he made his way around each mess, he then swiped the sheets from under you as you lay on the bed, then stamped all over them saying, clabby sheets, then stuffed them into his laundry bag, when you got back your sheets were all neatly folded and clean, ready to put on again.

He always asked if you wanted a suit, we used to say OK just to get rid of him, as you still had a hangover from the night before. He then started to measure you for a suit as you were still lying in your bed. "F**k off Peanuts I've still got a hangover", was our usual response. At lunch time Peanuts came round again with your neatly folded laundry and a half made suit, with the stitches still all around the seams, and in the evening he came round again with your completed suit, ready to wear. We all had extra pockets, special linings, and dragons on the inside, we were proud of our suits. He even made new uniforms for us as well, with the dragons on the inside of our cuffs so that you saw the dragon when you turned the cuffs up.

In the evenings Peanuts had a food stall down in Sambewang, he made the best egg banjos in the whole of the world. An egg banjo is a long bread roll with an omelette, but with his special recipe. We used to get one from him after the pubs were closed, then we would stagger back to the barracks munching in to this banjo on the way. They were so big you hardly ever finished them, I don't know how many times I used to wake up in the morning with half an egg banjo still stuck to my head and the pillow.

I know every sailor that ever passed through Sambewang will remember Peanuts. My brother Bill told me a few stories about Peanuts before I even met him, and Bill was there years before I even got there.

Whilst we were in the Singapore area, our divisional officer asked for volunteers to go on a trek through the Malaysian Jungle for two days, and staying in the jungle for one night, there were about ten volunteers altogether including myself. I've no idea where we actually went, but it was somewhere in the jungle. We were dressed in a full green jungle outfit with the floppy hat, and a machete knife attached to our belt, we had tight lace-up boots that went up our legs to stop the snakes and leeches from biting us. We didn't get bitten by any snakes, but when we took off our boots in the evening, we all had leeches stuck to our feet. They must be amazing creatures, you never see them get you, and you don't feel them either, we just burned them off with a cigarette and that was that.

We pitched our tents in a jungle clearing, and there was this monkey up in a tree close by us, and we couldn't get any peace for it screeching all the time, so we got our machete's and chopped down it's tree, and it went away somewhere else.

There were four of us in my tent, and after we had something to eat we tried to get some sleep, as we had to get up early the next morning. All the lamps were out, and I felt something touching my feet, I thought it was one of my pals playing a joke on me. When I shone my torch down to my feet, there was a jungle rat sitting at the bottom of my sleeping bag. They are not rats as we normally know them, these creatures are quite friendly, and they have great big eyes so they can see in the dark, I think it just came in for something to eat, but we scared it off anyway.

The next day we came to a waterfall, a few of the lads went in for a swim, but I didn't like the idea, so I just watched from the riverbank. We didn't find much in the jungle except jungle, but it was a good experience, and a lot of fun. We rendezvoused at a pre-arranged meeting place in the evening, where we got transport back to our ship. It was quite a tiring few days and we covered a lot of miles, so we were glad to get back to the ship for a shower and get the rest of the leeches off ourselves.

HONG KONG

After we left the Singapore area, we sailed for Hong Kong. I remember sitting right up at the bows of the ship, looking over the side at the Porpoises keeping pace with us. The sea was flat calm, and you could hear a steady shhhh sound as the ship sliced its way through the water. Every now and then the water surface would be disturbed as a shoal of flying fish suddenly leaped from the sea and glided for what seemed to be hundreds of yards, and then dived back into the sea again. It was fascinating to watch.

I remember entering Hong Kong harbour at night and being amazed at the millions of lights, not only from the hills all around, but also from all the small junks and ships buzzing round the harbour.

When I went ashore the next day, I went over the harbour to Kowloon by ferry with a few of my friends; we just had a look around the shops and sampled the oriental atmosphere with the local Chinese people.

We went into a restaurant for our lunch, and we all decided to have T-bone steaks. The chef asked us how thick we wanted them, and he chopped them in front of us to our individual requirements. I had one about one and a half inches thick, and cooked to perfection. This was the first time I ever had a sizzle steak cooked on its own cast iron plate and placed on an oval block of wood, it was so big I couldn't get anything else on to the plate. We had separate plates of French fries and side salads as well. It was all washed down with bottles of red wine, and I can honestly say that was the best T-bone steak I have ever eaten anywhere in the world.

I didn't manage to go up to the top of the hill that overlooks Hong Kong harbour whilst I was there. "But I saw it on a postcard" and sent some home to my mother.

My Life On The Ocean Waves – Douglas Freeman

YOKOHAMA - JAPAN

We knew we were going to Japan before we left Singapore, and it was said that if you gave a Japanese girl an Opal Gemstone she would love you forever. So a lot of sailors thinking they would be on to a good thing, bought loads of Opals in Sambewang before they left, as you could buy them very cheap there. In fact, I saw a man sitting cross legged against a wall on the pavement selling diamonds. Some of them were uncut but others looked like real shaped diamonds, and he was selling them for about five pounds each. He even had a piece of glass to scratch the diamonds on, to prove to you they were real, but I couldn't be convinced you could get real diamonds that cheap so I never bought any. But thinking back, I wish I had bought one for curiosity sake, as I have always wondered if they were genuine.

The ship arrived in Yokohama, and the thing that I remember most about Japan is the Taxis. When we flagged one down and the driver pulled over to the kerb, both front and rear passenger doors opened at the same time, this amused me, as the driver was in the taxi alone. It turned out that the driver had a lever down by his seat, and when he pulled it up both front and rear doors opened. I never saw anything like that anywhere else in the world.

Another unusual thing I remember is when we were standing on a street corner, all the streets around the junction were quite quiet, I heard a train arriving from a nearby station. A minute later there were thousands of commuters rushing out of the station, and you heard this loud sound of all the voices, and you couldn't get moved for about ten minutes, then all of a sudden they were all gone, and the street was quiet again. About fifteen minutes later it all happened again, it was like watching armies of ants on the move, it was so funny.

I did notice that the Japanese liked there drink though, they reminded me of Scotsmen, they drank their beer out of British style pint mugs with the handles, and most of them also had a whisky along with their beer, I expected them all to be drinking their own local drink called Sake.

I found the Japanese people very polite and courteous, but I didn't find a sailor who was loved forever by a beautiful young Japanese girl by giving them Opals.

I had a girlfriend in Aberdeen that I had been going out with for quite a while; I used to write home quite often to her. I bought her a Kimono from Japan, in fact she asked me to get her one if I went there, so I did. I'd only been back home in Aberdeen a few days, when we had a small argument about something trivial, she stormed out of the pub we were in, and I never saw her again. I could have went round and made it up with her, but I thought it was best that we parted anyway, as I was hardly in Aberdeen, and what's the point in staying in a relationship If I was never there.

We left Japan and headed back to Durban South Africa via stops at Gann in the Pacific, Singapore, Bahrain in the Persian Gulf, and Mombassa East Africa, almost back tracking the route we took to get out here.

DURBAN - 2

There we were again, all lined up on the starboard side of the ship, dressed all in white, we were expecting to see the Lady in White standing at the entrance of the harbour singing for us, but she wasn't there. When we got alongside, we found out she had died a whilst we were away. I can always say I witnessed the passing of a living legend.

I went on a tour round Zulu land and Natal, which we found very appropriate, with our ship being named H.M.S. Zulu. We had a ship's song which we used to sing whenever there were a bunch of us together and usually half drunk. It went like this.

Hold em down, you Zulu warrior,
Hold em down, you Zulu chief,
Hold em down, you Zulu warrior,
Hold em down, you Zulu chief, chief, chief, chief,
I kaka zumba, zumba, zumba, I kaka zumba, zumba zay,
I kaka zumba, zumba, zumba, I kaka zumba, zumba zay.

We repeated that words until we either got tired, or fed up of them. But during the singing and clapping there was always one drunken sailor who used to start stripping off his uniform until he was completely naked, where upon we used to drench him with whatever we had left in our beer glasses. I can't begin to count how many times I've seen that done in pubs all over the world, even on different ships where they adopted our song. I've even seen it done since I came out of the navy. Anyway the Zulu's were impressed with our song, without the striptease of course.

My Life On The Ocean Waves – Douglas Freeman

We bought a lot of useless souvenirs from them, like shields and drums, but we later found they were all infested with insects and bugs, so we threw them all away.

I went for a night out with a bunch of my mates to a big hotel. There was a group playing on the stage, and during their break one of my pals went up to them and said, one of our lads sings and plays the guitar, can he go up and play during your break. I didn't really want to go up and sing as there were hundreds of people there, and I was unprepared. Anyway, I went up on stage and sang for about half an hour. I really enjoyed myself, and I got a great response from the audience, especially from a table of beautiful young girls, which pleased my mates, and gave them an opportunity to go over to their table and chat them up.

When I got off the stage the hotel manager offered me £100 a night to sing at his hotel, as the present group was leaving soon, I couldn't accept his offer because I was in the navy, but a £100 a night was an awful lot of money in 1968.

I re-joined my mates at the same table as the girls of course, I thought they all looked like models, in fact they were. I trapped one of the girls with long blond hair, or should I say she trapped me, she was so impressed with my singing she made it perfectly clear that she wanted me, and none of my mates.

We danced and drank a lot, and then she took me back to her place. She lived in a flat of her own with two young children. I woke up next morning with this loud noise coming from the living

My Life On The Ocean Waves – Douglas Freeman

room. I put on a dressing gown and wandered through, I saw her sitting on a chair having her hair blow dried by this obviously feminine looking bloke with long blond hair, and wearing a sky blue suit with pink shoes. She told me he was a world famous hairdresser, and he did her hair for free because she was in the modelling business and a friend. She told me he sued Sandy Shaw for missing an appointment, I thought Sandy Shaw had straight hair anyway, so I thought that comical. After I had breakfast, she drove me back to the ship in time for 07:00 hrs.

I was on duty the next day, so I couldn't get ashore, but she took me and a friend of mine and a friend of hers on a tour round a Safari Park the following day. I took a few photographs of some of the animals whilst we drove around in the car that day, but I didn't realise it was only a 12 exposure film and I ran out of film so I never got any photos of her.

In the evening she took us for a meal to one of her favourite restaurants, but they wouldn't let me in because I wasn't wearing a tie. She tried to explain to them that you don't wear ties with this type of sailor's uniform, but they wouldn't listen, so she fell out with them and said she wouldn't use that restaurant again. We eventually went to another restaurant where we had a wonderful meal, not only that, she paid the bill.

We were all lined up on the port side of the ship as we left Durban harbour, all the girls that had met sailors were waving to us and crying as the ship left the jetty. I was waving to the girl I had been with during my stay, and the guy with the sky blue suit and pink shoes was by her side crying and waving a handkerchief.

My Life On The Ocean Waves – Douglas Freeman

He wasn't waving to me, he was waving to one of the Royal Marines who were lined up just down from us, he must have met some of them when they were ashore, we killed ourselves laughing at that. She gave me her address and I promised to write to her, but I lost the piece of paper I wrote her address on, and I never went to South Africa again, so that was the end of that.

We were now on our final journey back to Portsmouth. We were only at sea for one day when I came down with great big spots all over my body from head to toe, I was worried, as I didn't know what it was and neither did our medic. The medic put me in the sick bay, and I lay there for days looking through all the medical books on spots, looking up things like leprosy and smallpox. I was crawling up the wall with the severe itching; the medic wouldn't even give me a few codeine's to kill the pain until I complained strongly. I eventually remembered there was chickenpox going round the kids in Durban so I must have caught it off of one of them, but I was in the sick bay for ten days till we reached Portsmouth harbour. I was examined by a real doctor and he confirmed that I had chickenpox.

I was covered in spots that were healing, and I was feeling a bit miserable and sorry for myself when I received a phone call on the ship. It was my brother Bill, he was in Portsmouth, and when he heard the Zulu had just come in he gave me a call to drag me ashore for a pint. I told him what state I was in and he killed himself laughing. Half an hour later I met him in the Sailors Home Club just outside the main dockyard gate. When he saw me he killed himself laughing even more, and so did I, it was great to get ashore after being stuck in bed and in isolation for ten days and have a few pints with my brother whom I hadn't seen for over a year.

One of the ship's crew gave me this comical notice of return to send home to our families before we returned from the Far East.

NOTICE OF RETURN

To the neighbours, relatives and friends of......................

LOCK UP YOUR DAUGHTERS IN THEIR ROOMS
FILL THE FRIDGE WITH COLD BEER
GET HIS CIVVIES OUT OF MOTHBALLS

Very soon the above named sailor will be once more in your midst, radio-active, dehydrated and demoralised, eager to resume his place in society as a human being, entitled to liberty and justice whilst engaged on the somewhat delayed pursuit of happiness.

In making your preparations to welcome him back to civilisation, you must make allowances for the crude lack of environment, which has been his lot unfortunately for the past .... months. In brief, he may have become a trifle oriental in his outlook on life, be suffering from rashitis, sweatitis, and dogitis or even the shakes, (a common complaint brought on by the consumption of too much Tiger or San Miguel beer).

My Life On The Ocean Waves – Douglas Freeman

Therefore show no alarm if he prefers to sit on the floor instead of a chair. Always kicks his shoes off against the step before entering the house, wears only his towel and flip-flops when visiting the neighbours, has an epileptic fit at the sight of a coconut, or has the tendency to salute anyone of importance. Side-track him away from partially filled coaches for he will think they are organised parties to visit a local brewery.

His diet, to which he has grown accustomed, should, for the first few days at least, consist of tinned fruit, tinned milk (watered down considerably) dehydrated potatoes, or other canned foods. Fresh or rich foods, especially milk should be avoided at first and then introduced gradually. His only meat should be corned beef.

DO NOT allow him on the roads unaccompanied. It will be his undoing. Traffic he has forgotten, and rather than walk anywhere he will sit on the pavement for hours waiting for some kind sympathetic motorist to take pity on him and give him a lift.

Do all your purchasing yourself, gradually establishing in his mind that bartering, arguing, cajoling and even threatening the shopkeeper is taboo in your land of civilisation.

His language may be rather embarrassing at first, but in a comparatively short time he can be brought to speak good English again. Never ask him why the lad down the road has a higher rank than him, and never make flattering remarks about the Army, R.A.F. and in particular the Royal Marines in his presence.

For the first few months (until he has become house trained) be particularly watchful when he is in the presence of women, especially young and beautiful specimens. After seeing women on the screen being wooed by handsome men of the cinema world he thinks he is a master of the art himself. His intentions are sincere, but dishonourable. Keep in mind that beneath his tanned exterior, there beats a heart of gold.

Treat him with kindness, tolerance and the occasional quart of rum, and you will be able to rehabilitate that which is now only a hollow shell of the happy man you once knew.

(Signed) E. B. Cumming.

We left Portsmouth for Rosyth, and we were soon back in Scotland getting ready for to go on leave once more.

JOKE - 2

I was travelling in a train from Edinburgh to Aberdeen, and the sailor with me was only going to Stonehaven, a small town fifteen miles South of Aberdeen. I told him this was a straight through train to Aberdeen, and it didn't stop at Stonehaven, he wasn't very happy about that as he had been away for almost a year and was looking forward to getting home as quickly as possible. I told him the train did slow down as it went through Stonehaven. And what he could do is open the train door, throw his bags out on to the platform, hold on to the door and keep running, slam the door and still keep running along the platform to stop from falling over. He thought that was a great idea and decided to try it. When the train came to Stonehaven and slowed down, he opened the door and threw his bags out on to the platform, held on to the door and kept running, slammed the door and still kept running along the platform to stop himself from falling over. As the rear carriage of the train was passing him, the guard opened the door and pulled him in saying, bloody hell Jack, you almost missed this train!

LEAVE - 3

Here I was again, back home in Aberdeen after a long trip away, I was accustomed to being away by this time but it was still great to come home. I was as brown as a berry after having been sunbathing all round the world for almost a year. I was a fully-fledged royal navy matelot now and I was telling sea stories to my friends and family like old father time himself, you could see the lamp shades swinging as I brushed the salt off my shoulder. I sometimes went down to my local pub, Royal's Bar, with my father for a few pints and a game of darts. Other times I went down town with my friend Bert with whom I went to both Primary and Secondary school. We often ended up in the Palace Ballroom because it had a late drinking licence till 1 am.

In the early days, I had to wear my uniform whenever I went on leave from my ships, and as soon as I got home I used to get changed into my civvies, I felt more relaxed without everybody staring at me in my uniform. It also stopped it getting dirty, since I only had one No.1 best uniform, it had to be looked after. My mother didn't realise I had become independent and able to look after myself, until she saw me putting spit and polish on my shoes, and ironing my uniform. I had to iron five creases in each leg of my trousers, some sailors had seven, but it all depended on your height.

ROSYTH - 2

Back at Rosyth dockyard, the ship was having another refit after the long trip to the Far East. We were put up in H.M.S. Cochrane just outside the dockyard whilst all these repairs were going on, and we had to commute to the ship every morning and lunch time, and back to the Barracks in the evening. It was just like having a civvy job. We had to do a lot of the painting ourselves, whilst all the heavy electrical and mechanical jobs were carried out by the dockyard workers.

I used to go home to Aberdeen on some weekends when I was not on duty, and other times I went ashore with my friends to Dunfermline or Inverkeithing.

One Saturday morning I went to the Central Bar in Inverkeithing for a game of darts. I was to meet my friends there later on in the day. I was the only person in the bar, and I was having a game of dart by myself. Another person came into the bar and asked me if I wanted a game. I said OK, so we started a game of 501 straight off. After being absolutely thrashed for about four games in a row, I said, you are a brilliant player mate, getting all those 180s, you should play for Scotland. He said I do, and I asked his name. He said, Jocky Wilson. No wonder I got thrashed!

When my mates arrived later on, they didn't believe me when I said I'd been playing against Jocky Wilson.

After the refit was finished, the ship set sail again. First we did the usual sea trials to prove the sea worthiness of the ship, and after they were completed, we sailed for Portsmouth.

PORTSMOUTH - 2

The ship went down to Portsmouth for about a week before we went to the other places in the UK that we were going to visit. My ship was in Portsmouth dockyard alongside the jetty not too far from the main gate. My friend from Aberdeen, Bert, came down to Portsmouth, and he found out that my ship was in Portsmouth harbour, so he gave the ship a phone, I was surprised to find out that he was in Portsmouth. I arranged to meet him just outside the main dockyard gate, but there was another dockyard gate, and he went to the other one. He eventually realised he was at the wrong gate and made his way to the main gate where I was waiting. We went for quite a few drinks around Portsmouth, as I was trying to show him a few of the pubs that I frequented. In the evening we went to the Mecca dance hall. We had quite a good time there, Bert thought it was a lot better than the dance places we had in Aberdeen at that time, and he was right. He still recalls that situation to me every now and again when we speak about the old times.

CARDIFF

After Portsmouth, we went for a visit to Cardiff. Nothing special happened at Cardiff that I can recall, so why I am giving it a mention I don't really know, but I do remember having a quick visit round Cardiff Castle, only because it was in the centre of town, how exciting! We did have a good few runs ashore there though, as the pubs and people there were quite friendly far as I can remember.

LIVERPOOL

Our next port of call was Liverpool. I was out on the town one evening with my friends as usual, and we were walking down a very busy road in Liverpool town centre. Because it was an official courtesy visit by the ship, we were all dressed in our sailor's uniforms. A fight started up ahead of us between sailors from our ship and sailors from a Venezuelan ship that happened to be visiting Liverpool at the same time as us. The traffic had almost come to a standstill, due to all the fights going on in the middle of the road, the sailors seemed to be oblivious to all the cars on the road. It was very windy that evening, and the wind blew my hat off. I chased after it, and when I caught it I bent down to pick it up, just then I felt this hard dull thump on my head. A Venezuelan sailor had kicked me in the head as I was bending down to pick up my hat. I stood up and my white front went red with the blood rushing from my nose. I felt my nose, and it was half way over the right side of my face, it had been broken. My friend that was with me saw what had just happened. He grabbed the Venezuelan sailor by the back of the neck and shoved his head out on to the road, where it was hit by a passing car, which saw the end of him for a while. The police were on their way by this time, so we all disappeared. The thing that really annoyed me about Liverpool was the fact I went to about three hospitals around Liverpool to see what they could do about my broken nose, and they never even took the trouble to wipe the blood off my face, or check my over for any other injuries, like concussion etc. I hate them for that, and I will never go back to Liverpool again. You can imagine I wasn't feeling very happy with myself, and to be treated like dirt really pissed me off.

I got no sympathy from the ship's medic either, he just said it's broken now and you will just have to put up with it. The next day the Captain of the Venezuelan ship came round to our ship and asked for the return of the hats of his crew. Apparently we had them all, so our Captain gave an announcement over the ship's tannoy, "anyone with a Venezuelan hat must bring it to the gangway immediately". When the hats were counted, there were about a hundred of them. We were reluctant to hand back our war trophies, after having won them so well, especially since I suffered a broken nose during the conflict.

THE MED - 2

After a while of hanging about UK waters we were destined for the Mediterranean once again. We left Portsmouth and headed straight for Gibraltar, our normal first port of call to the Med.

NAPLES

Our next journey took us to Naples in Italy. I remember the same things happening there as happened elsewhere in the Med. The chef was throwing food rubbish over the side, and there were always a bunch of small rowing boats with a couple of grown-ups and a few children on board picking up the biggest pieces of food out of the water. When you hear the stories about the back streets of Naples being poor and deprived, they are true. The poverty was pretty bad, but some areas were better off, It was just like a lot of other poor and rich places that existed side by side that I saw throughout the world.

We went ashore as usual, but we never went alone, always a bunch of us. We were told not to go near the back streets of Naples, and where did we end up, the back streets of Naples. It was always pretty useless telling us where not to go, as nine times out of ten, that was where we would end up. There were a few shootings and stabbings in the area whilst we were there, but nothing to worry about.

We went on an organised visit to Pompeii near Mount Vesuvius. It was one of the most interesting historical visits I have ever been on. It takes you back to the way life used to be around the time of Jesus. When you walked round Pompeii, you were actually walking in the same footsteps the people of Pompeii walked two thousand years ago. You saw the grooves the chariot's made along the narrow streets, and there were worn away marks where people put their hands when they leaned on the well to get a drink. Going through some of the buildings, there were bodies lying where they fell when the eruption happened. I remember a couple wrapped in each other's arms at the very last moment before they died. There were male sexual organs carved out of stone on the pavement pointing to a doorway, where you would find the oldest profession in the world. We were also shown this real painting that was found in one of the houses when it was excavated. It was of a nude man standing with his huge organ on a set of scales, and on the other side of the scales were bags and bags of gold, and the gold was high up in the air, meaning something was worth a lot more than gold. They only showed it to the men, and we thought it was a good laugh.

After we spent about four or five hours touring all round Pompeii, we had our lunch and then went for a walk up to the top of Mount Vesuvius. We got a good look of the Bay of Naples from the top of the Volcano. The Volcano was still smoking in a few places when we were up there. We were not allowed to take any souvenirs from the Volcano, but I did manage to take a round lump of volcanic rock back with me, I thought I'm sure the Volcano can produce more when it needs to, and I don't think it will miss this one piece of rock.

When we were leaving the gates of Pompeii there were small stalls selling souvenirs of all kinds. The funniest souvenir that I saw was the Flying Fid. A Flying Fid is a male organ with wings on the top, they were made in gold or silver and were sold as necklaces. A lot of the sailors got them and put them through their jacket button holes so you could only see the wings from the front of the jacket, they looked like RAF wings, and it gave people a shock when you showed them the reverse side of the lapel. We used to laugh with anticipation, knowing there would be shock in the faces of some of the women. They used to say, oh, what a nice badge, where did you get it, and as they were having a closer look at it you would turn it round, and there were instant red faces as they realised what it was, it was a really funny practical joke.

MALTA - 2

The ship was a few miles off Malta and we were preparing to enter Grand Harbour. We were all in our white uniforms and mustered along the port side of the ship. There must have been somebody important watching us enter the harbour that day, as we were all fitted out with rifles and bayonets. The sun was very bright, and my eyes were watering with the glare from the water and the white buildings as we entered the mouth of the harbour. We had to look our smartest, and the Petty Officer was going round everybody with a hand brush and brushing their collars, and any other tiny speck of dust that he could see. We were still a few miles out and everybody was standing about getting themselves ready. We all got our bayonets fitted to the top of our rifles and were checking each other for any dust etc. The lad in front of me asked me to brush his collar for him and he handed me a brush. I spotted some marks on his trousers so I decided to brush them off. I put my rifle between my legs to stop it falling over, and bent over to brush him. As I bent over my bayonet stuck right in to my chin, as I stood up and pulled the bayonet out, the blood flowed all over my white front and uniform. The cut wasn't too bad, but it did get me out of standing up on deck for ages with my eyes in pain with the sun. The things some people do to get out of duty! In fact it really was an accident, and I had that scar on my chin for years afterwards.

My Life On The Ocean Waves – Douglas Freeman

FISHING IN THE MED

We were now heading West along the Mediterranean on our way back to the UK. We were a bit short of fresh supplies, so the skipper decide that we should catch some fish. There was no way we could catch enough fish with fishing lines for the whole ship's company, so we did it a different way. We picked up a shoal of fish on our sonar, just like we would track a submarine, and when we got to the correct distance from the shoal, we fired a Mk10 anti-submarine mortar right in to the centre of the shoal of fish. There was a massive explosion, and a huge plume of water rose up just off the starboard side of the ship. When the water settled, there were hundreds of fish floating on top of the water. We then sent the ship's boat to go and pick up as many as we wanted. So we had a big variety of fish to choose from that day, and the next day, and the next day! I suppose the firing of an expensive anti-submarine mortar was put down to some kind of training exercise for the TAS anti-submarine crew.

We had our usual stop in Gibraltar to pick up some more rabbits for the ship's crew on our way back to the UK, then we crossed the Bay of Biscay, up along the English Channel and in to Portsmouth. Home again!

GLASGOW RECRUITING OFFICE

There was a memo up on the ship's notice board, asking if anyone was interested in going to a Navy Recruiting Office for a while, there were vacancies all-round the country, so I thought I'd apply, as I saw Aberdeen on the list. You had to give a second and third choice in case you didn't get your first preference. I was surprised when a week later I was accepted for Glasgow Recruiting Office which was my second choice, I was also delighted as it was something new for me to do.

The ship was still in Portsmouth when I left for Glasgow. I packed all of the kit I would require and left the rest on board. All of my mates were jealous as they were going up to Rosyth soon to start another refit. Most of the ship's company would also be leaving the ship at Rosyth and a new crew taking over the Zulu before the refit had finished.

I was an Able Seaman by this time in my career, and I had also passed for "killick", that is a Leading Seaman. Although I had passed the exams for Leading Seaman there was always a long delay before you actually picked it up, it was like dead man's shoes, it was the same with all other promotions in the Navy. I never actually picked up my Leading Seaman's Badge, but I'll come to that story later.

I arrived at the Navy Recruiting Office in West Nile Street, Glasgow, with all my kit. The other sailor at the Recruiting Office then took me to the guesthouse where I was to stay. I was introduced to the Land Lady Mrs Motyl, and she told me the times we had to be there for our meals. I think it was 08:00 for Breakfast and 18:30 for the evening meal. It was good to have some real home cooking again, she was just like a mother to us.

My day consisted of the following. Getting up in the morning, and getting dressed in to my uniform. Catching the electric train form Pollock Shields Station to Queen Street Station, walking about half a mile through the streets of Glasgow to the office, sitting at the front desk in the office and dealing with anybody who came in to the office who wanted to join the Navy. I'd hand them some forms to fill in and hand the completed forms to the Chief Petty Officer, he would then interview the candidate and decide if he or she was initially suitable to go for further interviews. When my day at the office was done I'd make the return journey to the guest house for my supper.

We had to let Mrs Motyl know if we weren't going to make it back for our supper, because normally it would be all cooked and ready to serve by the time we arrived at the guest house. I got a telling off a few times for not informing her I was going to be late. I sometimes went for a pint of beer to the Red Lion Pub just up the street from the office, and after a few pints, I just forgot, but I sure got reminded when I got back to the guest house.

Mrs Motyl's husband was ill, and they lived at the top of the house. I think I only saw the back of him once all the time I was there. They had two daughters, one was about eight and the other was about ten, they were two little devils, they used to try and torment us, and we used to chase them round the room. It reminded me of when I used to play with my own young Nieces, it was a real family atmosphere.

Mrs Motyl also took in other lodgers, and I remember one day after supper, we were still sitting in the dining room when one of the new lodgers came in. He was one of those con men who organised those special sales in church halls etc. He came in with his day's takings in about five large brown paper bags and emptied them on the floor to count his money. He must have had about three thousand pounds in £1 and £5 notes, and he just sat there and counted up his money.

One day at the office, I was going for my lunch to the pub next door, when I heard a loud crash. I looked down West Nile Street and I saw a double decker bus that appeared to have had an accident. Apparently there was a window cleaning trolley halfway up a building, and one side of its lifting wires snapped and the trolley came swinging down and hit the front of the bus. It smashed through the front windows of the upper deck and killed a man sitting in the front seat. It made me think, the poor man couldn't have known his time was up, when he was just sitting on a bus going to his work in the morning minding his own business.

I met an old man in the Red Lion Pub next door, he must have been well over eighty years old. He was drinking whisky, so I decided to give him a recital of a poem that I knew which was written by Watt Nicol, called the Whisky History. It has the names of about fifty seven brands of whisky's in it, so I thought he'd appreciate this poem. He liked the poem very much, and he decided to give me a recital of a poem that he knew called Doo's Delight. It was about two old pals who went fishing together all of their lives, and there was always rivalry about who could make the best salmon fishing fly. One of them made a fly and called it Doo's Delight. His mate said he would never catch a fish with that fly. Anyway, Jake died, and one day his pal was fishing with his special fly, when he caught this big salmon. He looked at the salmon and thought it was his pal Jake, he got such a shock, he put the fish back in to the river. The last line of the poem goes like this, He hisnae touched a rod again, For fear o' catching' Jake again. Oh by the way, the whole poem was written Doric, an old North of Scotland dialect. The old man gave me a hand written copy of the poem, and I typed out properly for myself. I don't know who wrote this poem, but it is a very good one. I often hand it out to friends who are keen on poetry and fishing, and it does help if they can understand Doric as well.

I was sitting at the front desk at the office one day, when a man came in wanting to join the navy. I gave him the usual forms to fill in, and I had a look at them to see where to direct him. He was a fully qualified accountant, and he had a list of O-Levels and A-Levels as long as your arm. All he wanted to be was a seaman, I told him he could become an officer with all his qualifications, but didn't want to become an officer, he was sick fed up of office work and he wanted to work out in the open. I sent him through to the officer in charge of the officer recruits to see what he thought of this man. When the man came out after seeing the officer his eyes were filled with tears, I asked him what was wrong, he said they would only let him join as an officer but not as a junior rating, as he was too qualified. Officers would not like a junior rating being more educationally qualified than them, that's why they would not let him join.

I sometimes used to wander around central Glasgow in my uniform after I had finished work, I went to quite a few different pubs in the town centre, and I never once came across any trouble. Glasgow had a reputation for being a bit rough, but I was always treated with respect. My uniform collar was always being touched by old ladies for luck, and I was often treated to a free pint of beer by people who respected the services, and that has only happened to me in Glasgow, so it shows you how friendly the people really are there.

I often went home to Aberdeen on the weekends, so I didn't see much of the weekend Glasgow nightlife, I had to take advantage of the fact that I was quite near to home.

During my two and a half years on H.M.S. Zulu, I applied every six months for a branch change to the electronics branch of the navy, and every time I got told there were no vacancies. My divisional officer told me not to give up, and to keep trying, so I did.

I spent about six weeks in the Glasgow Recruiting Office, and just as I was preparing to go back to the Zulu, I was told I had been accepted for training at the electrical school called H.M.S. Collingwood. I was absolutely delighted. I was at last getting what I had always wanted, all I had to do now was try my best.

I left Glasgow and went back to the Zulu for the rest of my kit. I then went on two weeks leave to Aberdeen and then on to H.M.S. Collingwood, near Fareham in Hampshire.

H.M.S. COLLINGWOOD - 1

I arrived at H.M.S. Collingwood just like a new recruit, I was an Able Seaman RP "Radar Plotter", passed for Leading Seaman, had been in the Navy for years, and I had to go back to the lowest of the electrical branch. All the rest of the lads that were with me were brand new in to the royal navy, so I was put in charge of them all. Although I was starting from the bottom in this training, I still didn't lose the rate of pay I was on as an Able Seaman, so that was OK.

Our first electrical training was on basic electricity and electronics. I studied hard at this, as I didn't want to fail having waited for so long to get here. I got about 98% in my exams.

There were three kinds of electrical branches we could go in to, (REM), Radio Electrical Mechanic, which maintains Radio, Radar, and Computers. (CEM) Control Electrical Mechanic, which maintains Sonar and Gunnery Control Systems. (OEM) Ordinance Electrical Mechanic, which maintains Electrical Motors and General Electric's.

We all went in separately to see a Wren Careers Officer, who tried to make me go in to the Control or Ordinance side, which I refused to do. I knew I had passed my exams with the highest percentage to get the branch of my choice. I said If I do not get to go in to the Electronics Branch I would just go back to being a seaman. After waiting and worrying for about an hour, I was told I had been accepted for the Electronics branch just like I wanted. I was relieved and delighted, now I can get on with my new electronics career just like I wanted to do when I first joined the navy at sixteen. It had taken me about four years but I did it!

I was put in charge of my class, being the most senior one there. Every morning we had to muster on the parade ground to be counted and to make sure we were all there. There were sixteen people in my class, which gave me three rows of five people and me standing in front of them in charge. With me having done years of training in marching already, I knew how to get my class in to shape to be the best. There was a Gunnery Instructor "G.I." put in charge of all the classes to make sure they got up to a reasonable standard of marching, but we hardly needed him. All the other classes only had another new recruit in charge of them, so they knew nothing. Even though all the classes did get parade instruction, we were always the best, but some of the other classes really did need their parade instruction as they were so bad. Some of them marching with the left leg and the left arm out at the same time, it was comical to see.

After we had mustered in the morning, we then all marched to our various classes for instruction. Our lunch break was from 12:00 to 13:30, then we mustered on the parade ground again and marched to our afternoon instruction. At the end of the day we marched back to our mess.

We had to do a tour of duty once every four days, which consisted of almost anything. First of all we had a fire drill then we were detailed off to different things, like sweeping the streets round the establishment, peeling spuds for the chef, doing guard duty on the front gate, or guard patrol round the establishment, and cleaning out the mess decks. And that is only a fraction of the things we had to do.

There were regular sailors who did the Main Gate duties, they always thought they were somebody, it was normally those who had finished their training and was waiting to be drafted to a ship. One day I was detailed off to be on Main Gate duty, which lasted all night till the morning. With me being new, they put me outside by the gate, standing in the freezing cold, to check the Identity Cards of those wanting in. When the regular guy's did it they knew a lot of people, so just waved them through. Well, when all the people started arriving in the morning to start their work at H.M.S. Collingwood, me being very security conscious checked every I.D. card very closely before they got through the Main Gate. Within about half an hour there were queues of cars about a mile down the road, and queues of people hundreds of yards long down the pavements. A lot of people were arriving with no I.D. card, so I sent them over to the guardhouse to see the Officer of the Day before they could get in. But the Officer of the Day was not there so there were also queues of people all round the guardhouse till he arrived. I checked the I.D. card of every Lieutenant, Lieutenant Commander, Commander and Captain that came through that gate. They eventually had to change me out, as the whole Naval Establishment would come to a standstill if they kept me out there. There would be hundreds of people late for their work in the morning, including a lot of officers. I was only doing my job as a security conscious sailor, but I wasn't the green young electrical recruit that they thought I was, I was an ex Able Seaman who was having the last laugh on them! Ha! Ha!

My Life On The Ocean Waves – Douglas Freeman

FAREHAM - 1

We sometimes went ashore to Fareham, which was the nearest small town to H.M.S. Collingwood, it was about four miles down the road. It was a sunny Saturday afternoon and we had been sitting at the outside tables of this pub drinking and having a good laugh. We decided to go back to Collingwood early to get our supper and come out again in the evening. We left by the back door of the pub, and just across the lane was the back door of a cafe, we saw all these cardboard boxes piled up, and we saw they were those big fresh milk cartons with gallons of milk inside them. In our drunken state we decide to steal one for the stray cat that came by our mess. We carried it all the way back to Collingwood but we couldn't go through the front gate with it, so we found a hole in the outer perimeter fence round the back and sneaked in with this gallons of milk for the cat. What a disappointment, we put the milk out for the cat feeling pleased with ourselves, but it wouldn't drink it! So we ended chasing the cat all round the place trying to catch it, and there was us thinking we were being good to this stray cat.

Another time I was in Fareham, I was on my way back to Collingwood after another Saturday afternoon session, and I decided to take a short cut through some small lanes. I got a bit lost, so I decided to cross this garden to a road on the other side. I stood on top of this wire fence and jumped on to the grass, but the wire fence gave way as I jumped and I landed on my bum as my heels skidded along the grass. When I stood up after catching my breath, both the heels of my shoes were gone, sunk deeply in to the ground, I had to leave them there as I had to get out of that garden as quickly as possible in case I was caught trespassing. I had to walk all the way back to Collingwood with no heels to my shoes, it was quite painful as the nails were coming through the bottom of the shoes and into my feet. The really funny and unusual thing about all this was, the following week I was walking down the main street in Fareham and I found both of my heels lying in the gutter. I thought that was really strange, giving the circumstances I lost them in, anyway I picked them up, took them back to Collingwood and nailed them back on to my shoes. So I had my shoes back again, isn't that strange?

One Saturday I decided to walk to Fareham instead of catching the bus, I only went ashore there at the weekends as we had no studies at the weekends. I arrived at the first pub on the route to Fareham, there were a few of my mates sitting outside having a drink in the sunshine. This pub was just across from Fareham Creek, and I saw a bunch of sailors down by the water's edge. There were a lot of small yachts anchored in the Creek, and there was a sailor was hanging off one of the anchor cables. Apparently he had swam out to the yacht, but the current of the fast flowing Creek was getting too strong for him, and he tried to hold on to the slippery anchor cable. All his drunken friends could do was laugh at him struggling. I saw what was happening, and I ran down to the Creek and waded out up to my waist, I was slightly downstream from him, and I asked him if he could still swim, he said yes, so I asked him to swim to me. He let go of the anchor and swam towards me, I grabbed hold of him and waded with him back to the water's edge. He had swallowed quite a bit of water. Somebody saw what I was doing and called an ambulance, so he was taken away when I got him on to the grass bank. I gave his friends a telling off for being so stupid and for laughing at his predicament instead of helping him. A week later I was summoned to the Commander's office, somehow he found out it was me who rescued that young sailor from Fareham Creek, the Commander praised me for saving his life, then gave me a telling off for not reporting it to the navy. I just didn't think about reporting it. Later I met the chap that I had rescued at a disco in Collingwood. He thanked me and bought me a pint of beer for saving his life. He told me he was on the verge of letting go the anchor cable and he would have certainly been swept down the fast flowing Creek and drowned.

Some of the older sailors at Collingwood were married and had married quarters half way between Gosport and Collingwood, here is a joke that was going around at the time about them.

JOKE - 3

This joke is about a matelot who lived in married quarters and was up in front of the Officer of the Day on a charge of being adrift (late) in the morning. He was waiting outside the office with a bunch of other sailors that were late that morning, and he was listening to the other lad's excuses.

When the first matelot went in he was asked why he was late in the morning. Well it was like this sir. My alarm clock never went off on time and my car wouldn't start with the cold weather, so I jumped on to my bicycle and cycled down the road as fast as I could, but I hit a large stone in the middle road which buckled my front wheel. There was a field of horses nearby, so I jumped on to a horse and galloped along the road as fast as I could. The horse took a heart attack with the strain and died, so I had to run the rest of the way, and that is how I was late.

The officer never having heard that excuse before and always on the lookout for new ones decided to let him off with a verbal warning.

As the first sailor came out of the office he smiled to his mate to let him know that he got away with it.

The second sailor hoping to get away with it as well decided to try the same excuse, but because the officer had heard that excuse before, gave him seven days stoppage of pay, and he come out of the office looking miserable.

The third sailor realising what had happened, decided to change the story. Well it was like this sir. My alarm went off in plenty of time, I got up and had my breakfast, kissed my wife goodbye, jumped into my car and it started first time, and I set off down the road. The officer then asked, if everything was going so well, why the hell were you late? Well sir, I couldn't get down the bloody road for broken down bicycles and dead horses!

PORTSMOUTH - 3

I went on many runs ashore to Portsmouth whilst I was at Collingwood. A few of the pubs we used to go to were the Albany, the Fleece, the Mucky Duck, "real name the White Swan", and the Yorkshire Grey. These pubs were all in and around the Centre of

Portsmouth, of course there were other pubs we used to go to but you used to get some real characters in those pubs.

There used to be a prostitute who frequented the Albany and the Fleece, and her name was Big Sylve. As the name suggests, she was a big woman. I never ever saw her go away with anybody, but you used to see stacks of sailors coming in to the pubs and handing Big Sylve a £5 or £10 note. They weren't paying Big Sylve for her services as you might think, they were paying her back money that they had borrowed from her the week before. She was good to the sailors, she used to lend them money when they were broke, and they used to pay her back as soon as they got their wages. They never failed to pay her back as they could always borrow from her again when they were short.

One day I was in the Fleece and Big Sylve was standing at the bar having a drink. A guy came into the bar whom she didn't like, she went up to him, hit him on the chin with powerful right hook, and knocked him flying through the front double swinging doors of the pub, just like you used to see in the Westerns, she then went back to her drink although nothing had happened.

Occasionally I went dancing at the Mecca dance hall after closing time, and it was open to 01:00 in the morning. We sometimes got a taxi back to Collingwood via Fareham, which was almost a twenty-mile journey, or we would stay in the Sailors Home Club just round the corner from the Main dockyard gate in the Hard. It only used to cost us about £1.50 a night, then we would catch the ferry across to Gosport in the morning, then either a bus or a taxi to Collingwood from there.

My Life On The Ocean Waves – Douglas Freeman

I went to a small pub called the Railway at Fratton Bridge near Southsea on Monday's where there was a Folk Club. This club was more of a traditional type, where you sometimes got people up singing through their nose unaccompanied with a hand over their ear.

Most of the time there were no microphones used, but the quality of folk singers and musicians that used to come there was just brilliant, I saw some entertainers play in that small folk club that went on to become famous. Just like all the other clubs that I went to, I always had my turn up on stage. Although I thought of myself as quite reasonable, and always got a good round of applause, there were sometimes singers who went up for a song and they were not very good, but they always got a round of applause for trying.

Another bar we used to go to was The Fleece, it had two doors, one said Saloon Bar, and the other said Lounge Bar. We often arranged to see people in the Fleece, and for the people who hadn't been there before, we said we'd see them in the Lounge Bar of the Fleece. You used to see them coming in the Lounge Bar door and looking round wondering if they were in the right Bar, the comical thing was, it was all the same bar, there was just two different doors to the same place.

A lot of the time we used to drink Scrumpy instead of the usual Brickwoods p*ss, the real Scrumpy always had things floating round in the drink we called grollies, it wasn't a real pint of Scrumpy unless you got grollies. The Scrumpy was also cheaper and stronger than the pints of bitter they served in the pubs.

There were always a few gays in those pubs around the town centre, they never bothered anybody, they preferred to sit on a stool at the bar looking at themselves in the mirror behind the counter, they were more comical than anything else. The gays and the prostitutes seemed to stick together and keep themselves to themselves.

GOSPORT - 1

I used to go to a pub in Gosport called the Queen Charlotte, I went there every Sunday evening to a Folk Club that was held in the pub. I first met Jasper Carrot there, he was hilarious as usual. I saw him quite a few times around the area, I saw a few of his shows on South Parade Peer in Southsea. I always went to see him whenever he came to the area, as the tears used to roll down my cheeks with laughter every time without fail. He gave me a lift back to Collingwood in his red sports car after the pub had closed, he always drove all the way back to Birmingham after each show. He once gave me a signed LP, I still have it.

I also saw Robin Hall and Jimmy McGregor the Scottish Duo in the same pub. I never used to like them as a kid myself, but I must admit they did put on a very professional show, their timing was spot on, which you don't see all that often with groups now a days.

H.M.S. EXCELLENT

I passed all my exams with flying colours, and I was now qualified as an (REM) Radio Electrical Mechanic. I was now on the waiting list for a ship, and I was just hanging around waiting.

What happened next was not what I expected. I was detailed off with the rest of my class and other classes to go to H.M.S. Excellent at Whale Island to train for the royal navy's contribution for the Cenotaph Guard. I suppose my class was chosen because I had done such a great job at training them to be the smartest and best class in Collingwood.

H.M.S. Excellent is the Naval Gunnery School, where you get Gunnery Instructors (GI's). They were the people who trained the entire navy to march properly, and to execute rifle drill, they were renowned for being extremely strict, even with themselves.

The parade ground was made of gravel so you could hear yourselves marching. All other parade grounds in the navy were made of Tar. I remember the GI giving us our first lecture in the shelter at the edge of the parade ground. He said you always double across the parade ground if you have to cross it. There is only one person allowed to walk across my parade ground, and that is GOD! And that is only because I can't see him!

There were full length mirrors in the parade ground shelters so that you could inspect yourself. They were also there to help you perfect your saluting technique. Our uniforms had to be immaculate, our white belt and gaiters had to be blankoed, and our boots had to be spit and polished till you could see your face in them. No matter how hard you tried to spit and polish your boots, the GI's boots were always better, I know they had their own secrets for getting them that good.

One morning the Chief GI doubled across the parade ground to the shelter, he then proceeded to inspect himself in the full size mirror, he gave himself a telling off for having a minute speck of dust on his boots after having doubled across a dry dusty parade ground. He then ordered himself to go once round the parade ground at the double, then came to us and tore us to shreds. We knew it was going to be like this, so we just took everything he said to us with a pinch of salt and not personally.

We marched round and round the parade ground every day with the GI screaming at us, he taught us all the different kinds of rifle drill, and we also went through the whole Cenotaph Ceremony lots of times to make sure we knew every order and command off by heart. We even marched round and round the Island to mimic the long march we were to do through the City of London. By the end of our period there, we were the smartest you could ever see.

At the end of our training I pulled a muscle in my left arm, and I could not do the rifle drill without great pain in my left arm. I had to get infra-red heat treatment from the doctor, but I still had to be there.

Whilst at Whale Island I remember seeing Shep Woolly. He was a GI and he sometimes sang folk and comedy songs in the main mess in the evenings. He was quite good and funny. I will give you one of his songs that he wrote about the Navy at the end of this book, called "Ram It I'm RDP".

My Life On The Ocean Waves – Douglas Freeman

My brother Andrew was a bandmaster in the Army, and one-day he and his band came to Whale Island to play. He was driving, and he didn't know his way round Portsmouth, so he ended going round one of those huge roundabouts in the wrong direction, he wondered why all those idiots on the road were on his side of the road. He got stopped by the police, and he told them he was in the Army. He explained he had made a mistake because he didn't know the area. They asked where he was going, and he said I'm going to see Douglas at H.M.S. Excellent, it was although he expected them to know me personally, anyway, they said follow us, and they showed him all the way to Excellent Main Gate.

It was time to go up to London for the Cenotaph Parade, we went up there on the Friday because some of the lads were detailed off to be at the Lord Mayors Banquet on the Saturday. We were put up in terrible accommodation. I don't know London, but I'm sure this must have been a doss house to tramps and hobo's, as the place was in a terrible state. There were rows and rows of those double angle iron bunk beds. I slept on top of the bed because I didn't want to go between the dirty looking sheets with black spots all over them, some of the sailors did catch crabs after sleeping there, It was a disgrace.

We all went out on the town on the Saturday evening and got drunk, we were told not to take too much to drink, but sailors being sailors, the inevitable happened. On the Sunday morning we had severe hangovers and bloodshot eyes. We then got dressed into our uniforms and marched through the crowded Streets of London to the Cenotaph. We had to stop every so often because of the delays in the parade, and every time we stopped we were being chatted up by girls in the crowd along the pavements. We eventually arrived at the Cenotaph, and I was told to stand behind the Navy Guard up against the wall, because my sore arm was playing up again, and I was there in case I was needed to replace anybody who collapsed etc. We stood there for ages just like we had trained for at H.M.S. Excellent. All around us there were servicemen collapsing, the RAF, the Army, the Guards right across from us, but not one Sailor collapsed. We just stood there like Zombies with bloodshot bleary eyes. It turned out that the Royal Navy were the only service that was allowed ashore the night before, none of the rest were, and we were the only service that didn't have anybody collapse. Something to be proud of I'd say.

When the Cenotaph service was complete, the Navy came to attention, right turned, and marched away into the distance down Whitehall. I was left standing in the crowd with a rifle on my shoulder and a bayonet fixed to the end of it. The funny thing was, I didn't know where they were going, as I expected to be in the guard with the rest of them, so I didn't need to know. I ended up marching through the centre of London with a rifle on my shoulder and a bayonet fixed to the end of it, looking for the Royal Navy Guard! I was half way across one of the London bridges, when I decided it was a bit ridiculous marching around London with a huge bayonet fixed to the end of a rifle. Everybody was looking at me, and wondering what I was up to, so I put the bayonet back into its scabbard, and carried on looking for the Navy. I eventually found them, don't ask me how, just instinct I suppose, I was accustomed to finding my way back to my ship when I got lost in all those foreign places, so London was no different. The rest of the lads had a good laugh when I told them what had happened. I must have been the only sailor in the whole of the royal navy that had marched through the streets "pavements" of London with a rifle and bayonet in peacetime.

After all this was finished, we went back to Collingwood where we waited for our real drafts to come through.

JOKE - 4

The three-badge matelot was in a train going from London to Edinburgh. In the carriage with him were a soldier, an airman and a priest. A young woman came in to the carriage holding a baby and sobbing heavily. The priest asked her what she was crying about, and she said her baby didn't have a father and she didn't know how it was going to cope in life. The priest said, don't worry about it my dear, I don't have a father either, and I went on to become a priest. The airman sitting opposite said don't worry love, I don't have a father either, and look how well I got on in life. The soldier sitting next to him said, what a coincidence, I was born out of wedlock too, and just look at me, a sergeant in the army. The drunken matelot, who was sitting in the corner by the window, took a swig of rum from out of his hip flask, pulled out a blue liner cigarette from its packet and said, "have any of you B*****ds got a light"?

H.M.S. BELTON

The drafts were coming through a few at a time, some to Destroyers, some to Frigates, and I was wandering what kind of ship I was going to get. I got a Mine Sweeper called H.M.S. Belton, I didn't know if that was going to be a good or a bad thing for me, but it turned out to be a great experience that none of the sailors who got drafted to big ships would ever experience.

I left Collingwood and was heading for Scotland once again. H.M.S. Belton was based Port Edgar by South Queensferry, which is quite close to the Forth Rail Bridge on the South side of the Forth, so I was back in familiar territory again.

I remember joining the Belton at South Queensferry, I was met on the gangway of the ship by the ship's dog, called Doogal. He wasn't going to let me on the ship till another member of the crew took me on board, Doogal was the ship's mascot, pet, quartermaster, and guard dog all rolled in to one.

H.M.S. Belton was a Mine Sweeper, but was mostly used as a Fisheries Protection Vessel. It's hard to think where to start with the stories of the Belton, as we were forever on the move, sailing round Britain looking for fishing boats that were fishing illegally.

I would like to mention that we also had two other pets on board, we had a Budgie called Cedric and a Rat called Crappers. There are a few stories to be told about them later on.

My job on the Minesweeper was to maintain and repair the Radio and Radar equipment. The radio equipment never went wrong all the time I was on board, and the radar only ever had a few minor problems. I spent some time servicing the radar equipment, but most of the time I was doing normal watch keeping duties. Here is the watch-keeping schedule of the navy.

00:00 - 04:00 Middle Watch
04:00 - 08:00 Morning Watch
08:00 - 12:00 Forenoon Watch
12:00 - 16:00 Afternoon Watch
16:00 - 18:00 First Dog Watch
18:00 - 20:00 Last Dog Watch
20:00 - 24:00 First Watch

You had to do one or two of these watches every day on a rota, you were also split into Port and Starboard watches. When we were at sea, everybody had to do the general type of duties like, lookout on the Bridge, or steering the ship from the Wheelhouse.

I was also part of the boarding party that went on the fishing boats to test the size of their nets. It was the duty of the boarding party officer to actually do the testing of the nets. We just assisted him with various things. The seamen on board always drove the rubber Gemini, the inflatable rubber boat that we used to board the fishing boats. We were out there in all kinds of rough weather, if the fishing boats were out there, then so were we. We were often called out in the middle of the night when we were sleeping to go and investigate suspicious boats that we suspected my by fishing inside the legal limits. They sounded an alarm like action stations, you used to leap out of your bunk, get dressed in about two minutes, and in about five minutes after being called, we were sitting in the Gemini ready to go into the water. Sometimes it was in the middle of winter and we were absolutely freezing.

The Forth Bridges became a regular sight when leaving and entering the Firth of Forth. The navigating officer had a train time table, and he used to try and judge the speed of the ship from miles out at sea so that the ship was directly under the Rail Bridge when a train was crossing, I suppose it gave him something to do.

LERWICK - SHETLANDS

Soon after joining the ship, we set sail for the North of Shetlands. When we got there I saw hundreds of Russian trawlers on radar, all heading in the same direction just sweeping the ocean clean. Behind them were a few factory ships, and they sucked up the fish from the trawlers with great big Hoovers. The fish in that area didn't have a chance. They were a long way from the Shetland so it was no concern of ours. We did however see a Russian fishing boat inside the Shetland 3-mile limit. We boarded it to see if it had been fishing illegally, when we had a closer look around we saw the fishing nets on the side of the boat were just a few metres long and nailed to the side of the boat. There was no smell of fish and no fish in the hold. There was however aerials all over the boat. It was one of those Russian spy ships, because it had not been fishing we just told it to get out of our waters, and sent it on its way.

Later on we had a close look round a huge Russian Cresta Cruiser that was escorting the fishing fleet North of Shetland. It was quite an impressive looking ship. We were taking photos her, and she was taking photos of us, I think we got the better deal out of the two. It was bulging with missiles and guns, and we had one Bofor gun on the forecastle.

My Life On The Ocean Waves – Douglas Freeman

We went into Lerwick for a few days because the weather was going to get rough, and there were no fishing boats around. Lerwick was quite a good run ashore in those days, the pubs were good and you had a good laugh. I went back there many years after I came out of the navy, and I never recognised anything, it was although I had never been there before.

I remember the ship's Coxswain, he was a Chief Petty Officer and a decent sort of chap, and he had been in the Navy for about 27 years. He came back drunk one night, and this young sh*t of a Midshipman who was Duty Officer of the Day, and who had only been in the Navy for about a few Months charged him with coming back on board drunk. The Coxswain got charged and demoted to Leading Seaman. Because he got demoted he got drafted off the ship soon afterwards, probably to save him any embarrassment.

We went to a Ceilidh in the local hall in the town centre, we went with some of the local girls we met earlier on. There was no drink allowed into the hall and we were searched as we went in, but we were fly, we got the girls to put half bottles of Vodka in their handbags, and we got the Coke from inside, so we had a great time in there after all.

A few days later we went back to sea. We had only been at sea for a few hours when the skipper got a message through the radio. The message was from a woman who wanted her cat back. Apparently one of our crew stayed with this woman for a few days, and when he left he pinched her cat, so the ship had to turn round and bring the cat back to her. The Skipper apologised to the woman, and the sailor said it must have followed him back to the ship without him knowing! Well I believed him!

OBAN - 1

We sailed round to Oban on the West Coast of Scotland, and we were quite glad to get alongside the harbour wall, as we had just come in from a gale. We were only alongside for about an hour and we were told we had to go to sea again, but this time with a detachment of the Territorial Army for an exercise on one of the neighbouring Islands. So we went back out to sea straight into that gale again. All the Army lads were violently seasick, it was lunchtime as well, so we just had to eat our lunch in front of them, what a shame! They were really glad when we reached the island, and they were all eagerly waiting to get their feet on to dry land. But guess what! The exercise was cancelled, and we had to take them all the way back to Oban through that gale again. They just wanted to die, there were bodies lying about everywhere rolling in their own vomit. I've never seen anybody so glad to be back on dry land again as those army lads, and glad they were in the army and not the navy.

Another time we were in Oban, we were coming back to the ship from a good drunken night ashore. On our way back to the ship we saw this huge tarpaulin covering something, when we looked under it, we saw it was great big boxes of prawns, about a hundredweight of them to each box. We thought they wouldn't miss one tiny little box, so we carried a box on board, and got the chef to cook them and store them for us. The skipper was wondering where we got all those prawns from at meal times. We said it was a gift from one of the local fishermen. We were eating prawns for ages, we had more than we could cope with. We came back in to Oban about a week later and we went ashore with carrier bags of cooked prawns, and we gave them away to the locals that we met in the pubs, and also to a few barmen as well. So we did a good turn after all, just like Robin Hood.

I was in Aberdeen for a weekend, and I was in the Malt Mill Pub listening to friends of mine Mike Keavy and Eddie Ross, who are the comedy folk duo called Bunion. I went back to my ship at South Queensferry on the Sunday evening, and we sailed on Monday morning. We sailed round the North of Scotland and down the West Coast to Oban where we arrived on Wednesday. That evening I went ashore with some of my friends, and we went into this pub for a drink. I heard live music coming from over in the corner, and when I looked over, I got the surprise of my life, it was Bunion! They got a shock as well when I shouted to them, " what are you doing here". Mike shouted back to me, never mind us, "what are you doing here". It was a bit of a laugh and a surprise to see each other unexpectedly in a strange place hundreds of miles from Aberdeen, having met them only a few days ago.

DOUGLAS - ISLE OF MAN

We sailed down the West Coast to Douglas Isle of Man. There was nothing much to do there but to visit a few pubs when we went ashore, so we did. In the evening we went to a hotel, and we ended up in the Casino which was part of the hotel. I lost most of my money gambling, but I did meet a girl at the hotel. I must have been drunker than I thought, because I went up to the girl's hotel room, and I must have flaked out, because I can't remember anything about being there, but I do remember waking up in the morning with the strong light shining through the window. I panicked when I saw the time, I was adrift. I looked around the room, but she was gone, then I looked out of the hotel window and got an even bigger surprise, I saw my ship sailing out of the harbour! This was early Saturday morning, and I didn't know what to do about the situation, I had no money, not even to get the ferry to the main land. I didn't want to go to the police in case they kept me in, so I wandered round Douglas all day in the freezing cold wandering what to do. When the evening came it was snowing heavily, so I went to the Salvation Army to see if they would take me in for the night. I knocked at this huge wooden door for ages, eventually somebody came to the door, and I asked if they would let me in, but they told me to go away and slammed the door in my face. I tried to sleep for a while in their doorway to shelter from the snow that was coming down heavily. I'll never forgive the Salvation Army for that night, and I haven't donated any money to them since.

I went to the police on Sunday, I explained what had happened and they issued me with a ferry and rail warrant to get back to my ship. The annoying thing about this whole episode was my ship was going to Aberdeen for the first time, and here was me adrift.

I caught the ferry over to the main land, and caught a train to Aberdeen to re-join my ship. I arrived in Aberdeen on Monday morning just in time to watch my ship coming in to harbour. My ship was berthed alongside Regent Quay, so I went into the Regent Bar to wait for some of my mates to come in. When they came in I got a few pints of beer down my throat to drown my sorrows before going on to the ship, as I knew I was going to be on a charge. I was still in the bar when the skipper came in, he said ah, Freeman, I see you have made it back. You are on a charge, you've got seven days stoppage of pay, seven days stoppage of leave, and you can buy a round of drinks for all she ship's company in the bar, and I'll have a double. The seven days stoppage of leave was no real hardship, as we sailed for a week's exercises at sea anyway, he knew that, that's why he only gave me a week stoppage of leave.

DOOGAL - THE DOG

I mentioned earlier we had a dog on board called Doogal. Doogal was a small dog, he looked like a golden Labrador, he was golden in colour, but he was half the size of a lab, just a good size for a ship our size. Minesweepers were the only ships in the whole Navy allowed to have pets, people would hardly believe me when I told them that we had a dog, a budgie, a rat, and even a gold fish on board a royal navy Minesweeper.

Doogal was treated just like member of the crew, I think he was an Able Seaman. Other minesweepers had dogs as well, but Doogal was the best known of them all. We used to have dog races along the jetty when we were back in our home Port of Port Edgar, which is what the base next to South Queensferry was called. A member of the ship's company from each ship would go to the far end of the jetty and call on their dog, whilst they were held at the other end by somebody. They were all let go together and the first dog to cross the winning line at the far end of the jetty was the winner, Doogal won it quite a few times.

I remember one time we were leaving Port Edgar harbour early one morning, and Doogal was adrift, he didn't make it back from his run ashore the night before. We were out along the Forth, when we got a telex from the Admiral "F.O.S.N.E." Flag Officer Scotland North East. The telex went something like this.

To the Captain H.M.S. Belton.

The good news is, I have found your dog Doogal, he spent last night at my house. The bad news is, do you think you could keep your dog under more control next time, and keep the randy little devil away from my female Goat!

Regards,

F.O.S.N.E.

Doogal got put under a charge just like anybody else, and wasn't allowed ashore for a while.

We were somewhere off the West Coast of Scotland in a severe gale. The Belton was an open topped Minesweeper, open to all the elements like rain and snow. When the ship rolled over in the rough seas, the waves used to lap over into the Bridge wings, it happened to me many times when I was lookout on the Bridge in rough weather. But this time I was in the Wheelhouse steering the ship through the rough weather, it was nothing to be 30 degrees off either side of the main ship's course in rough weather. It was in the middle of the night, and the officer of the watch on the Bridge was a Midshipman. He was violently seasick, when he was trying to communicate with me in the Wheelhouse, he was sick down the voice pipe, and it came flushing out all over me in the Wheelhouse. I was seasick myself that day, I had a bucket just down by my feet to spew into every so often. Doogal was in the Wheelhouse with me that night, he wasn't keeping too well either, when the ship rolled from side to side, he went skidding from one side of the Wheelhouse to the other in the water and spew that was all over the deck. I decided to take Doogal up on to my knee to comfort him and to stop him from skidding all over the place. So there was me, trying to steer a Minesweeper in a force 12 gale in the middle of the night, hanging on to the ships wheel with a dog on my knee, and being sick at the same time. I felt like dying, I don't think I had ever felt as bad as that before, or afterwards, but we survived to carry on another day.

We were on patrol off the coast of Northern Ireland for about six weeks, we used to board and search any ship that we thought may be taking in weapons to Northern Ireland. We did go in to Belfast a couple of times, but we were not allowed ashore. I actually got the Northern Ireland medal for doing that.

Whilst we were in that area we went over to Campbletown on the Mull of Kintyre for a day or so, then we went and did a Minesweeping exercise up the coast towards the Clyde for a few days. It was quite demanding during those exercises, we had to tow all those anti-mine things behind us. In the electrical side, we had to reel out this great big electrical cable which was used to generate a very powerful electrical field to blow up those kind of mines. That wasn't really my field so I didn't have much to do with anti-mine operations, I just had to make sure the Radar and Radio kept operational.

THE SHETLAND - FISHING BOAT

One day we were patrolling off the South West Coast of England, and we spotted a fishing boat on radar, and it was fishing just inside the limit. We went to investigate, but when we got there, it had lifted its fishing gear and started to run away from us. As far as I can remember the fishing boat was European, its name was the Shetland, and it was a very big stern trawler. We eventually caught up with it and it was doing about fifteen knots, but it wouldn't stop even after all out warnings. Our skipper was still determined for us to board her, so we all got armed with grapnel hooks and lines and stood all along the starboard side of our ship, and when we got close enough to the Shetland we threw the grapnel hooks over and caught the hand rails of the other ship and pulled her in towards us. When it was close enough we jumped on to the Shetland and went up to the Bridge, believe it or not, we were issued with SLR rifles and we had a loaded magazine in our pockets. The skipper of the fishing boat wouldn't let us on to the Bridge, but the door was open ajar, and one of our sailors slammed his rifle butt on to the toes of the guy that had his foot in the door. When our officer got into the Bridge, he managed to get the skipper to stop the ship, but when it stopped, it let out one of its anchor cables on to the seabed so we couldn't tow it away.

My Life On The Ocean Waves – Douglas Freeman

The skipper of the fishing boat had got in touch with his own company, and he was trying to get us charged with piracy. I suppose looking through his eyes we must have looked like pirates. We all had those black woollen hats on our heads, we were wearing round polo neck sea jersey's and Wellington boots, we all had a sheath of rigging knives round our waists, and we leaped on board his ship like pirates from the days of Long John Silver.

A few hours after we stopped the ship, the news media were flying round us taking video for the 5 o'clock news. Eventually the owners of the ship told the skipper to comply with our orders, and we escorted them into harbour for the courts to deal with them. The skipper got fined, his nets confiscated, and they were allowed to go.

CRAPPERS THE RAT

I mentioned earlier that we used to have this White Rat called Crappers. He lived in a drawer in the Port side of the Wheelhouse. I remember when I first saw him, I opened up this drawer and it came to meet me, I didn't know whether to touch it or not, as I was new to the ship. I gave it a prod with the plastic Biro pen I had in my hand, and it bit clean through the clear plastic with no effort at all, it was then that I realised how sharp a rat's teeth really were. Eventually it got to know me, and I used to let it crawl up and down my arm and along my shoulders.

Sometimes we used to take Crappers ashore with us. Crappers had a habit of going into your top jacket pocket and popping it's head out when it was least expected, to look around. It was a good laugh when we had ordered a round of beer in a pub, and when you handed the money over to the bar maid, Crappers would run down your arm, and the bar maid would go out with a scream! Crappers got his photo in one of the local papers one day, he was photographed with one of the crew in a pub down the South of England somewhere.

Crappers developed a skin infection and had to be put down. What we actually did, was put him in an old budgies cage and we buried him at sea with full military honours somewhere in the Irish Sea.

CEDRIC THE BUDGIE

Cedric was a blue budgie, and he used to live in the seaman's mess. There was a budgie cage just behind the door where he used to live. There is nothing much I can say about Cedric except he was quite a good speaker. I made a tape recording of him speaking and took it home to let my mother hear him. I still have the tape of the recording, but I don't have a reel to reel recorder to play it on now. One day when we were in Rosyth dockyard having a refit, somebody left his cage door open and he flew out of the mess and through an open hatch and away. We never saw him again.

THE HORSES CLUB

A stoker had just came out of the shower one day, and his mates made a comment about big he was down below, they said it was so big he was rigged like a horse. For some reason known only to them, they decided to start a horses club, to qualify you had to lay it on to, and measure it over a certain amount of holes on a crib board, probably about 15. Because this restricted the club to only a few, the rest of the stokers complained and got the amount of qualifying holes reduced to about 7. But one stoker complained he would never be able to become a member of the horses club because he only had about 2 holes on the crib board, so eventually they did away with this ridiculous crib board idea and just made it a horses club. They made up small membership cards, with your name on it, and you also had to have a name of a horse, there was a Clydesdale, Racehorse, Palomino, Shetland Pony, when they ran out of names of horses to give themselves, one of the stokers called himself a Clothes Horse. It was ridiculous some of the things they got up to just to amuse themselves.

ANTWERP - BELGIUM

I remember one time when my ship went to Antwerp, we had never been there before. About fifteen of us went ashore together this evening and we got quite drunk on the local beer as usual. We separated into smaller groups as the evening went on, and then into pairs as we got lost from each other in the various bars. I ended up on my own, so I had a look round the pubs for some of my mates, but I couldn't find them. I went into this pub and I saw the Jimmy, "who was second in command of the ship" standing at the bar, so I went up to him and said hello. We ended getting absolutely paralytic together. We went from pub to pub, arm in arm, singing all the usual sailor type of songs. Eventually I made my way back to the ship and went to my bed.

The officer of the day was doing his nightly rounds of the mess decks, and he was shining his torch around to see if everybody was asleep. He shone his torch on to my eyes but I didn't blink, I was lying there on my back with my eyes wide open and he thought I was dead, because my eyes didn't react to the torch he was shining in my eyes. But he realised I was still breathing, so he got the sailors on night duty down to the mess, and they tied me in to a Neil Robinson's stretcher, that is the one which binds you together with about four tight straps the full length of your body. They then started to pull me up the ladder out of the mess deck and up to the upper deck, with all this going on, I woke up and shouted, what the f**k is going on. They said you are going to hospital, I said what on earth for, there is nothing wrong with me, but the officer wouldn't listen to me. By this time an ambulance was called to take me to hospital. They put me into the ambulance and drove me away at full speed with the sirens going. The funny thing about all this was, they didn't have an Accident and Emergency department to take me to, and the only hospital they could find to take me in was a Mental Hospital.

When I arrived at the hospital they bound my ankles and wrists to each corner on the bed with leather straps, and a bolt through the straps, I had a lot of trouble trying to convince the doctors I wasn't in here as a mental patient. I eventually persuaded them to take two of the straps off my wrists, but it was difficult, because they could not speak very good English. I was feeling a bit tired, and I knew I was not going to get any farther with them, so I decided to put my head down and go to sleep. They let me out of the two remaining wrist straps in the morning, and I told them to phone my ship to come and collect me. I didn't have any clothes with me, so I asked them to bring some with them.

Whilst I was sitting around this ward looking at all the patients, an old man came up to me and asked if I could speak English, I said yes, and he gave me a letter that was written in English. It was from a girl friend of his that he met during the war, he couldn't read English, and it had never been read to him before, he was really delighted when I read it to him, and the tears came to his eyes when he heard what was in the letter. I didn't think there was much wrong with the old man, he was just stuck in an old system that he couldn't get out of.

The officer came to get me, but he never brought any socks or shoes, so I had to leave on my bare feet. "They must have thought I was mad." I was told it only took one signature to get me in here, but it took me about ten signatures to get me out. No wonder the old man was stuck in there for the rest of his life.

WILLEMSHAVEN - THE NETHERLANDS

I remember the time we went to Willemshaven. As usual again, we had been out on the town all night, and we had been in this hotel, when we came out, a few of the lads stole the hotel sign, this was no ordinary sign, it was about 12 feet long, and it was illuminated. I didn't approve of it being stolen, but I couldn't stop them taking it, one of the lads actually plugged it in, and laid it along the Port side of the ship, this was about 03:00 in the morning so nobody saw it happening. When we got up in the morning, there was amazement all round at this illuminated hotel sign on our ship.

The skipper went spare, but not only about that, there was a full size Red Pillar Box on the Forecastle, God only knows how somebody managed to get that up there, as it was made of cast iron and must have weighed about four hundredweight. There was also a pushbike by the gangway, nobody would have found out about these things, but the pushbike belonged to the security guard on the dockyard gate. He came down, and we all had to muster on the jetty to explain where these things came from. The skipper threatened to charge us all if the people responsible didn't own up. They did own up, and the items were returned to their original locations.

INTER-MESS COMPETITIONS

We used to have inter-mess competitions every so often. One of the competitions we had was Kite Flying. We used to make kites out anything we could get our hands on, from old card board boxes to old tea shirts, and fly them from the aft end of the ship. Some of them flew, but most of them ended up in the Oggin (sea), with a spectacular suicidal nose dive into the waves, but it was good fun whilst it lasted.

We also had Beard growing competitions, you had to be able to grow a complete beard in six weeks. I tried, but I was not very successful, some of them only lasted one week and they had to shave it off as it was so bad. I have a photo of myself standing on top of something at the back of the ship flying a kite and having a beard, it wasn't exactly what you could call a beard. It looked more like something that Bob Dylan would grow just before a concert.

THE THAMES ESTUARY

We used to do a lot of Fishery Protection duties around the Thames Estuary, and we were forever catching French fishing boats fishing well inside the limit. The Thames estuary is the breeding ground for all kinds of fish, but the French were catching these fish before they had a chance to grow. We would catch them with holds full of Cod, only the size of Sardines, apparently these small fish were sold over the counters of the French Cafe Bars as a delicacy.

Some of these French fishing boats were well prepared for encounters with the fishery protection vessels, some were equipped with powerful engines to escape from us when they were spotted.

Because of this, we used to try some devious methods of our own to catch them. At night time we'd put all of our normal lights out on the ship, and we'd put fishing lights up our own mast. These are a sequence of lights that lets other ship know that a fishing boat is actually fishing and to keep clear in case they get in the way of the nets. Then we'd go along at the same speed as other fishing boats in the area, they would be looking out on radar for us, but they'd think we were one of them. When we got close to the fishing boat we were after, we'd switch on all of our superstructure lights and also a 20" search light and illuminate them. They'd get the biggest scare of their lives when this happened, it was like a flying saucer suddenly appearing right above you. They still used to try and get away by instantly cutting their nets and speeding away with their fast engines, and some of them actually did. We were getting fed up of this, so one night we went right up alongside one of them and we dropped our anchor on to their Bow, saying, try getting away now you B*****d! We would then board the fishing boat and escort them round to Dover, where their catch would be confiscated, their nets costing thousands of pounds would also be confiscated, and they would also get fined thousands of pounds. The fishing boat crew held no animosity towards us. They would give us Brandy in cups of coffee, so we were quite happy, and they were also pleased to get a run ashore in Dover themselves.

Our skipper used to leave Dover harbour at a high speed, but the unusual thing was, we were going astern at the time. We used to call it, "leaving harbour manoeuvres". I think we were the only ship in the navy to do it like that, It was quite impressive.

RUNNING AGROUND - LOCH MADDAY

We were anchored in a horseshoe bay called by Loch Madday, North Uist, Outer Hebrides, off the West coast of Scotland. The captain was ashore meeting with some people, but whilst he was ashore, the weather blew up to about a force 13 storm. We were keeping a continuous watch on the weather, and also a continuous radar watch on some fixed points on the land. I noticed that the radar echoes were moving slowly, which meant we were dragging anchor, this was due to the strong wind blowing against the ship. I reported this to the officer of the watch, and he got the whole ships company on watch in preparation for going to sea again. The captain was recalled from shore as the ship was still dragging anchor. When he arrived back on board, the captain decided to lift anchor and head back out to sea to ride out the storm. We went to our special sea duties, that is the special duties that you have when you enter and leave harbour. My special sea duty was on the depth recorder in the chart house. I had to read out continuous depth readings into a microphone, which came out on a loudspeaker on the Bridge. Five fathoms, four fathoms, three fathoms, two fathoms, one fathom, just then I felt a jolt and the ship came to a sudden stand still, and I said, NO FATHOMS!

I then realised we had run aground, but I didn't think it was too serious. We tried to go astern and pull ourselves off the rocks, but unfortunately for us, we ran aground dead on high tide, and as the tide started to go down, the more we got stuck on the rocks. Eventually, after hours of trying, the skipper realised we were not going to get off the rocks that night, so the order to abandon ship was given.

The wind was blowing strong, and it was very dark, we threw jumping ladders over the side, and we even managed to put down the ships gangway, so we could just walk down the gangway on to the rocks. The first members of the crew off the ship was Doogal the dog, Crappers the Rat and Cedric the Budgie, the rest of us followed later. After we had all mustered on the rocks wondering what was to happen next, the First Lieutenant decided he would try and salvage some of the ammunition of the ship, a bloody stupid decision if you ask me, endangering the lives of the crew again. He got all of the crew back on to the ship, which was leaning heavily on its side by now, and filling up rapidly with water, and commenced to unload shells and ammunition. The ammunition locker, which was below our mess deck, and also below the water line, was half full of water. It just so happens that the ammunition locker was also the Beer locker, and there were dozens of cans of beer floating around as we were passing the shells up the ladders. So we drowned our sorrows by opening a few cans of beer whilst we were up to our waists in water and passing the heavy shells out of the hatch. After about half a dozen cans of beer, we were slinging those shells up the hatch without a care. We were frozen to the bone, submerged in cold sea water, and our lives being put at risk by doing what we thought was a bloody stupid exercise throwing live ammunition about in the dark, lit only by a few torches.

We got a lot of ammunition on to the rocks before it was called to a halt and everybody had to get off the ship again. I managed to get a few photographs of us sitting on the rocks in the dark, and also of the ship on its side during day light.

When you saw the ship during the day, you'd wonder how it managed to get stuck so high up on the rocks, it looked like Noah's Ark, sitting high and dry on top of a hill. A tug eventually arrived, but it took quite a few turns of the tide before it managed to pull the ship off the rocks due to the high tide when we ran aground.

Eventually we were transported down to Greenock on the Clyde to await the arrival of the ship after it had been towed from Loch Madday. We were put up in horrible dump of a Salvation Army Hostel, why they didn't put us up in some decent accommodation like a B&B or Hotel, or even at the Royal Navy base at Faslane across the water I'll never know or understand.

All of our belongings were ruined with the salt water and was written off, we had to put in a claim for all the items of clothing we lost, and we were given money to buy new clothes and uniforms etc.

We didn't stay in Greenock very long, and we were transferred over to H.M.S. Cochrane at Rosyth till they decided what to do with a whole Minesweeper's crew without a ship to go to.

We were given about a week's leave to get over our ordeal, so I went home to Aberdeen to relax for a while and tell everybody my story of how I ran aground in a royal navy Minesweeper. I also got all of my photos developed to show the lads when I returned to H.M.S. Cochrane. I took orders from members of the crew who wanted copies of my photos, including the skipper.

H.M.S. CHAWTON

When I arrived back at Cochrane after my leave, I was told we were to get another Minesweeper and keep the whole crew together. We were absolutely delighted. There was a Minesweeper in mothballs out in Gibraltar called H.M.S. Chawton, and we were to fly out there and sail her back to the Firth of Forth.

We flew out to Gibraltar from RAF Brize Norton, and when we arrived, we proceeded to get the Chawton Sea worthy, she was a good ship, and there was even an enclosed Bridge, which we thought was a luxury.

We obviously had a few runs ashore in Gib before we sailed back to the UK. But there was one thing comical that sticks out in my mind, and that is the extremely cheap bottle of Vat 69 Whisky that I bought to take back with me to the UK. We arrived back in Port Edgar at South Queensferry on the Forth after a few days sailing. I then went on a weekend home to Aberdeen, but before I went, I collected my bottle of Vat 69 Whisky to take home with me. When I had a closer look at the label on front of the bottle, it said, "Bottled in South Queensferry Scotland". So I went all the way to Gibraltar to get a bottle of Whisky that was bottled just up the hill, but I bought it for about half the price.

After we got settled in to our new ship, we re-commenced our fishery protection duties. We were at sea one day and the weather was a bit rough, the swell was also quite big and the ship was going up and down quite a lot. It was early morning when I went out to the upper deck with my pal, I was climbing down a ladder, and my pal was standing at the top. He was feeling happy with himself, so he threw his arms up and jumped up in the air, saying "good morning world". Just then, the ship went down, and left him stranded about twenty feet up in the air, he came back down with a thud half way down the deck when the ship came back up again, he was very lucky not to have landed over the side.

We were in bad weather once again, the rain was pouring down, the visibility was very bad, and we were heading in to Oban for another visit. My opposite number was on special sea duty on the echo sounder this day, he was dying for the toilet so he asked me to take over from him whilst he went for a "P". I started reading out the depth readings once again, five fathoms, four fathoms, three fathoms, two fathoms, one fathom, just then I heard the skipper shout, "full astern both engines", and he came rushing down to the wheel house to look at the echo sounder. He was sh**ing himself, as he thought we were just about to hit a sandbank. My pal forgot to tell me he was on the 20 fathom scale, and to add 20 fathoms to the actual depth readout, and I forgot to check, so we were both at fault. We got a rollicking from the skipper for not doing things properly, but he was sure relieved there was 20 fathoms to add to the one fathom reading I last gave him. He didn't want to run aground again.

We had a really good skipper, he loved his ship, and his crew, and we couldn't have asked for anybody better. He got court-martialled for the Belton running aground, but he only got a severe reprimand, although that probably went against him for future promotion.

Whilst I was in Minesweepers, I passed some electrical exams, which gave me promotion to REM3, so I had one star above my badge. That is equivalent to an able seaman like I was before I changed branches, I didn't get a pay rise because I was on that rate of pay already, but at least it was a step forward.

RAF PITREAVIE - THE PIT

When I left the Chawton I went back to H.M.S. Cochrane, but I was to work at an underground communications centre at

Pitreavie Castle, although it was called RAF Pitreavie, "The Pit". Civilians and Navy personnel mostly manned it. I worked a shift type of system there, doing days and nights, and then I'd get about four days off, so I'd go home to Aberdeen in my time off. I was doing a high security job in The Pit so I can't say any more about that.

Whilst I was there, I did do some singing around the area, and I used to go again to the pubs that promoted the folk scene. I was introduced to this female that sang folk songs, and we sang together for a short while, going to barbecues etc to sing, she was quite good but I'm really a solo singer so that partnership didn't last very long.

BILLY CONNOLLY

I went to Kirkcaldy to see Billy Connolly one evening, and I brought my guitar along with me just in case. I asked the organisers if it was OK for me to go up and give a song during the break, and they didn't mind. I don't know why I did this, because it happened to be a Billy Connolly concert, and there were thousands of people there to see him, and not to see me, I was wondering what I was letting myself in for. I was watching his show, and it was quite funny, it was the time he was doing his Jesus jokes and the audience was in stitches. When it came to the first half interval Billy Connolly introduced me. And now ladies and gentlemen, just back from a successful tour of Europe, put your hands together and please welcome the one and only Doug Freeman. A big round of applause went up, I didn't actually expect to get called up, so you can imaging the shock I got when Billy called out my name, I could have died, my mind went blank, what am I going to sing. Anyway I sang about four numbers and they went down well with the audience, so I was relieved about that, then I went back down and watched the rest of the show. I was walking around like a celebrity, with strangers coming up to speak to me and saying, where in Europe were you singing? "Time for a quick sharp Harp"!

HELENSBURGH - SCOTLAND

My brother Bill also changed branches whilst he was in the Navy, he changed from being an RP2 to a PTI, Physical Training Instructor, and he was at H.M.S. Caledonia just up behind Rosyth Dockyard whilst I was at Cochrane. We sometimes went for a few drinks together to the pubs in the area, but mostly he used to go back to his Wife Jenny and daughter Lorraine at the weekends. He lived in Helensburgh, and I used to go over with him on occasional weekends. He'd pick me up in his car and we'd drive over to Helensburgh, and drive back over to Rosyth early on the Monday morning. We'd have quite a heavy session at his house over the weekend, and I'd be singing and playing my guitar all the time, he'd get friends and neighbours round for the party, and I would always end up with the biggest hangover you could ever imagine. I'd wake up on the Saturday morning with my head under the blanket to keep the light out of my eyes, and Bill would sneak up and take a close up photo of my head in the morning. We used to collect "heeds" as we'd call them, and I would take a few "heeds" of him as well, when he flaked out.

MY FATHER DIED

One day I was called to the main gate at H.M.S. Cochrane, Fife, Scotland. The Officer of the day told me my father "Da" had died. He had been ill in hospital for some time with Silicosis of the lungs. He was a building stone mason and he must have developed that disease whilst dressing granite stones and getting the stone dust in the lungs over the years.

Bill also phoned about the same time to inform me in case I hadn't been told the news. We arranged compassionate leave, and Bill drove me up to Aberdeen for the funeral. All the family were there, that's the only time my Brother's and Sister's get together, when somebody dies, which is probably just as well, with all the usual family arguments. All the Brother's went down to the White Horse Lounge Bar for a few drinks, which ended up more than just a few, but we had a good laugh together as we hadn't seen each other very often with being in the services.

My father lay in the small bedroom of the house for people to come and see him. The day of the funeral I was last out of the bedroom and watched the undertakers nail the coffin lid. I apologised to my father for using his black tie, I didn't have one of my own, so I used his, and it was only ever used at funerals anyway.

H.M.S. GLAMORGAN

After my time at Cochrane was complete, I was drafted to H.M.S. Glamorgan, which is a County class Destroyer. Before I joined the Glamorgan, I went back to H.M.S. Collingwood for a

PCT, that is Pre Commissioning Training, for a couple of weeks as I was to work in the ship's computer room, so I was given a special course on the Poseidon computer that the Glamorgan had. I joined the Glamorgan down at Portsmouth whilst the ship was in for a refit. I boarded the ship in the middle of the night, all the crew from the mess deck was ashore, and the mess was in darkness. I was given the only spare bunk in the mess, there was no mattress in it, so I had to go and get one. I was told somebody had died in that bunk, that's why it was always empty. I was feeling tired so I just went to bed and fell fast asleep, but it did feel a bit eerie.

    I awoke with a start a few hours later thinking I was drowning, I switched on my bunk light, and there was a drunken sailor standing there pissing all over me. I said what the f**k is going on here, he thought that bunk was still empty, and decided to relieve himself there rather than going to the heads. I almost thumped him, but he apologised to me as best he could in his drunken state, so I thought it was best just to let things go. That sailor turned out to be Frank Cripps, who ended up being one of my best friends on the ship.

    After the ship was painted and fit for sea again, we went to Portland to do our usual pre commissioning exercises, and after sailing around for a while in UK waters, we set sail for the Mediterranean again.

THE MED - 3

The ship arrived at Gibraltar, it was good to be in the Mediterranean sun again. I had passed my exams for Killick whilst I was at Cochrane and I was due to pick up my rate the next day, so my mates took me for a run ashore in Gib. We went round nearly every pub in Gib, and I got extremely drunk as you'd expect. The next thing I remember was waking up on a pavement bench seat just outside the dockyard gate at 06:30 in the morning. I was adrift, I had to be back on board by 06:00, and the ship was sailing at 08:00. Needless to say I never got my promotion that day, thanks to my friends. My promotion was suspended for six weeks but I eventually got made up to acting L.R.E.M. "Leading Radio Electrical Mechanic".

There was a song that some sailor wrote about the pubs in Gib, those who could remember it used to sing it, so I think this is an appropriate time to mention it, having been to Gib and all round them many times myself.

THE GIBRALTAR NATIONAL ANTHEM

Oh please daddy will you take me to Gibraltar
I want to see the rock and the big baboons
I want to go out there at night
To see if what I've heard is right
I want to see if chiefy can fly around the moon

cho
Eros, Tivoli, Spitroast and Pulxerine
Spinning Wheel, Smoky Joe's and Oliver Twist

My Life On The Ocean Waves – Douglas Freeman

Horse Shoe and Devil's Tower
Chimney Corner after hours
By four in the morning we will all be pissed

Oh please daddy will you take me down to main street
I want to spend a fortune in the flashy stores
I want to buy a postcard of
A pretty looking Geisha girl
When you tip it sideways she winks and drops her drawers

Oh please daddy will you take me to the Eros
I want to see nudes without their clothes
I want to see if Henry's there
His pants and bra up in the air
I don't know what you call it but I think he's one of those

Oh please daddy will you take me to the ape den
I want to see the rock apes large and small
They say that we shall leave the rock
When there's no apes left at all
I think I'll set a Bren gun up and shoot them all

Oh please daddy will you take me back to England
I've had about enough of this rock you know
I know I should be dutiful
But Henry's looking beautiful
That's a certain sign that it's time to go.

My job on the Glamorgan as I said earlier was in the Computer Room. I tried to get moved to some other departments on the ship during my time on board, to gain experience on other types of equipment. The chief in the computer room wouldn't let me go, because nobody else knew about the equipment I was working on, so I was stuck there all of my time on the Glamorgan. It was a pity, as I would have liked to see how the other departments were, especially in the Operations Room with me having been an Radar Plotter in the past.

THE MAG DRAIN ARMS

The electrical mess I was in held about 60 people. I spent quite a while in the same bunk that I was put in to when I first joined the ship, which was in the central part of the mess deck. This part of the mess was also used for the main recreational part of the mess for everyone, which had tables and chairs where they played cards etc, and generally just sat around. There was not very much privacy where I was situated. Each bunk area had three bunks, top, middle and bottom. If you had the top bunk you could lie up there out of the way. The middle bunk was folded down to make a back rest, and the bottom bunk was used as a seat. So if you had the middle bunk and especially the bottom bunk, you couldn't always get to your bed when you wanted to, not without complaints from the sailors that were sitting there anyway. With me now being a killick, I managed to get moved to another part of the mess deck on the port side of the mess. This part was slightly segregated from the main part of the mess and there were just killick's there, I managed to get a top bunk so I was happy about that, I could go and lie down any time I wanted to, great!

I used to play my guitar in this part of the mess, we would sit down with our cans of beer that we had for our daily ration, and have a sing song for an hour or so. Everybody had at least one verse of a song that they knew, and I used to play along with them which made them happy.

We decided to decorate our mess and give it the theme of a pub. There was a round handle in the corner of our part of the mess, and it was a control for the Magazine Drain, and just above it were the words Magazine Drain. So we called our mess the "Mag Drain Arms", I don't suppose it was the best name in the world we could have chosen, but it gave us a laugh anyway.

MALTA - 3

Our next port of call was Malta, I had been there a few times before and I knew the place well by now. We had a bit of general ship's maintenance to be done to the ship, so the ship ended up staying in Malta for about two or three weeks, I can't remember how long exactly but it was quite a while.

We were in tropical routine, which means we only worked in the morning, then we had the afternoon and evenings off. Some of the ship's crew even took some leave there, they hired a flat and lived ashore for a week. I just went ashore to go swimming in the afternoons at a RAF base along the coast and came back to the ship for supper. I went snorkelling a lot, and I gradually developed the ability to hold my breath under water longer and longer each day. One day I was lying on the seabed about fifteen feet below the water just watching the fish go by. I felt I had been down under the water for ages and I had to make a conscious decision to swim back to the surface. The unusual thing about this was I didn't want a breath of air, so I got a bit worried about that, I thought I could not possibly stay under water this long and not want air. So as I said, I swam to the surface and took a breath of air just for the sake of it, not because I felt I needed it.

JOKE - 5

The three badge Matelot was walking down the Gut one evening Malta, when he heard this sound coming from a dark doorway, Pssst! Jack, Pssst! Jack. Being curious, he went over to see what the sound was, and there standing in the shadow of a doorway was this big fat Maltese Prostitute. She said Pssst! Jack, would you like something you've never had before. He thought for a while and said, why, have you got Leprosy?

THE MALTESE HILTON

One evening we decided to have a posh night out instead of going down the Gut. We went to the Hilton Hotel, the beer cost more than we were used to paying down the Gut, but we managed to sink quite a few. My friend and I ended up having a stupid argument about the singer who was singing by the piano. I said he sounded like Frank Sinatra, and my friend said he didn't, anyway we were arguing so loud the bouncer threw us both out by the scruff of the neck, we landed in the bushes outside the front door in a fit of laughter. So much for our posh night out, getting kicked out of the Hilton. Where can we go from here we thought to ourselves? Back down the Gut!

We enjoyed our stay in Malta, and after our ship was gleaming again, we set sail once again for Greece.

GREECE - 2 KAVALLA

I went ashore with one of my friends Frank Cripps, although we were always arguing about something or other, we were the best of friends. We spent the evening going from pub to pub, but it was a funny place, there didn't seem to be anything to keep us amused, so by the end of the evening we decided to go back to the ship. We were walking back along the main town road, which runs parallel to the water, and we were commenting on all these beautiful millionaire's yachts and cabin cruisers that were moored alongside. We heard party music coming from one of them, so we had a closer look to see what was going on, when the people on board saw us they invited us aboard. We were delighted to oblige, after having spent a boring night in town. The party was great, there were stacks of beautiful girls, stacks of music, and stacks of free drink, what more could you ask for.

We were partying all through the night till the early hours of the morning. Frank and I were drinking white rum so we got rather drunk. I must have flaked out, because when I woke up nearly everybody had gone, even Frank. I was almost late getting back to my ship. I told the guy who owned the cruiser I had to be back to my ship in about half an hour, and it was anchored off Kavalla and I had almost certainly missed the liberty boat to take me back on board, so he gave me a lift back to my ship in the small outboard dinghy that hung off the back on the cruiser.

As we were speeding through the water he was telling me about Frank. He must have taken off his uniform, because when he woke up it had gone, and Frank was last seen walking along the jetty with a towel round his waist heading for the liberty boat pick up point.

I was actually back before him, and it was a laugh seeing him coming back on board with only a towel round his waist, and all the ship's company having a good laugh about it, but Frank got charged for coming back without his uniform.

GREECE - 3 THE FIGHT

I had another run ashore in Greece with Frank Cripps. We went ashore early in the day, and we had a great time soaking up the atmosphere. We sampled the kebab's from the numerous small stalls dotted all around the small town centre. We were sitting in an open-air cafe knocking back the Ouzo. We ordered two Ooze's to start with, and the waiter came up with two small bottles of Ouzo, two glasses of water and two empty glasses to mix the Ouzo and water in together, as they regarded the Ouzo as a strong drink. After two drinks like that we thought to hell with it, and when we got the next orders we just drank the Ouzo's right out of the bottles. Needless to say we got pretty drunk.

We lay off the drink for a while and started again when we went to some other pubs. I can't remember the details, but we started arguing over some female, we weren't even with her, we were just arguing about her. And for some reason we started fighting. There was an open-air park nearby and we ended swapping punches all around this park, he pulled down a tree and hit me over the head with it, I ripped up a park bench and hit him over the head with that, we were going berserk. The American Naval Police were driving by and saw us, they tried to restrain us but we were like two wild animals. They put us in the back of their meat wagon and we were at each other's throats in the back of the van as well. They put us on to a landing craft to take us back to our ship as it was anchored offshore. We started fighting all over the landing craft as well. These Yanks had never seen anything like it before. Then one of the Yanks said, you are approaching your ship now, and I said, hey Frank, were home. When we realised where we were, we immediately stopped fighting and put our arms round each other like the best of pals, and climbed up the jumping ladder to the ship. Our uniforms were in tatters, and we had lost our hats. We never got charged for fighting, but we did get charged for coming back to the ship with our uniforms all ripped to pieces, I think the charge was bringing the Navy in to disrepute.

ISTANBUL -TURKEY

After Greece, we sailed for Istanbul, through the Dardanelle's, which was a very interesting place, with a lot of ancient fortresses and castles along the way. Across the Sea of Marmara to Istanbul, which is located by the Bosporus leading to the Black Sea.

When we went ashore in Istanbul, we went mainly to the big hotels. All the sailors behaved themselves whilst they were there, I think mainly because we had recently watched the movie Midnight Express, and none of the lads wanted to end up in one of those Turkish jails. Especially with the terrible conditions and also with the thought of staying in one of them for years.

As far as I can remember, I just did a bit of sightseeing and had a few beers there, but nothing unusual sticks out in my mind worthy of a mention.

RETURN TO THE UK - 2

Our next destination was back to the UK via our usual call at Gibraltar. I remember I had one of these unusual Special Sea Duties whilst I was on the Glamorgan, and this particular one was up inside the forward mast just behind the radar's. I never really knew why I had to be up inside a mast whilst entering or leaving harbour. I just sat on a coil of rope and looked out of a small hatch on the mast at the scenery. That's exactly what I did when we entered Portsmouth harbour on our return from the Med. It was great up there. I saw all the families lined up along the jetty waving to the sailors they recognised, and most of the sailors were all lined up along the side of the ship in their best uniforms for the occasion. But I was quite happy with myself looking at them all out of my little crow's nest up the mast and thinking about my run ashore in a few hours' time.

After a while, my time on the Glamorgan was up and I was drafted to H.M.S. Collingwood again, but this time was it to do my L.R.E.M.s (Leading Radio Electrical Mechanic) course.

H.M.S. COLLINGWOOD - 2

I was pleased at last to be commencing my advancement in electronics. I learned more about radio and radar and about certain kinds of radar in particular during these courses. I passed all my exams with flying colours and I was given my new badges to sew on to all my clothes. I can't remember how many times I have had to replace all my badges, but it is a bit of a pain if you have to sew them all on by hand, so usually I got my ones sewn on by machine.

There were two Kenyans in my class, one was called Ndungu, he was a boxer in his own country, and he boxed and won for the royal navy against the army whilst he was here. He was quite a small guy, and quiet too. The other one was called Philip, but was always called Makanyanga after a Kenyan comedian. He was always happy and joking, so he was well named. He also had a way with the women too, he seemed to be with a different one every night, and he used to return to the base in the morning after a good night in the town looking knackered and rough. He must have been quite intelligent, because he never studied, he was always too tired in class to show any real interest, yet he came joint top of our class.

Makanyanga was blacker than Ndungu, but we used to say it was the other way round, and they ended up having an argument about who was the blackest, because back in Kenya, the blacker you were the sexier you were to the women, but it was all taken in fun.

My Life On The Ocean Waves – Douglas Freeman

There was a killick on the same floor of my accommodation named Bruno Cozzi, nick named Swim. I was playing my guitar to myself one day, and he being only in the next mess up heard me playing, so he came round to see who it was. It turned out that he also played the guitar, so we ended up having a few songs together. Eventually we managed to get moved into the same mess together, so we often had a song or two at lunch times and in the early part of the evenings. One Saturday we were sitting on our bunks having a practice session and Swim decided to record us on his big reel to reel tape recorder. It was just set up on a table in front of us, and we sang any song that came in to our minds at the time, at the end of our session we played it back and we were surprised how well the recording came out. I eventually copied that tape on to a small cassette, I also gave a copy of it to Swim. I still have that cassette tape to this day and I play it every so often, my wife also used to play it in the car when she was travelling to and from her work.

We eventually got around to playing at a few places. We played a few songs in Collingwood N.A.A.F.I. for some sort of show they were having at the time.

Swim met this Wren called Sally, she was also interested in singing and also in the sort of songs we did. She sang with us for a few songs but it was difficult for us to get the practice in together, so swim and I mostly did all the singing. I think Swim was more interested in Sally herself than in her singing voice.

Swim was a good friend of mine, but I never saw him again after I got drafted from Collingwood, but I did hear somewhere that he got married to Sally.

I can't remember where Swim got drafted to, but when I finished my training I got drafted to H.M.S. Nubian, this ship as you can gather by its name is another tribal class frigate. I was particularly delighted to hear that it was based in Rosyth and that it was destined to go to the West Indies.

LEAVE - 4

I was due another spell of leave, so I went straight to Aberdeen from Collingwood, with my kit bag, cases, guitar, and everything else that I owned. I was soon home again and settling in to a few beers with my friends.

I remember one Saturday afternoon I was in the Continental Lounge of the Masada Bar, and I was told a chap called Bob Richardson was coming in later on, and he was also joining H.M.S. Nubian at the same time as myself. We decided to play a joke on him when he arrived, and to say that I was joining the Nubian as a Regulator, that is the Naval Police.

When he arrived he was introduced to me, and he was told that I was a Regulator in the navy. I kept up this act of pretending to be a Regulator for about an hour, but I couldn't stand the looks and sarcasm he was giving to me anymore, so I relented and told him I was the same rate as him and in the same electronics branch as himself. We all had a good laugh about it afterwards, all except Bob of course!

My friends in Aberdeen were forever borrowing money off each other. One day there was about eight of us around a table in the Masada Bar. My friend to the left of me asked for the five pound note he loaned to me the week before, so I put my hand in my pocket and gave it to him. Just then, the person to his left asked for that same five pound note from him that he had borrowed from him. That same five pound note went round everybody at the table and eventually came back to me, because the guy to my right was due me a fiver. So I had my own original five pound back in my pocket, and the whole eight of us were clear of the five pound debt to each other. Some body shouted, now that you are the only one with money, it's your round!

I had been to an Indian Restaurant for a meal after a night on the town with my friends, and I was making my way home down along Union Street. I decided to take a short cut along Union Terrace, but half way along I sat down for a while because I was feeling a bit weary. I must have fallen asleep, because I woke up about 05:30 with the birds chirping all around me. I found myself lying on a very narrow ledge, and all I could see was the sky. A kind of shock went through me, as I thought I was lying on some narrow ledge on the top of some tenement building. I slowly turned my head round to the right, and I was so relieved to see I was only 18 inches off the ground and I was lying on a ledge about 9 inches wide that goes round the base of the Robert Burns statue half way along Union Terrace in the middle of Aberdeen.

H.M.S. NUBIAN

I joined H.M.S. Nubian at Rosyth dockyard. The ship had been in for a refit and most of the crew were also new to the ship just like myself. We all spent a few weeks getting to know each other by working hard and getting the ship up to standard. I spoke about what it was like during a ship's refit earlier on in the book, and this refit was no different. Everything was in complete chaos till the end. We had to get the ship up to a very high standard of cleanliness, and the captain, to make sure we were on schedule, regularly inspected the ship. Finally the admiral came round when everything was complete to give his seal of approval.

As mentioned earlier, we also had to do ships trials, first of all out in the Firth of Forth, and again down at Portland. When the ship's seaworthiness was passed, we eventually sailed for the West Indies for a nine month trip.

BERMUDA

Our first port of call was to the sunny island of Bermuda. The ship arrived in the early morning and anchored a few miles out in the bay. I think we had to wait for the tide or something before the ship was allowed to go alongside the harbour wall.

Because of the shifts they were working, quite a few stewards and other sailors were allowed to go ashore early. A liberty boat was arranged to take them ashore a few hours before the ship was due alongside the jetty. We were envious of them getting ashore before the rest of the ship's crew.

The only mode of transport to get around the Island was mopeds, and there were a few shops just across the road with dozens of them lined up outside for hire. Most of the sailors who were first ashore hired a moped and zoomed away for a sight-seeing trip around the local area, stopping off at every pub they came across for a few beers.

It was about lunchtime, and I was off shift when the ship was making its way sideways towards the jetty. I was standing on the upper deck looking at what was going on, when I heard the loud sound of mopeds racing round the sandy surface of the jetty. The next thing I saw was about three or four Evil Kinevil drunken sailors' zoom straight off the jetty right into the water. We killed ourselves laughing at them. A few minutes later a few more drunken sailors came skidding down the road, crashed into something and went sliding along the gravel surface of the road on their sides. The amazing thing about this was we were watching all this unfold and the ship was not even alongside yet!

I was on duty that first day so I didn't go ashore. The next day I went to an American Navy PX club for a few beers with some friends. We went by a mini bus, which was laid on by the Yanks; you weren't going to get me on one of those mopeds.

The third day the captain mustered all of the ship's crew on the jetty. They looked like something out of World War 2. About half the ship's crew had been injured on mopeds in some way or another. They were standing on the jetty on crutches, with broken legs, broken arms, and bandages round their heads, I only wish I had a camera to take a photo of that sorry looking lot. We called that condition "Mopy Rash".

The captain gave the crew a severe telling off and cancelled all shore leave. He said, I have no other option but to stop all shore leave because half of my ship's crew are injured or incapacitated, and if I allow the other half of my crew to go ashore today I would have no crew left to sail with tomorrow. He was right of course!

We set sail from Bermuda on our way to Fort Lauderdale in Florida. I can't remember why, but I got quite drunk on cans of beer. I'd never done that on any of my previous ship's, it must have been someone's birthday or something. A very strange thing happened to me that evening; I disappeared for a few hours without knowing where I'd been. All my friends had been looking for me for hours. When I eventually came back down the mess, they asked me where I had been. I didn't know, and I didn't even know I'd been missing. We all had a good laugh about it. Doug went missing in the "Bermuda Triangle"!

FORT LAUDERDALE - AMERICA

The weather was bright and sunny when we arrived at Fort Lauderdale. There is one thing that really stands out in my mind, and that is the ship's main notice board. There were dozens of letters from American families wanting to take a sailor home with them and treat him just like one of their own family for a day or two and to show him a good time sight-seeing etc. We were overwhelmed with their kindness and generosity. Some people asked for a sailor from a particular part of the United Kingdom as they probably had friends or relations in that area and they wanted to hear that accent again.

I didn't take up any of those offers, I just went ashore to the local pubs for a few games of pool. We found one pub in particular that was very friendly, so we just kept going back to that pub every day to play the locals at pool. I was quite good at playing pool at that time, and I used to thrash the locals all the time. They eventually gave me the nick name "JAWS", meaning I was a pool shark.

One day I was playing a game of pool with a guy in the pub I had never seen before. I noticed he had a different accent from the locals, so I asked him where he came from and what he was doing here. He said he came from New York and that he was here looking for somebody called Jaws! I said that's what the locals call me because I beat them at pool all the time, not because I am all that good, it's just because they are crap at pool.

I told him I was off the visiting royal navy ship in the harbour and we had been here for about ten days, and I was leaving in a few days' time. It turned out that he was a real pool shark and he came here to play me "JAWS" because he thought I was a real pool shark. We had a good laugh about how the rumour got round about me in just ten days, all the way to New York.

I don't normally play for money, but he persuaded me to play doubles with him at $5 a game against the gullible locals. Needless to say we won all the games all night till they got fed up losing. Well it was not my fault they were stupid enough to play us for money, wasn't it?

GUATEMALA AND BELIZE - WEST INDIES

It was whilst I was in Fort Lauderdale that we got news that Guatemala was threatening to invade Belize. I hadn't even heard of Belize up until then, or even where it was, but the ship had been given orders to sail as soon as possible. We were all a bit apprehensive about the developing situation, as we were heading into a possible war environment, and we didn't know what to expect.

We arrived at the Guatemala and Belize border a few days later and set up a patrol, keeping an alert watch on our radar's for possible air or sea attacks by the Guatemalan forces. We later found out that Guatemala had only a few Cessna training aircraft in their airforce, which posed no real threat to us.

The Guatemalan army had formed all along the Belize border threatening to invade, and the British army was soon deployed to defend Belize. The immediate threat of invasion eventually subsided and things began to calm down a bit, so we were eventually allowed to go ashore to a small village in Belize, where we enjoyed a few beers.

The Royal Air Force was also deployed near the City of Belize further to the north with a squadron of Harrier jump jets. We were soon getting daily attacks from the Harriers to help them develop their attack skills and for us to fine tune our defence skills with our anti-aircraft missile and gunnery radar's.

After the British army got settled in along the Belize border, they invited a team of sailors to spend a few days with them in the jungle, and we reciprocated by inviting a few soldiers to our ship to see how the navy lived. I decided not to volunteer for the trip in the jungle, as there were too many mosquito's and all kinds of stinging insects, including scorpions and centipedes about a foot long who like to make their bed in the warmth of your sleeping bag. "Not for me thank you very much"!

There was a small village by the coast where we were patrolling, so we did manage to go ashore for a few beers now and again. I remember one day I went ashore with a few of my friends, we were met by a bunch of small kids on the jetty, all wanting to take you by the hand and saying they'll lead us to the village pub, which they did. We used to hand them bottles of coke out of the open bamboo windows, and we'd give them our loose change before we went back to the ship, so as you could imagine, they were always glad to see us when we next came ashore.

One day, one of the small boys who became like a friend to us, and who always met us when we came ashore, insisted that we come with him to visit his family at his house. It was a small hut somewhere in the jungle, but not too far away, so after we had a few beers we went along with him and met his mother and father and a few of his smaller brothers and sisters. He was the only one who could speak any English, but he must have only been about eight or nine years old. His mother was delighted to meet us and she made us some type of scones on an open fire griddle along with a soft drink, the scones were quite good actually. The family were obviously very poor, and the small boy was keen to show his family his new found friends, I suppose his mother was wandering where he was getting all this loose change from. Anyway, they were very pleased to see us.

The ship always anchored a few miles from that village, and we had to go ashore and return by liberty boat every time. One day, I was standing looking over the side of the ship where the jumping ladder was, and I saw a liberty boat coming along side, returning with a load of drunken sailors. I saw my mate Bob struggling to climb up the jumping ladder and singing to himself. I heard what I thought was the clanking of glass bottles, but I couldn't see anything. I went with Bob to the place where he worked, and I found out what the clanking was. He had cello taped coke bottles full of dark rum to the inside of his bell bottom trousers. That was a good way to smuggle the drink he wanted on board without the bottles being seen sticking out of his uniform. Bob was in charge of the Sea Cat anti-aircraft missile radar system, and he used to hide his rum bottles there. He hid them in the ventilation shafts or behind the high voltage valves of the radar, knowing the officers wouldn't search behind the great big glowing humming valves when they did their inspections.

We stayed on patrol there for about six weeks till we were relieved by another ship, then we continued our tour round the islands of the West Indies. I was a bit annoyed with the conflict between Guatemala and Belize, because we only got to visit about half of the Islands we were due to visit.

TRINIDAD - PORT OF SPAIN

We frequented Port of Spain in Trinidad quite a few times whilst we were around the Southern islands of the West Indies, and it was good to be returning to a familiar place every now and again, as we had made quite a few friends in the area.

We had a two-week refit in the Swan Hunter dockyard, so two weeks in port was just great, just like being on holiday. It was a tropical kind of climate with down pours of heavy rain every so often, and the steam used to rise off the streets like a sauna. The jungle also used to look fresh and green just after a downpour.

We always had to get a taxi to take us to Port of Spain from the dockyard, as it was quite some distance to travel every time we decided to go ashore. Occasionally we stopped off at some of the pubs that we usually passed on the way to town, and got delayed there for hours. Because we would be having such a good time there, we'd phone another taxi to take us the rest of the way to meet up with the friends we'd promised to meet earlier.

We usually started off in a pub called the Pelican. It was an English style pub with a dartboard, where the British community of Port of Spain congregated. I also had a few singsongs in the pub during my visits there.

I also used to frequent a café bar in town and I ended going out with one of the girls who worked behind the bar. She was called Sheba. She had a light coffee coloured skin, not like the black Caribbean women, and she was absolutely beautiful. When I had to stay on board my ship because I was on duty, the only thing the rest of the sailors heard from her was, "when is Doug coming ashore." Even though I'd already told her that I had to stay on board that night. The lads used to be envious of me because she would have nothing to do with them, and all she ever did was speak about me.

RAT

I was in the bar one day with Sheba working behind the counter, and I was sitting on a stool at the far side of the counter having a bottle of beer. A black guy with long black dreadlocks came into the bar and sat on a stool by the door and ordered a bottle of beer. After about twenty minutes I ordered another beer for myself and I also asked Sheba to give the guy at the end of the bar a beer also. Since we were the only two people in the bar we started speaking and having a laugh. He introduced himself as Rat and we bought each other a few beers before he eventually left.

After Rat had left, Sheba told me that Rat was one of the big guys in the underworld drug industry in Trinidad and that I should think myself lucky that he liked me.

A few days later Sheba took me to an open-air rock concert in the Port of Spain cricket ground stadium. I soon found I was the only white man there, but it didn't bother me as I felt like one of the locals anyway. I remember one of the groups singing one of Freddie Fender's songs called "Before The Next Teardrop Falls".

After we'd heard enough of the music, it was time to go to the Marquee for a few beers, like one must. The tent was mobbed, and we stood at the counter trying our best to get served. Just then, I spotted Rat down at the end of the counter, so I shouted out to him, hello Rat, how are you keeping. He shouted back, hello dare, Dougie man, how are you doing yourself. Just then a huge space formed round me and Sheba, and the barman rushed up to us with two beers from Rat. We just had to walk up to the bar again, and the barman rushed up to us with two more free beers. This happened till we decided to leave the concert. I was also very glad to have friends like Rat around. You know what I mean man.

SHEBA

The ship was sailing the next morning, so I spent the day going round Port of Spain with Sheba and some of my friends with their girlfriends. In the afternoon we headed back to a beach club called the Copacabana, which was on the way back towards where the ship was docked. I thought it best to head in that direction just in case we got too drunk to find our way back to the ship.

We had our swimming costumes with us so we had a lot of fun swimming in the pool. We spent some time sunbathing and drinking beers. We also had bottles of Bacardi and coke kept cool in buckets of ice at the side of our table by the pool.

We stayed there all through the night till the early hours of the morning. There was a small peninsula just along the beach jutting out into the sea, and I remember the sun rising up behind this piece of land, and the whole sky just illuminated in bright reds, pinks, oranges and blues. The sea was flat calm, and every little ripple turned all the colours of the rainbow, and every few seconds I'd hear the small waves making a "sshh" sound as they lapped over the golden sands of the beach.

I was sitting on a deck chair in my swimming costume with Sheba in her bikini sitting on my knee, and I remember thinking to myself, what more could a man want out of life? A beautiful girl on my knee, as much drink as I could consume, looking at the most beautiful sunrise I had ever seen, surrounded by my friends and all having a good laugh. I thought, this really feels like heaven!

LUNCH TIME - ON THE SHIP

After we left Trinidad, we stopped off by a neighbouring island to pick up some local army troops and transport them to another island for some training exercise they were doing. They came on board in the forenoon and were on board for lunch. We use large stainless steel trays to eat off, with a place in the tray for each part of the meal, soup, main course, and sweet. Our visitors were obviously not accustomed to such a large and varied choice of food. We were in the meal queue helping ourselves to whatever we wanted, and the visitor in front of me helped himself to a large portion of stew, potatoes, vegetables, and gravy. I didn't take much notice until he proceeded to place a large portion of apple pie on top of the stew and covered it all with custard. I couldn't help but laugh to myself, but he sat down, mixed it all together and proceeded to eat it. I know it all goes down the same way, but he was enjoying it so much I didn't have the heart to say anything.

We dropped them off at their island destination in the afternoon. I can't remember taking them back to where they came from, maybe they are still there!

ST. VINCENT - WEST INDIES

St. Vincent was a beautiful island used by holidaymakers from all over the world. We usually went to the beaches in the afternoons and went to the pubs, clubs and hotels in the evenings. We were just like holidaymakers ourselves, but we were being paid by the navy to holiday in all these exotic places.

I remember lying on the beach sunbathing one afternoon, and there was a small island called Young Island just about a quarter of a mile from the shore. We were so close, that we saw a beachside pub with a few people sitting round the bar, so we decide that we should go over to it. First we decide to swim over, but with us all already having had a few beers, we decided it was best to hire a small rowing boat to get over, I thought it would be safer, just in case there was a strong underwater current running between the islands.

We rowed over to the bar and pulled the boat up on to the beach, we then joined the people already at the bar and had a good laugh for a couple of hours. Most of the people there were American millionaires, and they were on holiday in the island's private challis.

So there we were with millionaires in the afternoon, and visiting the back street bars in the evenings. Typical matelots, we speak to anyone and treat everybody the same.

ROBINSON CRUSO ISLAND

One day we decided to anchor off a very small island for a banyan, that is another name for a beach picnic. We took all that we required with us in the ship's cutter. At least a dozen crates of lager, along with the bar-b-q equipment and supplies. The island belonged to Venezuela, and we were told there was one man living on the other side of the island to keep the claim on the island. Although we never met him, I suppose he was just like the real Robinson Crusoe, so we called it Robinson Crusoe Island.

Having enjoyed our bar-b-q, and consumption of beers, my mate and I started playing knifey. Knifey is throwing our knives outside of each other's feet into the sand, and moving your foot up to the knife each time, until you could not stretch your legs apart any further, to see who falls over first.

Getting fed up with that, we decided to try and get a coconut from one of the many coconut trees surrounding the beach. After scraping the inside of our thighs and feet, and getting only about 6 feet up the tree, and proving we were not as good as monkeys at tree climbing, we had a rest for a few beers.

Bob suggested we try and knock one of the coconuts down from the tree. We threw sticks and stones up at the tree but failed to dislodge one. Bob bet me that I couldn't hit any of the coconuts with my knife, so I took aim and threw my knife at this coconut, to my surprise my knife stuck in the one I aimed for, so I won my bet and the can of beer. Bob said that was great throwing but how are you going to get your knife back down from up there? That was a very good point, so it was back to throwing sticks and stones at the coconuts once again! I never did get my best knife back down from that tree.

To end the day, we went for a paddle on a big tree trunk we found on the beach, using coconut leaves to propel us along. Speak about Robinson Crusoe, after a day on that island I was beginning to feel like him myself.

JOKE - 6

I was a seasoned Sailor by this time, so one day I was lying alone sun-bathing on a deserted Caribbean Island beach, when out from behind the dense rows of coconut trees came this beautiful topless girl with long flowing hair wearing just a grass skirt. She came up to me and said in broken English, "man want drink", I was very thirsty, so I said YES! She then pulled out from under her grass skirt a 2L magnum of Champaign. I was swigging down and enjoying this drink, when she said to me, "man want food", I was starving, so I said YES! She then pulled out from under her grass skirt a massive barbecued chicken, so there was I lying on the beach, drinking Champaign, eating barbecued chicken, so I was well fed and watered. She then turned round to me and said in a very sexy voice, "man want fun and games", so I turned round to her and said, "you don't have a Dart Board up there as well have you"?

My Life On The Ocean Waves – Douglas Freeman

ST. PETERSBURG / ORLANDO - AMERICA

We went to so many Caribbean islands that I can't remember them all, but our tour had to come to an end sometime, so we began our journey back to England, but we had to visit a few places on the way. First we went back to Florida, but this time to St. Petersburg. We were there for about four days, and during that time I had to do my tour of duty on board the ship, so I only got two days ashore to look around because we sailed on the fourth day.

Most of us went to Orlando the first day, going to Disney World in the afternoon and out on the town in the evening. Most of the pubs in Orlando were very lively, with some kind of live entertainment going on, and every night was party night. I suppose that was to be expected especially being so close to Disney World.

Disney World was a great experience, there was so much to see and do and well worth the visit. The things that impressed me most were the future technology displays. There were video laser disks, and that was almost 25 years since I was last there, and they are only starting to come out with things like that now. I suppose the nearest thing today is the Karaoke videodisks. I can't understand why it has taken so long for that technology to reach the public, even things like the pedestrian people mover or mono rails are hardly ever heard of.

There was this guy in my mess who wrote letters to his wife 2 or 3 times a day, and he used to cut out those newspaper cartoons called "love is" and everybody thought they had never seen anybody so much in love before as him. One night whilst we were out on the town, he met a girl and instantly fell in love with her. The next day he wrote a letter to his wife telling her he had met another woman and was leaving her.

I could not understand how he could do that to his wife. He had been away from home for 8 months and he hardly ever went ashore with the other lads during that period. The girl he met was not even good looking, but he did say her dad owned a brewery.

I heard that when he got back home to England, his wife had sold the house and all his belongings too, and left him with nothing.

It also turned out to be true that his American girlfriend's father did own a brewery and she was very rich. He left the navy soon after returning to England and her father paid for his airfare back to Orlando to be with his daughter.

CARACAS - VENEZUELA - SOUTH AMERICA

The ship went to visit Caracas in Venezuela. We were told that it was a very dangerous place for us to go ashore, so I didn't venture into the city whilst I was there. However I did go on a trip organised by the ship to the top of a high mountain a few miles out of the city.

We went up to the top of the mountain by cable car. On the way up we passed over hundreds of small huts with corrugated iron roofs surrounded by mud. They were occupied by the millions of extremely poor people of Caracas. I would have hated to live on the lower levels of the mountain, because the people on the top just threw their rubbish and sewage on the huts below them, it was a disgusting sight to see.

I didn't realise that Caracas was such a huge place. On the way up I could see thousands of skyscrapers for as far as my eye could see in all directions. When I reached the top of the mountain there was a reception area with a mock-up of a cable car. A huge photograph of Caracas was on the wall behind it, making it look like the real thing. We all got our photo taken hanging out of the cable car, and the end result looked impressive.

I sent a photo of me hanging out of the cable car back home to my mother, and she wrote me a letter back, very concerned about me getting into dangerous situations by hanging out of a cable car thousands of feet up a mountain. I had to write back again explaining it was just a trick photograph, and that I was not really hanging out of a real cable car. I don't think I would have been that brave, or that stupid!

FORT LAUDERDALE - 2 AMERICA

When we were first in Fort Lauderdale, a family invited a sailor for a weekend. He accepted their hospitality, and enjoyed himself having bar-b-q's, sun bathing, and swimming in their pool. He ended up sleeping with the guy's wife while he was away at work.

During our tour of the West Indies she used to write to him saying how much she loved him etc. He must have been a bit stupid, because he wrote back to her. Needless to say, her husband found the letters he wrote back to her, and in one of her letters she said they were separated and getting a divorce.

When the ship returned to Fort Lauderdale, he went to see her at her house, but when he got there her husband was visiting his kids, and he went berserk when he saw the sailor again. A fight started, and the sailor ended up getting chased down the street with a huge lumberjack's axe. The police arrested the poor husband for his actions.

I know we all laughed when we heard the story, but you can't help but feel sorry for the man who tried to be good and invite a lonely sailor into his family life for the weekend, and ended up losing his wife.

BERMUDA - 2

Having left Fort Lauderdale, our next port of call was back to Bermuda for a few days before crossing the Atlantic. The weather this day was a bit breezy with not too much sun. A few of us got together and decided to have a small bar-b-q round by one of the rocky shores which was not too far from the ship, so we went to the place with long trousers on for a change. We had our usual supply of beer and food to take with us. I hadn't been to that place before and was not very impressed with it when I got there, especially since there are lots of beautiful beaches in Bermuda.

After a while somebody spotted a small octopus swimming close to the rocks and they wanted to catch it and cook it on the grill. I stopped them from doing that and they wandered away again. The octopus fascinated me so I followed it along till it came to a set of steps that went down into the water. I decided to go down the steps to try and get a closer look at this wonderful creature, I slipped on the seaweed and slithered down the steps and fell half into the water. I scratched my back a little during the fall but apart from that I was OK.

I looked down into the water, and to my surprise I saw the octopus coming up the steps below the water to see me. It came right up to the surface of the water and reached out to me with one of its tentacles. I reached out and shook it with my hand and said, hello octopus, and the octopus said, hello Doug, "not really", well I did have a few beers down me by this time, then it slid back down the steps and swam away into the distance.

When I went back up the steps and told the lads that I had just shaken hands with an octopus, they wouldn't believe me. They thought I was mad, they all laughed at me and said I must have had too much to drink. I showed them the scratch on my back to at least prove I fell down the steps, which was not enough for them. But I know the truth! The truth is out there!

RETURN TO THE UK - 3

On our return to the UK, we stopped off at Gibraltar for a few days to stock up on some more Rabbits. I was due out of the navy in a few months' time, and I knew this would be the last time I would be sailing across the Bay of Biscay and up along the English Channel. I remember passing Plymouth where I first joined the navy and sailed out into the English Channel in a Frigate for the first time. We then passed Portland, where I used to do the 3-day wars and ship's pre-commissioning trials, I had been there so many times. Then sailing round the Isle of Weight for Portsmouth, where I had sailed from and returned to a hundred times in all kind of ships. Like the generations of sailors of sailors before me, from the days of the wooden ships to the present day, I felt like I was finally returning home again, but this was for the last time, and another chapter of my life was coming to an end.

The usual hundreds of families were there to greet us when the ship pulled up alongside the jetty at Portsmouth harbour. It was a very emotional occasion for the families and the sailors alike. My family lived in Aberdeen, so they were never there to meet me on those occasions, so I often stayed on board the first night, to let somebody off who was on duty so that they could be with their families.

ALDERSHOT - ENGLAND

Some months before, I had applied for a pre-release course on Television Repair, which was run by the army and held in Aldershot. The course was for one week. I was due 3 weeks leave after the course so I took two suitcases with me full of my own personal stuff and rabbits, as I wouldn't be going in by the ship on the way home. I left the ship at Portsmouth and went directly to Aldershot as the ship was sailing to Rosyth in a few days. Later that day I settled into my accommodation in Aldershot. There were about 8 people on this course, some from the army and air force, but I was the only one from the navy. There was a small guy in my room, I think he was leaving the army because he was small and everybody picked on him. The second day of the course, he came in to the classroom with bruises and black eyes on his face. Apparently some trainee paras in the town had beaten him up the night before. I was going in to town that night so I said he could come in to the town with me if that would help, so he did. We were walking back up the road after pub closing time and it happened again. Some drunken trainee paras started picking on him because he was small, I couldn't stand by and just let this happen again, so I stepped in to protect him, being a good matelot that I was. I ended up flattening two of them and the rest ran away. The next day an army officer came round to our class complaining that two of his lads needed medical attention during a fight with me. When I explained to the officer what the situation was all about, he said he was going back to charge them for beating up the small army guy the night before. That'll teach them to mess about with the navy!

THE ADMIRAL'S HOUSE - PORTSMOUTH

The course finished at lunchtime on the Friday, so I decided to go back down to Portsmouth for the weekend and to see the place for the last time. When I arrived, I realised I had nowhere to stay, so I tried the Fleet Club, it was full up so I went round the corner and in to the King & Queen on the Hard for a pint of beer till I decided what to do next. There was I sitting in a pub with two large suitcases with no home to go to in Portsmouth for the first time in my life. Just then, an old friend of mine from years gone by came into the pub, so I shouted him over for a pint. We chatted about old times for a while, and I asked him what he was doing now. He said he was still an AB, but was now working as a steward for the Admiral. When I told him I had nowhere to stay for the night, he suggested I come back with him to the Admiral's house and stay there as the Admiral was away and nobody would know.

After a while we jumped into a taxi and drove through the main gate to the Admiral's house where I ended up staying for the whole weekend. There were 4 stewards working there, and quite a big room with 8 beds, the beds were still the old angle iron types with squeaky springs, I thought they would have had a better quality of bed for the Admirals residence.

Although there was a bit of a cold wind blowing, the high walls round the back yard was an ideal place for sun bathing, because we saw the Admirals daughter lying out there completely unaware we could see her from our window. I had to sneak out the house in case she saw me, as she would have known I was not one of the regular staff.

So there is one for me over the Admiral. I got one back on the navy, but if the navy ever asks me if the story is true, I'll deny it. I'll say I just made it up for the book!

LEAVING THE NAVY

On Sunday afternoon I left Pompey for the last time, catching a train to Aberdeen via London's Kings Cross Station. I had 3 weeks leave at home then went back down to H.M.S. Cochrane at Rosyth to complete the procedure for leaving the

My Life On The Ocean Waves – Douglas Freeman

navy. I had been put up in Cochrane many times in the past. During ship's refits, and also whilst I was working down the Pit at RAF Pitreavie. I began the day by signing a few documents and returning my ID card, it was all very informal. Before I could go, I still had to return some of my naval uniforms etc. I had left them in my kit bag on the Nubian which was in the dockyard, so I had to go back down to the ship to collect it. I had already handed my ID card back, so I had a bit of trouble getting into the dockyard without it, however I did manage.

There were a few other naval ships in the dockyard, including a few foreign ones. My ship was berthed at the very far end of the jetty. I was walking down the jetty dressed in civvies, a crowd of Admirals, Captains, and all other ranks of officers came walking up the jetty towards me. I got a funny look from them as I passed because I didn't salute them. It must have really pi**ed them off.

I did however salute the quarterdeck as I stepped on to the Nubian. The officer of the day standing by the gangway said in a loud voice, "Freeman" where have you been! I felt like saying, Mr. Freeman to you sir, but I didn't, then I explained I was now out of the navy and that I had come on board to collect my kit bag. I walked down the gangway and on to the jetty. I picked up my kit bag, threw it over my shoulder, smiled to myself, and started singing as I marched back along the jetty.

La, la-la, la, la-la-la, la-la, la, la-la-la, La, la-la, la, la-la-la, la-la, la, la-la-la, La, la-la, la, la-la-la, la-la, la, la-la-la, La, la-la, la, la-la-la, la-la, la, la-la-la. Ram It, I'm RDP!

My Life On The Ocean Waves – Douglas Freeman

To explain why I was singing that song, here are the words to Ram It, I'm RDP.

by Shep Woolly.

RAM IT I'M R.D.P.

I was walking through the dockyard
One morning bright and fair
When a sailor came towards me
With long and shaggy hair
And it looked to all the world
Although he didn't have a care
And he said why are you looking at me

I said well it's your uniform
You really look a scruff
He said see me in me civvies mate
I'm really quite the stuff
and when I put me Brute on
I smell just like a poof
I'm a smoothly from R.N.B.

I've been to Honolulu
And I've been to Tokyo
I've been to San Francisco
Most any place you'll go
I've done nine years in the navy
And there's just two days to go
So ram it I'm R.D.P.

My Life On The Ocean Waves – Douglas Freeman

There'll be no more get your hair cut
No standing out in rows
No more duty watches
No more R.P.O.'s
No killick's, pigs, or P.T.I's
Now they get up my nose
So ram it I'm R.D.P.

I've trapped polar bears in Iceland
Film stars down in Nice
Grizzly bears in Canada
And snappers in the Fleece
But now it's nearly over
And it's two days to release
So ram it I'm R.D.P.

Now I've returned my pusser's Dirk
I'm sure I've felt the loss
Two blue suits and steaming boots
And now I'll count the cost
But I'll stand outside the Barracks,
And make rude signs at the Joss
So ram it I'm R.D.P.

I've done my share of punishment
I've sweated in the sun
I've done nines and fines and D.Q.'s
But now it's nearly done

And now some silly ba****d's
Just asked me to sign on
So ram it I'm R.D.P.

But now I've stood here talking
For nearly long enough
I've got to go to Barracks mate
I've got to pack me stuff
Perhaps I might come in again
If civvy street gets rough
So ram it I'm R.D.P.

Cho la, la, la, etc.

HOME FOR GOOD - TO ABERDEEN

Now that I was home and out of the navy, I felt a great variety of emotions. I was glad to be free, and to be able to do whatever I want and go wherever I want when I want. I was also quite sad to be leaving behind my friends and the great comradeship I found in the navy. I was excited, thinking of the new challenges that lay ahead, just like the first day I joined the navy back in May 1966.

As the weeks passed, I used to wake up with a start, thinking I was still in the navy and that I was adrift or late for something, just like I had been so many times before. Then I realised I was finally out of the navy, and I could do whatever I wanted, so I rolled over and went back to sleep with a smile on my face, and started to dream of all the good times I'd had during my "Life On The Ocean Waves" as "A Very Ordinary Seaman"!

The End

Notes

The word **R.O.M.F.T.** in the title of my book is an old navy saying, and stands for

Roll **O**n **M**y **F*******g **T**ime.

Thanks

I would like to thank you all for purchasing and reading my book. I sincerely hope you enjoyed it. If you were in the Royal Navy yourself, you may have found some of the stories familiar and amusing, and they may have brought back some good memories of your own, maybe you should write your own stories down and put them in to print. If you did like this book, I would appreciate a Positive Favourable Review on Amazon. Thank you.

Douglas Freeman

Printed in Great Britain
by Amazon

FOLIO JUNIOR/**ANIMORPHS**

Même le livre se transforme !
Faites défiler rapidement
les pages et regardez...

Déjà parus dans la série

ANIMORPHS

1. L'INVASION
2. LE VISITEUR
3. L'AFFRONTEMENT
4. LE MESSAGE
5. LE PRÉDATEUR
6. LA CAPTURE
7. L'INCONNU
8. L'EXTRATERRESTRE
9. LE SECRET
10. L'ANDROÏDE
11. L'OUBLI
12. LA MENACE
13. LA MUTATION
14. LE MYSTÈRE
15. L'ÉVASION
16. L'ALERTE
17. LE PIÈGE
18. LA DÉCISION

K. A. Applegate
LA DÉCISION

Traduit de l'américain
par Mona de Pracontal

ANIMORPHS
FOLIO JUNIOR/**GALLIMARD** JEUNESSE

Pour Michael et Jake

Titre original : *The Decision*
Edition originale publiée par Scholastic Inc., 1998
© Katherine Applegate, 1998
Tous droits réservés
© Gallimard Jeunesse, 1998, pour la traduction française
avec l'autorisation de Scholastic Inc.
Animorphs est une marque déposée de Scholastic Inc.
Illustration de couverture : David B. Mattingly

CHAPITRE 1

Je m'appelle Aximili-Esgarrouth-Isthil.

J'ignore si mes frères andalites reconnaîtront un jour ce nom. A mon avis, l'histoire que je m'apprête à vous raconter sera en partie évoquée dans les publications scientifiques. Ce que je veux dire, c'est que l'incident qui m'est arrivé a radicalement bouleversé la science de l'extrusion de masse en Espace-Zéro pendant l'animorphe.

Mais je doute que mon vrai nom soit utilisé. Je doute que la vérité soit dévoilée tout entière. Et je crois que cela vaut mieux. Voyez-vous, il y a des traîtres parmi nous. Oui, des traîtres parmi nos frères andalites. Des Andalites au service des Yirks.

Je suis le seul Andalite vivant à avoir été témoin de l'incident de l'*Ascalin*. Moi seul – en dehors de mes amis humains, prince Jake, Cassie, Tobias, Rachel et

Marco – sais ce qui s'est vraiment passé à bord de ce vaisseau spatial, sur la planète Leira ravagée par la guerre.

Je le sais, il paraît inconcevable qu'un Andalite puisse trahir. Cette simple idée a de quoi rendre malade n'importe quel Andalite normalement constitué. Je dis la vérité, pourtant. L'incident de l'*Ascalin* s'est bel et bien produit. Nous avons été trahis par l'un des nôtres.

Je me nomme Aximili-Esgarrouth-Isthil, et je suis le frère d'Elfangor-Sirinial-Shamtul. Je jure sur sa mémoire que tout ce que je vais raconter ici est exact.

Je suis le seul Andalite présent sur la planète Terre à l'heure actuelle. Ne perdez pas votre temps à chercher des informations sur la Terre ; vous ne trouveriez pas grand-chose. La vérité, c'est que nous avons perdu un vaisseau Dôme qui stationnait en orbite au-dessus de cette planète. Les Yirks l'ont détruit. Nous avons également perdu mon frère, le prince Elfangor, dans ce combat. Mais avant de mourir, Elfangor a enfreint notre loi et révélé le secret andalite du pouvoir de l'animorphe à cinq jeunes humains.

Les Yirks s'attaquent à cette planète, maintenant. Ils envahissent la Terre en procédant de leur façon habituelle. C'est un jeu d'enfant, pour les limaces parasites yirks, de s'introduire dans la tête des humains et de se fondre autour de leur cerveau. De réduire les humains en esclavage, comme ils l'ont fait pour les Hork-Bajirs et les Gedds. Comme ils espèrent le faire avec nous, un jour.

Je vis parmi ces humains, désormais. Avec les jeunes humains qui ont reçu d'Elfangor le pouvoir de l'animorphe. Ils se sont donné le nom d'Animorphs. Ils luttent contre l'invasion des Yirks. Et ils sont les seuls, autant que je sache.

Je vis avec des humains. Je les respecte. Cependant, mes cœurs sont restés andalites. Quoiqu'on puisse jamais dire à mon sujet ou au sujet de ce qui s'est passé sur Leira, je demeure loyal envers mon peuple.

Pourtant, il m'arrive maintenant de me poser des questions : qui est mon véritable peuple ? Ma race, mon espèce ? Ma famille ? Mes amis ? Mes alliés ?

Mes amis humains tiennent absolument à me donner un diminutif : ils m'appellent Ax. Vous comprenez, les humains communiquent principalement par des sons qu'ils produisent avec leur bouche. (La plupart des Andalites comprennent le concept de « bouche », je pense.) Or, si mon nom entier est facile à prononcer en parole mentale andalite, il est un peu trop long et complexe pour l'outil primitif que constituent les sons buccaux des humains.

Je suis seul sur cette planète. Seul de mon espèce. L'unique Andalite parmi tous les humains de la planète. J'ai donc recouru à la technologie de l'animorphe pour créer une animorphe humaine. Parfois, pendant deux heures d'affilée, je me transforme en humain et je me fais passer pour l'un d'eux.

En toute modestie, je dois dire que je suis très fort pour jouer les humains. J'ai appris leurs us et coutumes à la perfection, de sorte que je parais entièrement normal et naturel en homme.

Cela me permet même de fréquenter les lieux les plus typiquement humains. Le centre commercial, par exemple. Un centre commercial est un lieu plein de magasins, qui vendent pour la plupart de la peau artificielle et des sabots artificiels – des vêtements et des chaussures, pour employer les termes techniques.

Le centre commercial abrite également les plus merveilleux des établissements d'alimentation. Car, voyez-vous, les humains ne se servent pas seulement de leur bouche pour produire des sons, mais aussi pour s'alimenter. Ils mettent de la nourriture dans leur ouverture buccale et la broient entre leurs dents, tout en y incorporant de la salive. Ce procédé, qu'ils appellent manger met en jeu un sens du nom de goût.

Le goût est quelque chose de très, très puissant.

Oh oui…

J'étais vêtu de peau et de sabots artificiels, comme un humain. Je me suis approché de mon magasin d'alimentation préféré.

— Bonjour, ai-je dit en actionnant ma bouche humaine. Je veux travailler pour de l'argent. Ar-gent. Rrrgent.

(Petite parenthèse : l'argent est une invention humaine assez abstraite. Vous donnez des quantités variables d'argent à divers membres de la société et eux, en échange, vous remettent des articles utiles.)

— Tu veux commander quelque chose ? m'a répondu l'humain.

— J'ai besoin d'argent afin de pouvoir l'échanger contre de savoureux beignets à la cannelle, ai-je expliqué.

L'humain a cligné des yeux.

— Bon, alors, tu veux commander quelque chose, ou non ?

De toute évidence, j'avais affaire à un spécimen sous-intelligent.

— Je souhaite accomplir un travail, tra-vail, aïe, ay-yeu, et recevoir de l'argent de vous. Je souhaite ensuite utiliser cet argent pour acquérir de savoureux beignets à la cannelle. Nelle, nelle.

— Je vais chercher la gérante.

— Beignets, gnè, ai-je répété.

Je trouve le son « gnè » particulièrement agréable : il roule dans la bouche. Beaucoup de sons buccaux sont divertissants.

La gérante est arrivée et je lui ai exposé ma requête.

— Bien, a-t-elle répondu. Je ne peux pas te faire travailler, à mon avis tu es trop jeune. Mais si tu as faim, tu pourrais débarrasser quelques tables et je te donnerais quelque chose à manger en échange.

Cela me paraissait tout à fait acceptable.

— Pauvre gosse, a-t-elle dit à l'autre humain tandis que je me dirigeais vers les tables, il a l'air un peu dérangé, mais c'est un beau garçon.

J'ai vite compris ce qu'elle voulait dire par débarrasser : dans cette partie du centre commercial, il y avait plusieurs tables, entourées de sièges sur lesquels on se place pour s'alimenter. Les tables étaient couvertes de choses délicieuses !

Sur la première, j'ai trouvé de fins triangles salés, gras et croustillants, recouverts d'une sécrétion jaune vif. Je les ai mangés, ils étaient excellents.

A la table suivante, il y avait des liquides. Je les ai bus. L'un était chaud, l'autre froid. A côté des liquides, j'ai trouvé un carré de papier froissé. Il contenait un produit rougeâtre et semi-liquide. Je l'ai léché. C'était bon, mais rien d'extraordinaire.

Puis, enfin, j'ai repéré ce que je voulais. Deux énormes beignets à la cannelle, brillants, tout chauds. Deux humains étaient assis très près de ces beignets.

Ils allaient les manger !

J'ai foncé aussi vite que me le permettaient mes jambes bancales d'humain.

– Je débarrasse ces tables ! Je débarrasse ces tables !

Les humains m'ont dévisagé.

– On n'a pas encore commencé !

– Bien ! ai-je répondu avec soulagement.

J'ai attrapé les deux beignets à la cannelle et je les ai emportés.

– Hé ! Toi ! Arrête-toi !

Vite, j'en ai fourré un dans ma bouche. Quelle joie ! Ah ! Comment pourrais-je expliquer cela à un Andalite qui n'a jamais possédé le sens du goût ? Cette sensation ! Un plaisir qui dépasse l'imagination. La tiédeur tendre et poisseuse d'un beignet à la cannelle !

– Qu'est-ce que tu fais ? s'est écriée la gérante, qui avait accouru.

– Ggueu guébarrasse les tabb... ai-je répondu.

Il est très difficile de parler en mangeant. Encore un des nombreux défauts de conception de l'organisme humain.

– Je suis vraiment désolée, a dit la gérante aux humains qui essayaient de me reprendre mes beignets à la cannelle. Je vais vous en apporter d'autres. Et toi – elle a tendu vers moi un de ses doigts humains, énergiques bien que ridiculement courts – viens avec moi.

Elle m'a tiré par le bras, ce qui m'a fait perdre un morceau de beignet que je mettais dans ma bouche. Elle m'a emmené à l'intérieur de l'établissement d'alimentation et m'a fait asseoir sur une chaise. Cela signifie plier les deux jambes et faire reposer le poids du corps sur une plateforme horizontale et légèrement en hauteur, par l'intermédiaire de deux coussinets charnus situés en haut des jambes. Un peu difficile à visualiser quand on ne l'a jamais vu faire en vrai.

– Bon, maintenant, écoute-moi. Si tu as si faim que ça, il y a là un plateau de beignets à la cannelle qui sont juste un peu rassis. Sers-toi, si tu veux. Pauvre petit.

Elle m'a montré du doigt un assortiment de beignets. Il y en avait peut-être une douzaine !

– Pour moi ? ai-je demandé d'une voix étranglée par l'émotion.

– Oui, mon petit. Vas-y, prends-en un.

Là, j'aimerais apporter une dernière précision : le langage buccal humain est parfois très vague. « Prends-en un », avait-elle dit.

Un quoi ?

Un beignet à la cannelle ?

Un plateau entier de beignets à la cannelle ?

Alors, est-ce ma faute s'il y a eu malentendu ?

CHAPITRE 2

– Je me promenais donc dans la galerie des snacks, raconta Marco. Gentiment, sans embêter personne, et je me suis dit : « Tiens, mon petit Marco, si tu t'offrais une petite friandise ? » A ce moment-là, j'ai vu la foule et les pompiers rassemblés autour de la Maison du beignet.

Marco est un de mes amis humains. Il est plus petit que certains humains de son âge. Il a les cheveux bruns, les yeux noirs, et il aime faire des plaisanteries. Les plaisanteries, c'est de l'humour. L'humour est plus fréquent chez les humains que chez les Andalites.

Je crois qu'ils ont besoin de recourir à l'humour. Ça les aide à surmonter leur gêne d'être aussi bancals sur ces deux jambes ridicules.

– Et je vous jure, ça m'a fait un de ces chocs. Je veux dire que j'ai tout de suite su que, d'une façon ou d'une autre, Axos était mêlé à l'affaire. Alors je suis allé voir et j'ai demandé à quelqu'un ce qui se passait. Elle m'a dit...

— Elle ? l'a interrompu Rachel. Laisse-moi deviner. Une jolie fille qui ne t'adresserait même pas la parole en temps normal ? Tu t'es dit que, comme il y avait urgence médicale, c'était l'occasion rêvée de l'aborder ?

— Exactement.

Rachel est un humain femelle. Elle a les cheveux dorés et les yeux bleus. Elle est grande pour son âge.

— En tout cas, elle m'a dit qu'un gosse avait pété les plombs et qu'il avait mangé un plateau entier de beignets à la cannelle. Alors je vous demande, qui connaissons-nous qui soit capable de manger un plateau entier de beignets à la cannelle ?

Marco, Rachel et les autres – prince Jake, Cassie et Tobias – m'ont tous regardé en étirant les coins de leur bouche pour produire des sourires. Tous sauf Tobias, qui est un nothlit : une personne prisonnière d'une animorphe. Tobias est un faucon, il n'a pas de lèvres.

J'ai eu le sentiment que je devais dire quelque chose.

< Je n'étais pas conscient des normes spécifiques de l'estomac humain. Il semble qu'il y ait un genre de

limite à la quantité de nourriture que l'on peut ingérer. Le dépassement de cette limite provoque une sensation déplaisante dans la zone de l'estomac. Ça m'a également donné des vertiges. >

— Le taux de sucre le plus élevé du siècle, a dit Cassie.

Cassie n'est pas plus grande que Marco. Elle a les yeux et les cheveux foncés. Cassie s'intéresse beaucoup aux animaux. Par animaux, les humains entendent tous les autres êtres vivants en dehors d'eux.

J'avais quitté mon animorphe humaine et repris mon propre corps. Nous étions dans la forêt qui commence à la lisière des champs qui entourent la ferme de Cassie. C'est là que je vis. Avec Tobias. Lui mange des souris, en général le matin. Moi, je sors de la forêt la nuit pour aller courir à travers les pâturages et absorber l'herbe par mes sabots, comme sont censées le faire toutes les créatures raisonnables.

Nous attendions dans les bois l'arrivée d'un étrange allié : Erek, le Chey.

Les Cheys sont des androïdes. Ils ont été créés par une espèce aujourd'hui disparue, les Pémalites. Les Cheys et les derniers survivants pémalites sont arrivés sur Terre il y a quelques milliers d'années. Ils fuyaient la destruction de leur planète natale. Les Pémalites n'ont pas survécu. Leurs androïdes, créatures non violentes dotées d'un grand sens moral et de remarquables pouvoirs, ont traversé les siècles*.

Prince Jake a regardé sa montre. Les humains ont un problème avec le temps. Ils sont sans arrêt persuadés qu'il est plus tard ou plus tôt qu'ils ne le pensaient. Je n'ai encore jamais entendu un humain s'exclamer : « Oh, regardez, il est exactement l'heure que je croyais. »

– J'allais dire qu'Erek était en retard, a dit prince Jake, mais il est plus tôt que je ne le pensais.

Vous voyez ?

< Le voici qui arrive, a prévenu Tobias. Il peut se déplacer très discrètement quand il le veut, mais je le vois d'ici. >

Les faucons ont une ouïe excellente, ainsi qu'une vision véritablement extraordinaire. Il n'empêche qu'ils ne peuvent regarder que dans une seule direction à la fois, comme les humains.

Erek s'est approché – parfaitement à l'heure bien sûr. Il avait l'aspect d'un garçon humain normal.

* voir *L'Androïde* (Animorphs n°10)

Naturellement, c'est juste une illusion holographique très sophistiquée. Sous l'hologramme se trouve un androïde métallique gris et blanc, qui ressemble un peu à un chien terrestre dressé sur les pattes arrière.

Les Cheys sont incapables de violence. La non-violence est un principe inscrit dans leur programme. Pourtant, avec notre aide, Erek a pu désactiver cette fonction. Il nous a sauvé la vie à tous lors d'un combat terrible. Mais ensuite, il a choisi de renoncer au pouvoir de se battre.

Cependant, bien qu'ils ne puissent pas se battre, les Cheys sont parvenus à infiltrer les activités yirks sur Terre. De temps à autre, Erek nous livre de précieuses informations.

– Bonjour tout le monde, a-t-il dit.

– Salut Erek, a fait Marco. Quoi de neuf ?

Il a haussé les épaules, exactement comme l'aurait fait n'importe quel garçon humain de l'âge qu'il semblait avoir.

– Pas grand-chose. Juste un truc bizarre, un truc qui ne tient pas debout. Ou du moins, que nous n'arrivons pas à comprendre.

Prince Jake a hoché la tête et levé les yeux vers Tobias.

– Personne en vue ?

Tobias a quitté sa branche et battu des ailes, puis il a disparu au-dessus des cimes d'arbres.

– Désolé, a dit prince Jake à Erek, mais je veux être sûr que nous sommes en sécurité.

Erek a souri, l'air amusé.

– Tu penses que je serais venu seul ? Trois des miens sont déployés dans le secteur et nous surveillent. Même Tobias, avec ses yeux, ne pourra pas les repérer.

– Ah oui ? Tu veux parier ? a demandé prince Jake.

A ce moment-là, Tobias est revenu à toute allure et s'est perché sur la même branche qu'il venait de quitter. Tranquillement, il s'est mis à lisser ses plumes.

< Tout va bien >, a-t-il déclaré.

– Tu n'as vraiment rien remarqué ? lui a demandé prince Jake, d'un ton déçu.

< Oh, j'ai bien vu deux Cheys qui projetaient des hologrammes d'arbres et un autre qui essayait de se faire passer pour un rocher mais, à part ça, rien d'inquiétant. >

Ils ont tous ri, Erek et les humains.

< Je connais ces bois, a repris Tobias avec suffisance. Tu t'imagines que tu peux planter un

hologramme de saule à un endroit où il n'y a jamais eu le moindre saule, et que je ne vais pas m'en apercevoir ? Enfin, franchement... >

Erek a fait une sorte de courbette devant Tobias.

– Rappelle-moi de ne jamais te sous-estimer, frère faucon.

Puis, subitement sérieux, il nous a expliqué ce qu'il était venu nous signaler.

– Le numéro deux des services secrets, un type dénommé Hewlett Aldershot, se trouve à l'hôpital, dans le coma. Il s'est fait renverser par une voiture en traversant la rue. Nous ne savons pas ce qu'il était venu faire dans le secteur. Mais nous savons ceci : tout le monde, même sa famille, ignore qu'il est à l'hôpital.

– Sa famille n'est pas au courant ? a insisté Cassie.

– Non. Personne ne le sait. Ni sa famille ni sa supérieure, Jane Carnegie. Personne. Cet hôpital est dirigé par les Yirks : la moitié du personnel se compose d'humains-Contrôleurs. Son nom ne figure même pas dans les ordinateurs de l'hôpital. A propos, vous savez, la voiture qui l'a renversé ? C'est un minibus qui appartient à notre cher ami Chapman.

Prince Jake a hoché la tête. Jake est le chef des Animorphs. Je le considère comme mon prince. Étant donné que je suis encore un aristh, un élève guerrier andalite, j'ai besoin de quelqu'un qui soit mon prince.

– Bien, bien, a répondu prince Jake. Je crois que nous devrions aller voir ce qui se passe.

CHAPITRE 3

< J'ai une question, a dit Marco. Quel genre de parents faut-il être pour infliger un nom pareil, Hewlett Aldershot, à un môme ? Le pauvre, il a dû se faire tabasser à la sortie de l'école tous les jours de sa vie. >

C'était le lendemain. Marco, Rachel et moi étions perchés sur un rebord de fenêtre, au deuxième étage d'un immeuble. Nous étions en animorphe de mouette. D'après mes amis humains, les mouettes sont comme les pigeons : elles peuvent aller n'importe où sans avoir l'air suspectes.

Ils ont certainement raison. Mais je n'ai aucune idée de ce qu'est un pigeon. Et je suis incapable d'imaginer à quoi peut ressembler un oiseau suspect.

< Ce que je pense, moi, c'est que Chapman a peut-être écrasé ce type rien que parce que son nom l'énervait. >

Rachel a soupiré.

< Pourquoi faut-il toujours que Jake m'envoie en mission avec toi, Marco ? >

< Quoi, je devrais me taire ? Je ne devrais pas bavarder ? Ça fait une heure et demie que nous sommes sur ce rebord de fenêtre minable. Toi, Ax et moi. >

< Une heure et demie seulement ? C'est marrant, j'aurais cru bien plus. Quand tu parles, Marco, le temps paraît long, long, long. Long, long… >

< … Très drôle. >

J'ai jugé bon d'intervenir :

< Ça ne fait qu'une heure et dix-huit minutes de votre temps >, ai-je rectifié.

< De notre temps ? s'est étonné Marco. Tu sais, c'est aussi ton temps à toi, maintenant. On est sur Terre, et tu es coincé ici, alors mets ta pendule à l'heure locale. >

Marco s'ennuyait. Comme nous tous, d'ailleurs. Seulement il devient facilement agressif quand il s'ennuie.

Nous étions à l'hôpital en train de surveiller la chambre privée de Hewlett Aldershot. C'était notre deuxième tour de garde sur le rebord de sa fenêtre.

Nous étions déjà venus en début de matinée, et nous étions restés jusqu'à la limite des deux heures. Ensuite prince Jake et Cassie nous avaient relayés et, maintenant, c'était de nouveau à nous.

< Ça n'a tellement rien à voir avec ce que j'aimerais faire par un beau dimanche comme aujourd'hui… quand je pense aux soldes qu'ils font un peu partout ! a gémi Rachel. C'est mon tour de me dégourdir les ailes, je reviens tout de suite. >

Elle s'est envolée en nous laissant seuls, Marco et moi. Nous avons un peu battu des ailes, remué la tête, fait les cent pas le long du rebord de la fenêtre. Nous nous efforcions d'adopter un comportement de mouette. C'est pour cette raison que Rachel avait dû s'envoler : c'est ce qu'aurait fait une vraie mouette.

< Y a-t-il quelque chose de bizarre dans le nom de Hewlett Alder… Regarde ! ai-je dit en changeant brusquement de sujet. Il y a un nouvel humain qui entre dans la chambre, et sa tête me dit quelque chose. >

< Rachel ! a crié Marco en parole mentale. Va chercher Jake, Cassie et Tobias. Nous avons de la compagnie ! >

< Qui ça ? >

< Vysserk Trois dans son animorphe humaine, ai-je répondu. L'Abomination ! >

Les mouettes ont les yeux placés sur les côtés de la tête. J'ai donc orienté un œil vers l'intérieur de la pièce. Pas d'erreur, c'était bien lui. Vysserk Trois, le chef de l'invasion yirk sur Terre.

Vysserk Trois est le seul et unique Yirk qui soit parvenu à infester avec succès un corps andalite. Lorsqu'il s'est emparé de ce corps, il a également pris possession de son pouvoir d'animorphe. De sorte que seul Vysserk Trois, de tous les Yirks de l'univers, est capable de morphoser.

J'ai ressenti la rage sourde que j'éprouve toujours en présence de cette vile créature, l'assassin de mon frère. Une fois, j'ai bien failli venger Elfangor. J'ai bien failli anéantir Vysserk Trois. Mais, au dernier moment, j'ai commis une erreur et il est toujours en vie.

La prochaine fois, je ne commettrai pas d'erreur.

< Oh ! Oh ! Vysserk Trois, en animorphe d'humain en plus. Il se passe quelque chose de grave, c'est sûr >, a commenté Marco avec une pointe d'inquiétude dans la voix.

Deux médecins humains sont entrés dans la pièce. Ils se sont adressés à Vysserk. Avec respect. Avec

crainte. En tremblant. Je ne pouvais pas entendre leurs paroles à travers la vitre, mais il était évident qu'ils savaient qui et quel genre de créature était Vysserk Trois.

Vysserk Trois a commencé à démorphoser. A reprendre sa forme d'Andalite. Sur sa tête humaine ont jailli les deux tentacules oculaires. De son torse d'humain sont sorties les deux pattes de devant. Et depuis la pointe de son coccyx s'est déployée la longue queue foudroyante des Andalites.

A ma gauche, un éclair brun et fauve, avec un reflet roux. Tobias, qui passait en flèche. J'ai gardé l'autre œil rivé sur la fenêtre.

Une fourrure marron et bleu recouvrit rapidement l'ancienne peau humaine. Vysserk Trois se tenait maintenant sur ses quatre pattes, la queue dressée et prête à frapper.

< Le Vysserk doit être vraiment certain de ne courir aucun risque ici, autrement il ne démorphoserait pas comme ça >, ai-je remarqué.

< Mais les médecins n'ont pas l'air très à l'aise >, a observé Marco.

Effectivement, les deux docteurs tremblaient de tout leur corps. Manifestement, il y avait un problème.

Tout à coup, rapide comme la foudre, Vysserk Trois a plaqué sa lame caudale contre la gorge d'un des médecins.

Il lui aurait suffi d'un tressaillement de la queue pour envoyer la tête de l'homme voltiger à l'autre bout de la pièce.

Maintenant qu'il avait retrouvé son corps d'Andalite, nous pouvions entendre les paroles mentales de Vysserk Trois, qu'il ne songeait pas à mettre en sourdine.

< Je vous ai ordonné de guérir cet humain ! criait-il rageusement. Il ne nous servira à rien de lui mettre un des nôtres dans la tête s'il est incapable de bouger ! >

Le docteur a murmuré une réponse. Une réponse très respectueuse, très prudente.

< Je me moque de son bulbe rachidien ! Je le veux sur pied ! Avez-vous idée de l'utilité qu'il peut avoir ? C'est le numéro deux des services secrets du président de ce pays. Il a accès à la moitié des secrets de cette planète. C'est pour cette unique raison que j'ai organisé cet accident et que je l'ai envoyé à l'hôpital. >

Prince Jake et Cassie approchaient à toute vitesse, tous deux en animorphe de mouette.

< Que se passe-t-il ? > a demandé prince Jake.

< Vysserk Trois, prince Jake. >

< Ne m'appelle pas prince. Ouais, j'entends sa voix mentale. Mais je veux dire, que voyez-vous ? >

< Vysserk est en train de terroriser deux docteurs humains >, ai-je expliqué.

Juste à cet instant, Vysserk Trois a écarté sa lame caudale. L'humain s'est effondré, à genoux sur le carrelage de la chambre. Son compagnon médecin l'a regardé avec pitié, mais n'a fait aucun geste pour l'aider.

< Vous ne me laissez pas le choix : si je ne peux pas me servir de cette créature comme hôte, je serai obligé de l'acquérir et de le morphoser. Je ne peux pas passer tout mon temps sous sa forme. Je ne peux pas vivre sa vie. Mais en me servant de lui, je pourrai me rapprocher de sa supérieure. Je pourrai me servir de cette animorphe pour m'emparer d'elle à la place ! >

Le docteur qui était resté debout a pris la parole. Il souriait. Il prenait l'air enthousiaste et optimiste. Avec le plat de sa lame, d'un coup de queue désinvolte, le Vysserk l'a projeté à l'autre bout de la chambre.

< Ne me raconte pas que tout s'arrange pour le mieux, a-t-il ricané. J'exige toujours que vous me

répariez cet humain. C'est l'unique raison pour laquelle je vous épargne. Si dans trois jours il n'est pas rétabli, vous deux, vous irez très, très… très mal. >

Alors un tentacule oculaire a pivoté et s'est arrêté juste dans ma direction. Vite suivie du deuxième tentacule. Et j'ai eu un horrible pressentiment.

CHAPITRE
4

Vysserk Trois est sorti de notre champ de vision.

< Est-ce qu'il nous a regardés ? > a demandé Marco, qui a aussitôt répondu à sa propre question.

< Il nous a regardés. >

< Prince Jake, ai-je demandé en contrôlant ma parole mentale pour que seuls mes amis puissent l'entendre, que devons-nous faire ? >

< Que s'est-il passé ? >

< Il nous a regardés, il nous a repérés, voilà ce qui s'est passé >, a répondu Marco.

< Le Vysserk est sorti de notre champ de vision >, ai-je ajouté.

< Bon, écoutez, a dit prince Jake. Il vous soupçonne peut-être de ne pas être de vraies mouettes. Alors ne faites rien de louche, continuez de vous comporter comme si vous ne l'aviez pas remarqué. Un de

vous deux décolle. Le second laisse passer quelques secondes avant de s'envoler à son tour. Comme le feraient… >

Craccc !

La vitre a volé en éclats, fracassée par un corps inconnu. Marco, déséquilibré, est tombé à la renverse et s'est mis à dégringoler vers le sol sans parvenir à se rétablir.

Quant à moi, j'étais trop choqué pour réagir.

Alors j'ai vu ce qui avait traversé la fenêtre : un *kafit* ! Un *kafit* à six ailes !

Il ne pouvait s'agir que de Vysserk Trois en animorphe. Mais comment ?

< Impossible ! > me suis-je écrié, complètement abasourdi.

Le *kafit* est un oiseau qui ne vit que dans un seul lieu au monde : la planète mère des Andalites. Le *kafit* a secoué les éclats de verre coincés dans ses ailes et obliqué vers moi en effectuant un virage à quatre-vingt-dix degrés. Son bec tranchant était pointé sur moi comme un missile. Ailes repliées, je me suis jeté du rebord. Le bec redoutable ne m'a manqué que de l'épaisseur d'une plume ! J'ai déployé mes ailes pour prendre appui sur l'air et je me suis mis à les agiter frénétiquement.

Le *kafit* m'attaquait ! Ses six ailes lui donnaient une vitesse extraordinaire.

< Ax, qu'est-ce que c'est que cette créature ? > a demandé Cassie.

Pas le temps de lui répondre. Mes amis humains ne comprenaient pas. Le *kafit* se nourrit en harponnant des animaux qui vivent dans les arbres. C'est un oiseau rapide, précis, et terriblement meurtrier pour les animaux de petite taille.

Or, pour le moment, j'étais un animal de petite taille.

< Tout le monde attaque cet oiseau ! a ordonné prince Jake. Il ne peut pas nous battre tous à la fois. Tobias, où es-tu ? >

< Trop loin >, a-t-il répondu avec dépit.

J'ai tourné la tête pour repérer le *kafit*. Erreur ! Agissant comme un gouvernail, ma tête m'a fait pivoter, me plaçant en travers de sa trajectoire !

J'ai battu des ailes en redoublant d'ardeur. Trop faible, trop lent ! Le bec du *kafit* m'a entaillé le dessous de l'aile.

< Aaaarrgh ! > ai-je hurlé.

Pris d'une panique abominable, j'ai changé de cap et piqué vers le sol pour voler en rase-mottes, à une petite vingtaine de mètres d'altitude. Je savais que le *kafit* était plus rapide que moi. Serait-il également plus agile ?

Néanmoins, dans un coin de ma tête, je ne cessais de me demander : « Comment ? Comment ? Comment ? »

Comment Vysserk Trois avait-il acquis l'ADN d'un *kafit* ? L'Abomination avait-elle réussi à mettre le pied sur le sol andalite ?

Je survolais une grande artère, maintenant. En dessous de moi s'alignaient ces établissements d'alimentation que les humains appellent des fast-foods. Vysserk me suivait de près. Il m'aurait rejoint dans trois... deux... J'ai déployé les ailes, coupé ma vitesse, et tourné la tête et la queue en un seul et même mouvement pour me projeter sur le côté. Le *kafit* a continué tout droit.

Il était plus rapide. Je pouvais le semer, mais seulement en comptant sur l'effet de surprise. Combien de fois parviendrais-je à le tromper de cette façon ?

< Jolie manœuvre, Andalite, a grogné le Vysserk, dont la voix mentale a résonné soudain dans ma tête. Montre-moi si tu peux recommencer. >

J'étais presque assez en colère pour lui répondre. Seulement bien sûr, Vysserk Trois ne pouvait pas savoir avec certitude que j'étais un Andalite en animorphe ; il se contentait de le supposer. Si je continuais à me taire, il finirait peut-être par se dire que je n'étais qu'une innocente mouette perchée sur un rebord de fenêtre.

J'ai alors aperçu prince Jake et les autres qui fonçaient à ma rescousse.

< Prince Jake ! Ne m'aidez pas. Si vous m'aidez, il aura la preuve que nous ne sommes pas de simples oiseaux. >

< Arrête de jouer les héros, a répondu prince Jake. Tobias ! >

< Je fais ce que je peux ! Je n'ai pas le moindre courant thermique pour m'aider ! >

Du coin de l'œil, j'ai vu le grand faucon à queue rousse qui faisait d'énormes efforts pour prendre l'altitude qui lui permettrait d'effectuer un plongeon meurtrier. Mais il n'était encore qu'à trois mètres au-dessus de moi, et beaucoup trop mal placé pour pouvoir intervenir efficacement.

J'étais seul.

« Bien, tant mieux », me suis-je dit, d'un ton qui se voulait courageux. J'ai battu frénétiquement des ailes pour me rapprocher d'une grande enseigne jaune formée de deux arches jumelles.

< Voyons à quelle vitesse ce *kafit* est capable de tourner. >

J'ai visé l'ouverture d'une des deux arches, je l'ai traversée comme une flèche puis j'ai aussitôt pivoté sur moi-même. Vysserk Trois est arrivé à toute allure et a contourné l'arche pour me rattraper. Alors, à ce moment-là, je me suis engouffré par la seconde arche. Le *kafit* était tout près de moi, mais sa vitesse supérieure ne lui servait plus à rien, maintenant. En revanche son envergure d'ailes le gênait pour passer à l'intérieur des arches.

Vysserk Trois décrivait des cercles rapides, mais je n'arrêtais plus de louvoyer, passant d'une arche à l'autre.

< Beau travail, Axos ! m'a félicité Tobias. Tiens bon ! Je l'ai dans ma ligne de tir ! >

Dans la rue, les gens s'étaient attroupés, bouche bée, et contemplaient notre étrange spectacle.

– Hé ! s'est exclamé quelqu'un, cet oiseau a trop d'ailes !

– Ça doit être un mutant. Sauve-toi, la mouette, sauve-toi !

Vlan ! J'ai cogné le bord d'une des arches du bout de l'aile et j'ai raté mon virage.

< Aahhhh ! >

Le bec effilé comme un rasoir venait de me trancher trois centimètres d'aile ! Je suis tombé. J'ai heurté le toit plat du fast-food. En titubant, je me suis réfugié dans un recoin, entre deux gros climatiseurs.

J'ai vu le Vysserk piquer en rase-mottes et j'ai compris que lui aussi se posait.

Je me suis mis à démorphoser à toute vitesse. Le toit était entouré d'un mur, de sorte que les humains ne pouvaient pas nous voir de la rue. Et une fois que je serais redevenu andalite, cet oiseau ne serait plus une menace.

Mes serres se sont changées en sabots. Les plumes de ma queue se sont fondues pour former le début de ma lame caudale. Mais à force de grandir, je me suis trouvé trop à l'étroit, coincé entre ces deux climatiseurs qui m'envoyaient des bouffées d'air gras.

Moitié Andalite, moitié oiseau, je me suis extirpé hors de mon abri en titubant sur des pattes informes. J'ai débouché au beau milieu du toit. Alors, je l'ai vu. Comme moi, il démorphosait. Comme moi, il était mi-oiseau, mi-Andalite.

Mais il n'était pas un véritable Andalite.

< Rends-toi, Andalite, a persiflé le Vysserk avec mépris. Et peut-être t'épargnerai-je. >

< Voyons ce que tu vaux en combat singulier >, ai-je répliqué, m'efforçant une fois de plus d'exprimer plus d'assurance que je n'en ressentais.

Il a dressé la queue. J'ai dressé la queue.

Deux créatures qu'on aurait pu prendre toutes les deux pour de véritables Andalites s'apprêtant à livrer un duel à mort.

J'ai plongé le regard dans les yeux de l'Abomination. J'y ai vu le mal.

Puis j'y ai vu autre chose, et mes cœurs ont tressailli de joie. Car j'y ai aussi vu la peur.

CHAPITRE 5

Cela faisait très longtemps que deux Andalites n'avaient pas combattu ainsi, queue contre queue, en dehors des entraînements militaires et sportifs.

Et là, ce n'était pas du sport.

Là, entre les climatiseurs, dans les vapeurs de graisse et les odeurs de viande grillée, Vysserk Trois et moi allions nous affronter.

Deux mouettes se sont posées avec un léger battement d'ailes. Suivies de deux autres. D'un tentacule oculaire j'ai aperçu le profil de rapace d'un faucon, perché sur une cheminée d'aération voisine.

< Démorphosons >, a proposé Rachel, en faisant en sorte que j'entende sa parole mentale.

J'ai espéré qu'elle avait veillé à ce que Vysserk Trois ne puisse pas l'entendre, en revanche. Les humains ont tendance à oublier qu'on peut adresser sa parole mentale à toutes les personnes présentes ou seulement à quelques-unes qu'on a choisies.

< Impossible, a dit prince Jake. Nous serions obligés de repasser d'abord par notre forme humaine. Nous ne pouvons démorphoser que si nous avons la certitude absolue que Vysserk Trois n'en réchappera pas vivant. >

< Si nous démorphosons, il n'en sortira pas vivant >, a rétorqué Rachel avec une détermination farouche.

Je gardais les yeux rivés sur le Vysserk, la queue prête à frapper. Le moindre mouvement de sa part, et j'attaquais.

< Prince Jake, suis-je intervenu, nous ne pouvons pas prendre ce risque. Si jamais il découvre que vous êtes des humains, vos jours seront comptés. Je peux venger Elfangor tout seul. >

< Ce n'est ni le moment ni le lieu, a estimé Cassie. Les gens dans la rue ont vu un oiseau à six ailes se poser sur ce toit. Il y a certainement quelqu'un qui va venir voir. >

Je l'ai à peine entendue. Le Vysserk se déplaçait en crabe, guettant la moindre faille. J'ai levé très haut ma lame caudale, prêt à parer son attaque.

< Ax, a repris prince Jake. Cassie a raison. Peux-tu

battre en retraite sans qu'il te blesse ? Ce n'est pas le bon endroit pour ce combat. >

Dans un coin de ma tête, j'avais envie de répondre : « Oui, oui, oui, laissons le Vysserk s'en tirer. » Il était plus fort que moi. Sa queue devait avoir une portée supérieure de quinze bons centimètres à la mienne. Il était également plus grand que moi, ce qui lui permettrait de me frapper plus facilement aux yeux et à la tête.

Mais j'avais vu la peur dans le regard du Vysserk. Il avait compris qu'il n'avait pas le choix. Il savait qu'il était sur le point d'engager un combat mortel, et qu'il n'aurait pas forcément l'avantage.

Je désirais voir de nouveau sa peur. Je désirais ardemment voir sa terreur lorsque j'appuierais ma lame caudale sur sa gorge en lui disant : < De la part de mon frère ! >

Un mouvement soudain !

J'ai frappé ! Ma lame caudale a manqué sa cible, mais j'ai entaillé l'épaule de l'Abomination.

Dans la confusion, je n'ai pas tout de suite compris ce qui se produisait. Tout s'était passé si vite : son mouvement brusque, mon attaque, puis le bond gracieux qui l'a emporté par-dessus le mur du toit.

Je ne le voyais plus. Je me suis précipité au bord du toit et j'ai tendu le cou pour regarder.

Dans la rue, une fillette criait :

– Je vous jure que j'ai vu un cheval bleu sauter du toit !

– Tu es folle. Et où a-t-il atterri, alors ? lui a demandé son amie.

J'ai vu, moi, où il avait atterri. Dans une grande benne à ordures.

– Là-bas, dans la benne.

J'ai regardé Vysserk. Sa patte arrière gauche s'était fracturée dans la chute. Il morphosait en humain à toute vitesse. Il m'a lancé un regard brûlant de haine.

Je voulais dire quelque chose. Je voulais hurler une menace. Prononcer un serment terrible. Mais je me suis contenté de fixer Vysserk Trois droit dans les yeux.

Alors, quand il a repris sa bouche humaine, l'Abomination a ricané.

< Allez viens, Ax, m'a dit prince Jake. Nous n'avons plus rien à faire ici. >

CHAPITRE 6

Cette nuit-là, j'ai couru dans les champs les plus reculés de la propriété de Cassie, en essayant de mettre de l'ordre dans mes émotions. C'était une nuit humide. Il pleuvait, mais une pluie fine selon les critères terrestres. L'herbe était gorgée d'eau. Je sentais mes sabots absorber les vers qui sortent du sol par temps humide. Voilà qui m'apporterait un supplément de protéines – et c'était bien la dernière chose dont j'avais besoin : trop de protéines m'empêchent de dormir.

Les nuages voilaient la lune et les étoiles. Cela m'attristait. J'aime repérer ma planète mère dans le ciel, la nuit. C'est devenu une sorte de rite personnel. Quelque chose que je fais pour moi. Pour me souvenir que j'ai ma place quelque part dans la galaxie. Je n'y suis pas, certes, mais ce lieu existe.

Mais si je me faisais des illusions, pourtant ? C'est

vrai, j'ai une planète mère. Et une maison sur cette planète. Un peuple qui est le mien. Mais y serais-je encore à ma place, aujourd'hui ? N'ai-je pas trop changé au contact des humains ?

J'ai vu de la lumière chez Cassie. Un soir, j'avais morphosé en prince Jake et j'étais allé dîner chez elle, avec ses parents. Je possède l'ADN de prince Jake depuis le jour où il s'est fait infester par un Yirk*.

C'est un souvenir qui m'est précieux. Le dîner chez Cassie, bien sûr, pas l'animorphe de prince Jake. Parfois, lorsque je suis seul dans les bois et que je pense à la maison, c'est cette image qui me vient à l'esprit, et non celle de mon foyer andalite.

Je me suis mis à courir plus vite ; je ne me souciais plus de me nourrir, maintenant, je voulais juste sentir l'impact des gouttes de pluie contre mon torse et mon visage. Si je parvenais à galoper suffisamment vite, l'eau me tomberait sur la figure et le torse, mais pas sur le dos. J'ai aperçu une clôture en bois. Presque trop haute à franchir. J'ai quand même continué mon galop, droit sur la barrière, puis je me suis propulsé en repliant les pattes avant, et j'ai décollé.

* voir *La Capture* (Animorphs n° 6)

Il y eut un léger chouff ! quand j'ai éraflé la barre supérieure du bout d'un sabot.

Je me suis posé en douceur, pour m'apercevoir alors que j'étais à bout de souffle. J'ai ralenti la cadence et suis reparti au petit trot vers les bois.

« J'aurais pu le battre, me disais-je. J'aurais pu l'obliger à m'affronter. J'aurais pu le frapper sans lui laisser le temps de fuir. »

Dans un autre coin de ma tête, une voix répondait : « Non, tu aurais perdu. Il est plus grand, plus fort. Le corps andalite que Vysserk Trois contrôle appartenait à un grand guerrier, et il profite de son adresse et de son expérience. Tu as affronté Vysserk Trois en combat singulier et tu l'as laissé filer. »

Je l'ai affronté et je ne me suis pas enfui.

« Ce n'est pas l'envie qui te manquait ! Tu avais peur. »

Il aurait fallu que je sois inconscient pour ne pas avoir peur. Mais je n'ai pas fui. C'est lui qui a fui.

Je me suis rendu compte que je m'étais arrêté sous un pin particulièrement haut, à peine en retrait de la lisière d'une clairière. La clairière de Tobias.

< Qu'est-ce qui se passe, Axos ? > m'a-t-il demandé, caché dans l'obscurité.

< Tu ne dors pas ? >

< Non. J'ai une légère tendance à me réveiller quand de grands centaures extraterrestres à queue de scorpion galopent à travers bois comme un troupeau d'éléphants paniqués. >

Tobias n'est pas toujours très aimable lorsqu'il se réveille. C'est une caractéristique humaine qu'il a conservée.

< Excuse-moi de t'avoir réveillé. Qu'est-ce qui peut paniquer un troupeau d'éléphants ? >

Avec un soupir, Tobias est descendu vers une branche plus basse, puis il s'est posé sur une souche morte, par terre.

< Tu rumines, c'est ça ? >

< Quoi ? >

< Tu rumines. Tu retournes les mêmes pensées dans ta tête, sans t'arrêter. Tu te poses les mêmes questions de la première à la dernière, et puis tu recommences, et ainsi de suite. >

< Comment le sais-tu ? >

< Écoute, Ax... la première fois que j'ai vu Vysserk Trois... et tu sais à quelle occasion... j'ai pleuré, tellement j'ai eu peur. >

< C'était un extraterrestre. Une créature inconnue de toi. >

< Elfangor aussi était un extraterrestre et une créature inconnue. Il ne m'a pas fait peur. Vysserk Trois, oui. Pas à cause de son aspect physique, mais parce que je sentais quelque chose qui émanait de lui. Comme un nuage sombre. Presque comme une odeur. C'était une sensation, je ne trouve pas d'autre mot. J'ai très nettement senti que je regardais quelque chose qu'il fallait détruire. Cette créature était maléfique, je le sentais. Et j'avais cette horrible sensation, cette conscience que, d'une façon ou d'une autre, ce mal allait m'atteindre et changer ma vie. Alors j'ai pleuré. >

< J'avais déjà rencontré Vysserk Trois, ai-je répondu, inébranlable. Je n'aurais pas dû avoir peur. >

< Qu'est-ce que tu aurais pu faire ? >

< J'aurais pu lui imposer le combat. >

< Et si tu avais perdu ? >

< Et si j'avais gagné ? Quel coup terrible pour les Yirks ! J'aurais vengé Elfangor. Et j'aurais rendu un grand service à mon peuple. >

< Écoute, Ax, tu l'as affronté. C'est lui qui a battu en retraite, pas toi. >

< Il était encerclé, seul contre nous tous. Il vous prenait chacun pour un guerrier andalite, prêt à

démorphoser pour l'attaquer. Il a battu en retraite avec honneur. >

< L'honneur ! s'est exclamé Tobias d'un ton sarcastique. C'est un tueur au sang froid, un envahisseur qui convoite la planète des autres. Ce n'est rien qu'une racaille, un assassin. Ces types-là n'ont pas d'honneur. >

< Je devrais te laisser dormir. >

< Comme tu veux... Si tu ne veux plus en parler, on laisse tomber. >

Il a regardé autour de lui en clignant des yeux, presque aussi aveugle qu'un humain dans la pénombre avant d'ajouter :

< Difficile de dormir avec cette pluie, de toute façon. >

< Tobias. Tu sais, cet oiseau que Vysserk Trois a morphosé ? C'est un oiseau andalite. Cela s'appelle un *kafit*. C'est un oiseau de ma planète mère. >

< Ce qui signifie ? Tu crois que Vysserk Trois a dû aller sur ta planète pour pouvoir l'acquérir ? >

< Oui. J'ai peur que l'Abomination ait mis les pieds sur la planète mère andalite. >

J'ai senti Tobias se contracter. Il commençait à comprendre. Pourtant, il m'a juste répondu :

< Mais quelquefois, les gens emmènent des

animaux hors de la planète mère, non ? Je veux dire, un peu comme chez nous, où tu peux voir des lions d'Afrique dans les zoos d'Europe, d'Amérique, ou de n'importe où. Donc voilà, si ça se trouve, quelqu'un a emporté cet oiseau en toute innocence en quittant ta planète, puis il s'est fait attaquer, voler, va savoir, et l'oiseau s'est retrouvé entre les mains de Vysserk Trois. >

J'avais envie de croire à cette possibilité. Alors j'ai dit :

< Oui, ça pourrait s'expliquer comme ça. >

Cependant, je n'y croyais pas. J'avais l'intime conviction que Vysserk Trois s'était rendu sur ma planète. Lui ou l'un de ses alliés.

Il fallait alors se rendre à l'évidence : les Yirks avaient accédé à l'unique endroit encore sûr de la galaxie, ma planète mère.

CHAPITRE 7

Nous nous étions réunis dans la grange où Cassie et son père soignent les animaux malades ou blessés. Ils l'ont appelée le Centre de sauvegarde de la vie sauvage. C'est une grande bâtisse sombre, en bois. A l'intérieur se trouvent de nombreuses cages métalliques. Et dans les cages, il y a les animaux malades.

Tobias était perché sur la charpente de la toiture. De là-haut, il peut surveiller les environs par une ouverture et nous prévenir si quelqu'un approche.

Tous les autres étaient en bas. Cassie travaillait : elle déblayait des tas de paille sale avec une très grosse fourche à trois dents. De temps à autre, prince Jake déplaçait une cage qui lui barrait le chemin.

Marco et Rachel ne faisaient rien, ils se relaxaient.

Relax, c'est ce que disent les humains. Je crois que cela signifie que quand ils restent assis sans rien faire, leur corps se détend : ils se relaxent.

Un jour, quand je serai vieux, trop vieux pour être un guerrier, j'écrirai un livre sur les humains, sur leurs habitudes étranges, leur langage et leur technologie. Par exemple, saviez-vous que les humains ont inventé le livre avant l'ordinateur ? C'est pour cette raison qu'ils persistent à voir dans l'informatique une technologie supérieure, en dépit du fait évident qu'il faut au moins trente secondes à leurs ordinateurs pour charger un document, tandis qu'une page de livre est accessible immédiatement.

On serait presque tenté de considérer l'humanité comme une race arriérée et négligeable. S'il n'y avait deux points capitaux. Tout d'abord, ce sont les humains qui ont porté l'art du goût à des niveaux remarquables. Ils ont beau avoir une technologie des plus primitives, ce sont eux qui ont créé le pop-corn, les barres chocolatées, le chili con carne et les mégots de cigarette. (Pourtant, les humains eux-mêmes sont rebutés par l'idée de manger des mégots de cigarette.)

Et n'oublions pas : les humains, malgré tous leurs

défauts, ont créé le beignet à la cannelle. Un jour, après la guerre, on organisera des excursions d'Andalites qui afflueront sur Terre pour morphoser une journée en humains et ne rien faire d'autre que manger des beignets à la cannelle.

Choisissez de préférence ceux qui sont fourrés, cela en vaut vraiment la peine.

– Ax, tu écoutes ? a demandé soudain Marco.

Je me suis arraché à ma rêverie.

< Oui, bien sûr. >

– Parce que ça fait deux fois que je te dis la même chose, et tu continues de regarder dans le vide comme si tu étais à des années-lumière d'ici.

< S'il te plaît, répète-la-moi une troisième fois et je ferai attention. >

– J'ai dit : en morphosant en oiseau andalite, Vysserk Trois nous adresse peut-être un message. Je veux dire, il croit toujours que nous sommes tous des Andalites. Il avait l'air certain de poursuivre un Andalite en animorphe, tu es d'accord ? Et il choisit de morphoser en oiseau andalite ? Ce n'est pas une coïncidence. C'est un message.

Et voici la seconde raison pour laquelle on aurait tort de considérer l'humanité comme une espèce négligeable : leur incroyable capacité à s'adapter. Il y a encore quelques mois, Marco ne croyait pas à la vie sur d'autres planètes. Aujourd'hui, il a accepté cette réalité et intégré une vision du monde radicalement différente ; il s'est retrouvé impliqué dans une guerre qui recourt à une technologie d'animorphe qu'il ne comprend pas, et il parvient même à entrevoir des choses qui m'échappent.

< Oui, ai-je répondu lentement. Oui. Mais pourquoi ? Quel message ? >

Marco a haussé les épaules.

– Il secoue les barreaux de ta cage. Comme s'il voulait te dire : « Regarde, mon gars, pendant que tu es coincé sur Terre, moi je vais et je viens chez toi, je traîne avec tes potes, je mange les gâteaux de ta mère ».

< Ma mère ne fait pas de gâteaux, lui ai-je rappelé. Le sens du goût est inconnu chez... >

– Vysserk agite tes chaînes, a dit Rachel.

– Il te provoque, a renchéri Cassie.

< Il veut te taper sur les nerfs >, a ajouté Tobias.

– Il essaie de te déstabiliser avec... enfin peu importe, a dit prince Jake. L'important, ce sont ces deux questions : comment Vysserk Trois a-t-il acquis cet oiseau ? Et pourquoi a-t-il morphosé en cet animal pour t'attaquer ?

– Non, ce n'est pas ça la vraie question, est intervenue Cassie. La vraie question, c'est : qu'allons-nous faire pour ce Hewlett Aldershot ?

Marco a levé la main.

– Lui suggérer de changer de nom ?

– Vous savez, a repris prince Jake, il est plutôt bon, le plan qu'a monté Vysserk Trois. Il acquiert notre ami Hewlett Aldershot, puis il se rend aux bureaux des services secrets, consulte tout ce qu'il veut sur les ordinateurs, assiste aux réunions et, pour finir, il apprend tout ce que savent les gens des services secrets.

< Que savent les gens des services secrets ? > ai-je demandé.

– Beaucoup de choses, m'a répondu Marco.

< Ah. >

– Il ne s'agit pas seulement de ce qu'il peut découvrir, il s'agit également des gens qu'il peut rencontrer et auxquels il peut parler, a continué Rachel. Il peut savoir si des informations concernant les Yirks parviennent à…

– Ah, trop mortel ! s'est écrié Marco en se levant d'un bond sur ses deux jambes bancales. (Quand je vois un humain faire ça, je ne peux pas m'empêcher de croire qu'il va tomber à la renverse.)

— Quoi, trop mortel ? a demandé doucement prince Jake.

— Trop mortel, comme dans trop mortel. Rachel a raison. H. A. peut parler à tout le monde, non ? Il parle avec sa supérieure, d'accord ? Donc s'il se pointait un jour en lui disant : « Chef, vous savez quoi ? Des limaces parasites venues de l'espace envahissent la Terre ! » Là, pas de problème, il finirait à l'asile direct. Mais, par contre, s'il se pointait en disant : « Des limaces parasites venues de l'espace envahissent la Terre, et vous savez quoi ? Je peux me changer en rhinocéros. » Et qu'à ce moment il se changeait vraiment en rhinocéros... eh bien soudain, bing ! Le secret éclate au grand jour. Les Yirks sont fichus.

— Sauf si sa supérieure est un Contrôleur, a objecté Rachel.

— Si c'était un Contrôleur, pourquoi Vysserk Trois irait-il s'embêter avec H. A. ? a fait remarquer Cassie, qui s'est alors tournée vers Marco : A quoi tu penses, au juste ? Serais-tu en train de suggérer de morphoser en M. Aldershot ?

— Eh bien... oui !

– Nous ne faisons pas ça, a-t-elle protesté. Je croyais que nous avions décidé de ne jamais le faire. Nous ne morphosons pas en humains.

< J'ai morphosé en prince Jake >, ai-je dit.

L'idée de Marco m'excitait. Mais parfois, mes amis humains ont des réticences à faire ce qui serait nécessaire pour porter atteinte aux Yirks. Parfois aussi, c'est moi qui hésite.

< Et Cassie a morphosé en Rachel, rappelez-vous >, a ajouté Tobias*.

– D'abord, Ax, tu n'es pas humain, donc ce n'est pas pareil si tu morphoses en Jake. En plus, Jake t'aurait autorisé à le faire s'il n'avait pas été infesté par un Yirk. Et Rachel m'avait donné la permission, a repris Cassie.

– Excuse-moi ! a rétorqué Marco avec une pointe de sarcasme dans la voix. Notre ami H. A. n'est pas en état de donner sa permission. C'est un légume. C'est une carotte. C'est une tomate.

– Je croyais que la tomate était un fruit, est intervenue Rachel, pour provoquer Marco.

– Cela s'appelle un coma dépassé, Marco, bravo pour ta délicatesse, s'est indignée Cassie. Mais nous

---

* voir *La Menace* (Animorphs n°12)

ne sommes pas sûrs que M. Aldershot aille si mal que ça. Il pourrait être juste dans un coma normal. Nous n'avons pas le droit d'aller voler son ADN.

– Cet homme est un chou de Bruxelles.

– De toute façon, a dit prince Jake, nous ne pourrions pas entrer dans l'hôpital. Vysserk Trois sait que nous savons. Nous devons être dans nos corps humains pour acquérir l'ADN d'Aldershot. Vous croyez qu'on y arriverait avec Vysserk Trois sur ses gardes ? Il y a peu de chances.

Prince Jake avait raison. Nous nous sommes tous tus, découragés.

Mais alors, Cassie a murmuré :

– Oh là là...

– Quoi ? a demandé Marco.

Cassie a soupiré :

– Je suis complètement contre, mais...

– Mais ? Mais ? Mais quoi ?

Cassie s'est tournée vers moi.

– Ax, peut-on acquérir l'ADN de quelqu'un à partir de son sang seulement ?

< Oui, ça devrait être possible. >

– Du sang ?

Rachel a fait la grimace.

– On va récupérer le sang de ce type ? Ne compte pas sur moi ! L'hépatite, le sida, non merci.

< Les maladies ne peuvent pas se transmettre pendant l'acquisition d'ADN, me suis-je empressé de préciser. Le processus d'acquisition ne concerne que l'ADN, et cet ADN est isolé, encapsulé à l'intérieur de votre propre sang à température très basse – donc avec une grande stabilité – dans une sphère de molécules naltron, et... >

– Je crois que mon cerveau vient de tomber en sommeil automatique, m'a interrompu Marco. Bon, d'accord, ce sang n'est pas dangereux. Alors, Cassie, comment fait-on pour le récupérer ?

Cassie a expliqué son idée.

Tous les autres humains, même Tobias, ont dit : « C'est immonde ! » Ils ont dit « immonde » très fort et à plusieurs reprises.

J'ai appris une chose au contact des humains. Lorsqu'ils disent : « C'est immonde ! » ils ont presque toujours raison.

CHAPITRE 8

– **A**lors comment je fais pour l'acquérir sans qu'il me suce le sang ? a demandé prince Jake d'un ton inquiet.

– Ne fais pas le bébé, a dit Marco. Tu ne t'es jamais fait piquer par un moustique, peut-être ?

– Jamais de mon plein gré.

Quelques jours s'étaient écoulés. Mes amis humains vont à l'école cinq jours d'affilée, puis ils ont deux jours de repos. Ils essaient donc d'accomplir les missions pendant ces deux journées sans école.

Nous étions dans la grange, rassemblés autour d'une boîte en verre transparent, qui contenait un certain nombre de petits insectes volants à l'aspect fragile.

– Il faut que tu en prennes un dans ta main. Ne se rre pas trop fort, tu risquerais de l'écraser, a expliqué Cassie. Comme ça.

Elle a plongé la main dans la boîte. Après deux tentatives infructueuses, elle est parvenue à attraper un moustique.

Elle a sorti la main de la boîte et remis le couvercle en place, puis elle s'est concentrée sur le moustique. Au bout de quelques instants, elle a rouvert les yeux.

– Bon, à qui le tour ?

– Passe-moi ton moustique, a dit Marco. Il t'a certainement déjà piquée, avec un peu de chance il n'a plus faim.

– Nous ne pouvons pas morphoser tous le même moustique, a objecté Cassie. Il n'y a que les femelles qui sucent le sang. Les mâles sont inutilisables.

– Tout à fait exact ! s'est exclamée Rachel en riant.

– Et celui que tu as dans la main, c'est un mâle ou une femelle ? a demandé Marco.

– Comment veux-tu que je le sache ? Je n'ai pas de loupe assez puissante. Et même si j'en avais une, tu peux me dire comment on reconnaît un moustique mâle d'un moustique femelle ?

– Facile ! Les mâles trouvent ça drôle de roter en public, pas les femelles.

– Pourrions-nous envisager de continuer ? est intervenu prince Jake.

< Oui, ai-je répondu. Je ne crains pas la morsure de ces minuscules insectes. >

J'ai mis la main dans la cage de verre. Mais je n'arrivais à capturer aucune des créatures. Les mains humaines sont plus fortes et plus rapides que celles des Andalites. Pour finir, Cassie a attrapé un moustique et me l'a donné.

< Merci >, ai-je dit.

Et j'ai acquis l'ADN nécessaire.

Lorsque nous avons tous fini, prince Jake a déclaré :
– Bien. Allons-y.

Nous avons morphosé en oiseaux de proie pour voler rapidement jusqu'à l'hôpital. Grâce à mes yeux de busard cendré, j'ai vu que l'humain Hewlett Aldershot était toujours alité dans sa chambre d'hôpital. Mais avec une différence de taille. Quatre grands humains étaient assis autour de lui. Dans la chambre de gauche, nous en avons vu quatre autres. Et autant dans celle de droite.

Des humains-Contrôleurs, il n'y avait aucun doute là-dessus. Dangereusement armés, aucun doute là-dessus non plus. Douze humains armés pour protéger Hewlett Aldershot de notre éventuelle intervention.

< Plutôt flatteur, en fait, a estimé Rachel. Douze

types ? Et il y en a peut-être d'autres que nous ne voyons pas. >

< Les Yirks doivent avoir des Contrôleurs haut placés dans cet hôpital, a remarqué Cassie. Mobiliser deux chambres privées rien que pour des gardes... >

< Alors comment on entre ? > a demandé Marco d'un ton perplexe.

< Et si on créait une diversion ? a proposé Rachel. Je morphose en éléphant, Jake fait son rhino, et on saccage l'hosto ! >

< Si j'ai bien compris, ai-je dit, nous espérons tous parvenir à piquer l'humain pour être sûrs de lui prendre assez de sang. Mais, Rachel, je pense que pour faire diversion, rien n'attirerait plus l'attention d'une bande de Contrôleurs qu'un Andalite. >

C'était tout à fait sensé. Prince Jake en est convenu. Alors, pendant que les autres allaient se poser sur le toit pour remorphoser en humains avant de se changer en moustiques, j'ai gagné le rebord d'une fenêtre ouverte et sans lumière, tout au bout de l'hôpital.

Je suis entré dans la pièce en voletant, attentif à tous les bruits. J'ai entendu une respiration humaine. Lorsque mes yeux de busard cendré se sont habitués à l'obscurité, j'ai distingué la silhouette d'une jeune humaine, qui paraissait très frêle dans le lit.

J'ai démorphosé à toute vitesse, mes plumes d'oiseau se transformant rapidement en fourrure.

Soudain, la fillette a ouvert les yeux.

– Qui es-tu ? m'a-t-elle demandé. Tu es une licorne ?

< Non, je suis un Andalite. >

Je n'avais rien trouvé d'autre à répondre. Et puis je n'aime pas l'idée de mentir à une enfant malade.

– Comment t'appelles-tu ?

< Je m'appelle Aximili-Esgarrouth-Isthil. >

– Drôle de nom… a-t-elle dit.

Puis elle a refermé les yeux et s'est rendormie.

J'ai pris une grande inspiration. Puis je me suis approché de la porte le plus silencieusement possible. Je l'ai entrebâillée et j'ai pointé un tentacule oculaire dans le couloir. Deux humains vêtus de blanc se trouvaient à son extrémité.

J'ai pris une nouvelle inspiration. « Bien, me suis-je dit, je suis censé créer une diversion. »

J'ai ouvert la porte et je suis sorti dans le couloir. Les deux humains ne m'ont remarqué que lorsque je suis arrivé pratiquement à leur hauteur. Alors ils ont ouvert très grand la bouche et leurs visages ont changé de couleur : l'un est devenu tout blanc, l'autre tout rouge.

J'ignore pourquoi.

– Nom de…

– Qu'est-ce que…

Manifestement, ce n'étaient pas des Contrôleurs car, en ce cas, ils auraient hurlé : « Un Andalite ! », au lieu de : « Nom de… » et de : « Qu'est-ce que… ». Ces hommes étaient d'innocents humains.

< Bonjour, ai-je dit. N'ayez pas peur. >

– C'est… c'est une espèce de cerf mutant !

– Il y a un truc, c'est obligé, il y a un truc. Ok, Terry, tu peux enlever ton déguisement, maintenant. Ha ! Ha ! Ha ! Très drôle.

Je suis passé devant eux et j'ai continué mon chemin en direction de la chambre de Hewlett Aldershot.

Un humain avançait en poussant un chariot chargé de plateaux de nourriture. Il n'a pas levé les yeux. Il est passé devant moi en gardant le regard fixé sur le sol. Ensuite, je crois qu'il a dû remarquer mes sabots.

– Aaaahh ! a-t-il hurlé, et il a sursauté si violemment que le chariot s'est renversé.

Cling ! Cling ! Vlan ! Cracc !

C'est ainsi qu'a commencé ma diversion.

Brusquement, des portes se sont ouvertes. Des têtes ont pointé, des hurlements ont fusé. Des gens ont accouru dans le couloir. La plupart détalaient en me voyant.

– Non mais t'as vu ? T'as vu ?

– C'est un monstre !

– Je le savais bien qu'ils faisaient des expériences génétiques au labo ! C'est un monstre fabriqué !

J'aurais pu le prendre mal, si j'avais été susceptible.

A ce moment-là, la porte qui se trouvait à droite de la chambre d'Aldershot s'est ouverte. Un humain est sorti. Il m'a regardé l'espace d'une seconde, bouche bée, puis il s'est écrié :

– Un Andalite !

Il est resté interloqué une seconde de trop. Le temps qu'il sorte son pistolet, j'avais projeté ma queue vers lui, et il s'est empressé de lâcher son arme.

– Andalite ! a-t-il crié de nouveau, cette fois-ci avec des yeux brûlants de haine.

Les autres gardes se sont tous précipités hors des trois pièces en même temps. Ils étaient trop nombreux et se bousculaient dans le couloir. J'ai vu qu'ils sortaient des pistolets humains. Et j'ai même aperçu deux lance-rayons Dracon yirks.

Dans une fraction de seconde, ils allaient se mettre à tirer. Les balles de plomb qui jailliraient des armes humaines seraient des plus dangereuses. Pas seulement pour moi, mais aussi parce qu'elles pourraient traverser les cloisons et faire des victimes innocentes.

– Tirez ! Abattez-le, imbéciles, ou Vysserk Trois va nous hacher menu ! a hurlé un des humains.

Vlam !

J'ai balayé l'air d'un coup de lame caudale, à un millimètre du premier rang des hommes armés. Ils ont reculé en bousculant leurs camarades.

Vlam !

J'ai asséné un second coup de queue, mais ils étaient prêts à se battre, maintenant. De plus, ils étaient beaucoup trop nombreux pour moi, et j'avais peur que d'innocents humains soient blessés dans la bagarre.

Manifestement, ma diversion n'était pas au point.

C'est alors que j'y ai pensé. L'unique moyen d'éviter de me faire abattre.

< Je me rends ! me suis-je écrié. Je veux être l'un des vôtres. >

CHAPITRE 9

– **Q**uoi ?

< Je souhaite déserter. Je désire rejoindre les rangs des Yirks. J'aimerais devenir Contrôleur. Avez-vous des renseignements sur les conditions d'accès ? Y a-t-il des frais d'adhésion ? >

Une douzaine d'armes étaient braquées sur moi. Derrière, à l'autre bout du couloir, d'autres humains discutaient.

– Qu'est-ce qui se passe là-bas ?
– Est-ce un cheval ?
– Regarde les yeux qu'il a sur la tête !
– Où sont les vigiles ?

Le chef des Contrôleurs a rapidement pris sa décision. Il m'a entraîné dans la chambre où Hewlett Aldershot dormait de son sommeil comateux.

C'était une petite pièce. Trop petite pour contenir

tous les gardes. Ils n'étaient plus que cinq, maintenant, ce qui valait beaucoup mieux pour moi.

– Tu veux rejoindre nos rangs ? m'a demandé un des Contrôleurs d'un ton sceptique.

< En fait, non >, ai-je dit à regret.

Vlam ! J'ai frappé un grand coup avec ma queue, et le garde le plus proche a sauté en arrière, bousculant les autres. Je disposais d'une demi-seconde avant qu'ils ne se ressaisissent et ne me tirent dessus.

Vlam ! Cracc !

J'ai fracassé la vitre avec ma lame caudale.

< Regardez ! Un truc que m'a appris Vysserk Trois ! > ai-je hurlé.

Là-dessus j'ai fait trois pas au galop, ployé le torse, plaqué mes tentacules en arrière, replié les pattes, et je me suis élancé par la fenêtre.

Je suis tombé dans le vide !

< Aaaaahhh ! >

De trop haut, de beaucoup trop haut, mais cela valait mieux que de me faire tirer dessus.

< La fenêtre est ouverte, prince Jake ! ai-je crié. Et l'attention des Contrôleurs... >

Boum ! Crac !

< ... est détournée ! >

J'ai atterri dans un taillis qui a amorti ma chute, mais qui m'a aussi fait perdre l'équilibre. Lorsque j'ai voulu me relever, je me suis rendu compte, aussi ridicule que cela puisse paraître, que j'étais complètement empêtré dans les branches épineuses des buissons.

Pan ! Pan ! Pan pan pan pan !

Les gardes tiraient depuis la fenêtre. Les balles traversaient les branches et se plantaient dans le sol humide, tout autour de moi.

Les armes humaines fonctionnent selon un principe de gaz explosifs qui propulsent une balle de métal solide le long d'un tube. Le tube guide le projectile, ce qui augmente la précision du tir. Cela ne vaut pas la technologie d'un lance-rayons Dracon yirk ou d'un atomisateur andalite, mais c'est tout de même un moyen très efficace d'infliger de grosses blessures béantes à sa cible.

J'avais un besoin urgent de rétrécir. Il fallait que je devienne assez petit pour échapper aux balles !

J'ai commencé à morphoser en moustique.

< Nous sommes entrés ! ai-je entendu prince Jake annoncer. Ax, tout va bien ? Nous avons l'impression d'entendre des coups de feu, mais l'ouïe de ces animaux est assez faible. >

< C'est exact : vous entendez effectivement des coups de feu >, ai-je répondu laconiquement.

< Tu vas bien, Ax ? > a demandé Tobias.

< Pas vraiment. Mais j'espère aller mieux très bientôt. >

« Si je vis assez longtemps pour ça », ai-je ajouté en mon for intérieur.

Je rétrécissais à vive allure. Maintenant, des sirènes retentissaient dans la rue, de plus en plus proches.

– La police ! s'est exclamée une voix humaine, en provenance de la chambre d'en haut. Nous ne pouvons pas prendre le risque de nous faire arrêter !

– Si nous laissons l'Andalite s'échapper, il nous arrivera bien pire ! Continuez de tirer !

– Je ne vois pas où je tire, dans ces buissons... En plus, ils sont à l'ombre.

Je rapetissais de plus en plus vite. Les feuilles qui m'avaient paru toutes petites étaient maintenant plus grandes que ma tête. Les minuscules branches noueuses semblaient s'allonger, s'allonger... Elles ne m'emprisonnaient plus. J'aurais pu m'extirper du taillis, sauf que mes jambes rétrécissaient encore plus vite que le reste.

Un jour, les chercheurs andalites parviendront à rendre la technologie de l'animorphe parfaitement logique et prévisible. Mais, à l'heure actuelle, le processus est souvent bizarre et complètement irrationnel. Surtout lorsque l'on morphose en d'étranges animaux terrestres.

Mes pattes arrière cessèrent de diminuer une fois parvenues à la taille de celles d'un chat. Alors le mouvement s'est inversé et elles se sont remises à pousser. Ensuite, elles se sont affinées au point de ressembler à de simples baguettes, mais en conservant une longueur ridicule : elles étaient plus longues que tout le reste de mon corps !

Mes pattes avant se sont transformées en petits membres courts, et une troisième paire m'est sortie des bras.

Je n'étais plus sur quatre pattes, mais sur six. J'avais des pattes d'insecte, mais mon corps était encore en grande partie celui d'un Andalite. D'un Andalite très petit, mais néanmoins beaucoup trop gros pour pouvoir se déplacer sur des membres d'insecte.

Mes tentacules oculaires ont glissé le long de mon crâne pour venir s'immobiliser juste au-dessus de mes yeux principaux. Ils se sont mis à pousser. Ils poussaient comme des arbres à la croissance horriblement accélérée. De longues tiges nues qui explosaient en une multitude de minuscules ramifications : comme des brindilles courtes et rabougries. Sur ma tête, à la base de ces tiges velues – qui étaient des antennes – des demi-sphères sont apparues et ont commencé à bouger.

Mes yeux principaux fonctionnaient toujours, mais j'étais assailli par un flot de nouvelles données sensorielles apportées par mes antennes. Température de l'air ! Direction du vent ! Ondes sonores des feuilles, des voix lointaines et confuses, les explosions aiguës et violentes des armes à feu et de l'impact des énormes projectiles tout autour de moi.

Les balles ne m'inquiétaient plus. A moins d'une malchance extraordinaire, j'étais devenu trop petit pour qu'elles m'atteignent. Je mesurais moins de trois centimètres, et je n'avais pas encore fini de rétrécir.

Le sol poussiéreux me faisait l'effet d'une étendue parsemée de rochers. Les troncs des arbustes me semblaient plus gros et plus hauts que n'importe quel arbre que j'aie jamais vu sur Terre ni même sur ma planète.

Mes narines se sont obstruées puis elles ont pointé

vers l'avant. Deux excroissances poilues et de petite taille se sont formées, fournissant immédiatement un ensemble de données nouvelles à mon cerveau.

L'odorat ! Rien à voir avec celui d'un Andalite ou d'un humain. Il s'agissait là d'un odorat spécifique. Il n'était pas du genre à attendre passivement les odeurs qui passent. Ces organes fouillaient les molécules du vent, cherchaient, analysaient…

J'avais faim.

Des ailes membraneuses ont surgi de mon dos qui se décharnait. Mon corps s'est sectionné en trois parties distinctes : une tête minuscule, un thorax musclé, un abdomen volumineux et bombé. Des plaques cuirassées ont recouvert le bas de mon abdomen en se chevauchant.

Malgré tous ces changements, je conservais encore une version miniature de mes yeux andalites principaux.

J'aurais préféré qu'ils cessent de fonctionner. J'aurais vraiment aimé ne jamais voir ce qui a suivi.

C'est de mon menton, de l'endroit où les humains ont une bouche, qu'elle a jailli. Une lance ! Une aiguille ! D'une longueur inimaginable. A son extrémité, elle était hérissée de dents minuscules, presque comme des dents de scie.

La lance était creuse à l'intérieur. C'était une paille. Un tube conçu pour aspirer le sang.

Une gaine rétractile était également apparue. Une gaine qui protégerait l'aiguille et l'empêcherait de s'abîmer.

Du sang.

J'avais faim de sang. Là était mon objectif.

Du sang !

J'ai agité mes ailes membraneuses et me suis élevé dans l'air, d'un vol instable, désordonné, m'efforçant de grimper vers l'endroit où mes « narines » avaient localisé l'odeur qu'elles recherchaient : le doux arôme d'un souffle animal qui m'indiquait la route de la nourriture.

CHAPITRE
10

C'est alors que mes yeux ont cessé de fonctionner. Pendant quelques secondes, le temps que l'animorphe soit finie, je me suis retrouvé aveugle. J'ai rétréci encore un peu et, tout à coup, deux yeux à facettes ont jailli sur mon front.

A travers ces yeux, je voyais la réalité fractionnée en plusieurs milliers de minuscules images. Des milliers d'images microscopiques et toutes différentes, comme autant de fragments de lumière déformée, de couleurs sinistres et de tourbillons d'énergie carrément cauchemardesques.

Je n'ai jamais perdu le contrôle de l'animorphe. Je veux dire que je n'ai jamais oublié qui j'étais réellement, ce qui arrive parfois lorsqu'on morphose en une créature pour la première fois.

Je ne peux donc pas dire que j'aie perdu la tête.

Simplement la faim du moustique était si grande, si puissante et si présente, que je me suis laissé emporter par elle. Je l'ai acceptée.

Je volais en toute conscience de ma véritable identité pourtant, quand l'instinct du moustique s'est mis à crier : « Du sang ! Du sang ! », j'ai répondu : « Oui ! Oui ! »

Les moustiques n'ont pas la vitesse ni le génie acrobatique des mouches. Pas davantage la précision ou la force d'un oiseau. Ils ont un vol désordonné, ils sont ballottés par les vents. Leurs pattes pendent dans le vide et agrippent l'air. Les ailes sont faibles. Il n'empêche, le moustique arrive à destination.

On dirait un insecte inoffensif, à première vue. Mais j'ai fait quelques recherches. Les moustiques transmettent des bactéries, des virus et des parasites. Ils sont porteurs des maladies nommées encéphalite, fièvre jaune et malaria.

A elle seule, la malaria tue deux millions d'humains par an. Les moustiques sont les plus redoutables tueurs en série de la planète Terre.

< Ax ! Ax ! Réponds-moi ! > a crié prince Jake.

Je me suis alors rendu compte qu'il m'appelait depuis un moment.

< Je vais bien. J'ai morphosé en moustique. >

< Bien, a répondu prince Jake. Écoute, je sais ce que tu ressens maintenant. Ne résiste pas. La faim se calme dès que tu piques. >

< Suis l'odeur, a conseillé Cassie. Tes palpes, ce qui te sert de narines, sentent le dioxyde de carbone. C'est une substance que dégagent les animaux, y compris les humains. Vas-y. >

Affamé, j'ai grimpé jusqu'à la fenêtre ouverte. Mais alors, je me suis senti perdu : il y avait beaucoup de créatures chaudes, émettrices de dioxyde de carbone.

Celle que je cherchais était couchée. Immobile et allongée. J'ai mobilisé mes sens de moustique. Avec un gros effort de concentration, je me suis servi simultanément des ondes sonores captées par mes antennes, de l'odeur de dioxyde recueillie par mes palpes et de l'étrange vue morcelée de mes yeux à facettes.

Ma cible était absolument gigantesque. Plusieurs centaines de fois ma taille, des millions de fois mon poids... Hewlett Aldershot gisait dans son lit telle une île d'où s'échappaient d'appétissants effluves.

J'ai actionné mes petites ailes et suis allé me poser sur lui. La surface de son corps était rugueuse et inégale. Sa peau rose formait des bosses et des plis ; çà et là, des poils se dressaient, comme des arbres clairsemés sur une plaine aride.

La chair était vivante. Elle palpitait, ce qui me faisait monter et descendre. L'humain respirait. Mais sous mes pattes, je sentais quelque chose d'encore plus fascinant que le mouvement léger de la respiration : un battement de tambour régulier.

Le pouls de l'humain. Le battement du sang qui parcourait ses veines et ses artères.

Et alors…

Pan !

CHAPITRE
11

Il y eut une petite détonation très nette et, brusquement, instantanément, j'ai cessé d'être un moustique perforant une veine humaine. Je me trouvais dans l'espace. Dans le vide blanchâtre de l'Espace-Zéro !

< Quoi ? Quoi ? L'Espace-Zéro ? >

Pas très brillant comme réflexion, je vous l'accorde. Mais j'étais complètement dérouté.

Instinctivement, j'ai donné de grands coups de pattes. Avec mes pattes d'Andalite, car j'avais réintégré mon corps. Mais je m'agitais dans le vide.

Je n'éprouvais aucune sensation de mouvement, ne percevais pas le moindre souffle d'air. Déjà, le manque d'oxygène affaiblissait mon cerveau. Mes yeux se voilaient. Mes membres s'engourdissaient.

L'Espace-Zéro ! Impossible ! Pourtant, c'était bien là que je me trouvais.

J'ai regardé autour de moi avec angoisse, en orientant mes tentacules oculaires dans toutes les directions. J'ai vu mon corps, de l'intérieur et de l'extérieur. On aurait dit un puzzle à plusieurs dimensions, déformé de manière à m'offrir une vue interne de mon propre organisme.

Et là, à côté, quatre corps humains étaient disposés de la même façon – comme des coupes transversales. J'ai vu le visage de prince Jake, mais aussi son cœur qui battait, le tissu musculaire de ses jambes et l'intérieur de son cerveau. Pareil pour les autres.

Ils se tordaient tous de douleur.

Il y avait également un oiseau, immobile.

< Prince Jake ! Tobias ! > ai-je crié.

Mais ils ne pouvaient pas répondre, bien sûr. Il n'y avait pas d'air pour porter les sons. Il n'y avait rien, pas même les atomes et molécules qui flottent librement dans l'espace normal. Pas d'étoiles, pas de planète. Il n'y a aucune vie dans l'Espace-Zéro.

J'ai aperçu une forme gracieuse et argentée, à peut-être huit cents mètres de distance. Un vaisseau ! Comme pour les corps, je voyais l'intérieur et l'extérieur du vaisseau en une seule et même image. J'ai distingué les silhouettes déformées des individus qui s'affairaient à l'intérieur.

Même perturbé et le cerveau engourdi, je savais avec certitude de quelle espèce de créatures il s'agissait.

Des Andalites. C'était un vaisseau andalite !

Ses moteurs zéro-spatiaux tournaient à fort régime, pourtant il ne s'éloignait pas.

J'ai compris en un éclair. J'ai compris ce qui s'était passé. Comme le sait tout Andalite, lorsqu'on morphose en une créature beaucoup plus petite que son propre corps, la masse excédentaire se trouve expulsée dans l'Espace-Zéro. Cela fait un amas de matière disposée au hasard, qui attend là.

Du moins était-ce la théorie qu'on nous enseignait. En réalité, rien n'était disposé au hasard, ici. Parce que nous étions hors de l'espace à trois dimensions, je voyais l'intérieur de tout, des objets comme des créatures animées. Et les corps étaient encore très nettement humains ou andalites ; ce n'étaient pas des boules de matière organisée sans logique.

Un jour, il y a longtemps, j'avais expliqué à mes amis comment l'excédent de matière se trouvait refoulé dans l'Espace-Zéro. Ils m'avaient demandé si ces bulles de matière ne risquaient pas d'être percutées par les vaisseaux qui naviguaient dans cette zone.

Cela m'avait fait rire. Après tout les chances étaient...

Eh bien, apparemment, les chances étaient assez fortes, maintenant. Le vaisseau andalite s'était approché et il nous avait pris dans son champ magnétique. Il nous entraînait dans son sillage en fonçant à travers l'Espace-Zéro.

< Ohé ! ai-je crié de toutes les forces que je parvenais encore à rassembler. Vaisseau andalite ! Vaisseau andalite ! Nous sommes pris dans votre sillage et nous mourons. Au secours, vaisseau andalite ! Au secours ! >

L'effort que je déployais pour appeler pompait mes dernières réserves d'énergie. Il n'y avait pas d'air. Je voyais mes poumons s'aplatir littéralement dans ma poitrine. Je voyais mes cœurs battre frénétiquement, s'efforcer de me maintenir en vie.

Peu à peu, mes cœurs ralentissaient, ralentissaient, ralentissaient...

< Vaisseau andalite ! Vaisseau andalite ! Au secours ! Au secours ! Au secours... >

Je n'ai pas de mots pour décrire la douleur que j'éprouvais à voir mes frères andalites de si près. C'étaient les premiers que je voyais depuis si longtemps...

Eux, bien sûr, ne pouvaient pas me voir. A l'intérieur du vaisseau, ils conservaient l'espace normal à trois dimensions. Les Andalites qui étaient à bord ne voyaient que les ponts et les cloisons du vaisseau.

A ce moment-là, j'ai distingué, aussi nettement que si je me tenais à côté de mon propre corps, les derniers battements de mes cœurs. J'ai vu l'afflux de sang en direction de mon cerveau ralentir et s'arrêter.

J'ai su que j'allais mourir. J'allais mourir avec mes frères andalites à portée de vue.

Mourir...

Tout s'est obscurci.

Et puis, tout à coup, je n'étais plus mourant. Et je n'étais plus étalé dans toutes les dimensions. J'étais en un seul morceau, vivant et couché sur une table à la forme spécialement conçue pour un corps andalite, où mes pattes et ma queue pouvaient reposer confortablement.

< Quoi ? > ai-je dit sans raison particulière.

< Quoi ne me semble pas la bonne question,

a répondu une voix andalite. Je pense que les questions sont : pourquoi ? comment ? et surtout qui ? >

J'ai tourné mes tentacules oculaires. Debout à côté de moi se tenaient trois guerriers andalites.

CHAPITRE
12

< Je suis l'aristh Aximili-Esgarrouth-Isthil >, ai-je déclaré.

< Le petit frère d'Elfangor ? > s'est exclamé un des Andalites.

< Oui, je suis le frère d'Elfangor. >

J'ai poussé un léger soupir. Je sais bien que c'est ridicule mais, même si j'adorais Elfangor, si je l'admirais inconditionnellement, cela m'agace un peu qu'on m'appelle toujours « le petit frère d'Elfangor ».

Ils étaient trois guerriers andalites. Cela se voyait à la façon dont ils se tenaient. Ils parvenaient à combiner un port raide et altier, avec une souplesse désinvolte sur leurs pattes arrière.

Cela, plus le fait qu'ils portaient en bandoulière des atomisateurs militaires et des téléphones portables ultrapuissants.

< Je suis Samilin-Corrath-Gahar, a dit le plus âgé des trois, le capitaine de ce vaisseau. Voici mon officier tacticien Hareli-Frodlin-Sirinial, et le médecin du vaisseau, docteur Coaldwin-Ashun-Tahaylik. Maintenant, au nom du *yaolin*, que fabriques-tu dans l'Espace-Zéro avec ces cinq créatures ? >

< Les avez-vous sauvées ? Sont-elles vivantes ? Les créatures, je veux dire ? >

Docteur Coaldwin a répondu :

< Oui, elles sont saines et sauves. Mais quelle physiologie insolite ! Quatre d'entre elles sont de toute évidence des bipèdes, mais sans queue. Ils marchent sur deux pattes, mais ils arrivent pourtant à garder l'équilibre sans l'aide d'une queue. Fascinant. La dernière créature est manifestement conçue pour voler et... >

< Oui, merci, docteur, a interrompu le capitaine Samilin. La question que nous posons à l'aristh, c'est ce qu'il fait dans l'Espace-Zéro en compagnie de ces... ces créatures fascinantes. >

Je me suis levé. Mes pattes étaient vacillantes, mais je ne pouvais pas rester allongé comme ça.

< Capitaine, j'étais en animorphe. Une animorphe de très petite taille. Puis j'ai entendu une détonation et, brusquement, je me suis retrouvé dans l'Espace-Z. >

< Quoi ? Tu es la masse extrudée d'une animorphe de petite masse ? Impossible ! s'est exclamé le docteur, les yeux brillants d'excitation. Enfin, ce n'est peut-être pas impossible, mais cela ne s'est encore jamais produit ! Cela anéantirait toutes les théories actuelles sur le déplacement de la masse lors des animorphes. Ce serait une découverte scientifique de... >

< Oui, certainement, a encore interrompu le capitaine, avec une pointe d'impatience cette fois-ci. Mais aussi fascinant que cela soit sur le plan scientifique, j'ai une question plus importante. Nous savons comment tu t'es retrouvé dans l'Espace-Z, aristh Aximili, mais comment ces créatures sont-elles arrivées ici, puisque seuls les Andalites détiennent le pouvoir de l'animorphe ? >

C'était une question directe, posée par un officier de grade élevé. De grade très élevé. Un capitaine de vaisseau est maître et seigneur à bord. En gros, on peut dire qu'un aristh est un être qui pourrait servir de paillasson à un capitaine de vaisseau.

Le ton du capitaine était lourd de menaces, pourtant je me suis senti pris d'une soudaine envie de rire. Je me sentais soulagé. D'abord, parce que mes amis étaient hors de danger. Et puis aussi parce que j'étais de retour parmi mes frères andalites.

Ils me ressemblaient. Ils parlaient comme moi. Ils se déplaçaient comme moi. J'avais envie de rire et d'être triste à la fois.

< Réponds à la question du capitaine ! > a rugi l'officier tacticien, qui prenait la parole pour la première fois.

En tant que gradé numéro deux du vaisseau, l'officier tacticien est chargé de la discipline à bord.

< Excusez-moi, lieutenant, ai-je répondu. Mais ça fait tellement longtemps que je n'ai pas vu d'Andalite. Et je pensais que... que peut-être... que je serais coincé sur Terre pour le restant de mes jours. >

L'expression sévère de l'O. T. s'est un peu adoucie. Très peu.

Le capitaine a hoché la tête et s'est contenté de dire :

< Fais ton rapport, aristh. >

Mais il l'a dit gentiment.

< Oui, capitaine. Je suis naufragé sur la planète Terre depuis à peu près 0,7 année andalite. Je pense être l'unique survivant d'une bataille qui a opposé le vaisseau Dôme où je faisais mes classes à un vaisseau Bassin yirk. Le vaisseau Bassin était escorté par un vaisseau Amiral camouflé qui appartenait à Vysserk Trois. >

L'O. T. a poussé un grognement de dégoût.

< Le Dôme a été détaché avant le combat et... je m'y trouvais. Ce n'était pas ma décision, j'avais reçu l'ordre d'y rester. >

Je me sentais idiot à me défendre de la sorte, mais je ne voulais pas passer pour un lâche.

< En tout cas, le Dôme a quitté son orbite et s'est écrasé au fond d'un des océans de la Terre. Je suis resté plusieurs semaines terrestres sous l'eau avant que les humains viennent me sauver. >

< S'agissait-il des humains qui sont à l'infirmerie en ce moment ? > a demandé le docteur.

< Oui. >

< Ils ont employé une technique de plongée humaine ? > a demandé l'O. T.

< Non. Ils ont morphosé en animaux aquatiques et m'ont sauvé. >

Le visage du capitaine est resté impassible, à peine a-t-il crispé légèrement le dessus de ses yeux principaux.

< Ils ont morphosé, dis-tu. Et où ont-ils acquis le pouvoir de l'animorphe, au juste ? >

Cela n'allait pas être facile. Quelque temps plus tôt, j'étais parvenu à entrer en contact avec l'état-major andalite. On m'avait clairement signifié d'endosser la responsabilité de la transmission du pouvoir de l'animorphe aux humains : il ne fallait pas entacher la réputation d'Elfangor le héros. Or transmettre la technologie de l'animorphe est un grand crime.

Qu'allais-je dire ? Devais-je mentir au capitaine ? Cela me paraissait impossible. Cependant, j'avais reçu des ordres d'une source bien supérieure.

< C'est moi, capitaine. Je leur ai donné le pouvoir de l'animorphe. >

Il m'a regardé.

< Je vois. Tu es un mauvais menteur, aristh Aximili. >

Mes cœurs ont battu plus fort.

< Capitaine ? >

L'O. T. a soupiré :

< Jeune imbécile, si c'était toi qui avais donné le pouvoir de l'animorphe aux humains, comment auraient-ils fait pour être déjà en animorphe la première fois que tu les as vus ? Il est évident qu'ils étaient déjà capables de morphoser quand ils t'ont trouvé. >

Que pouvais-je répondre ? Je n'avais pas eu le temps de préparer mon histoire. J'étais censé être un moustique à plusieurs milliards de kilomètres

de là. Maintenant, j'avais l'air d'un menteur doublé d'un imbécile.

Je n'ai rien ajouté. Je me suis juste efforcé de me tenir au garde-à-vous.

< Docteur, merci, a dit le capitaine pour le congédier. Peut-être souhaitez-vous aller vérifier l'état de vos humains ? Et voir si vous pouvez analyser ce problème d'Espace-Zéro qu'a révélé le jeune Aximili. >

Le docteur a quitté la pièce. Alors le capitaine s'est penché vers moi.

< Aristh Aximili, j'aimerais savoir pourquoi tu me mens. >

< Je ne mentirais jamais si… >

< Si quoi, misérable petit aristh de rien du tout ! s'est écrié l'O. T. Tu parles à un capitaine de vaisseau ! >

J'ai hoché la tête.

< Oui, je le sais.>

L'O. T. allait se remettre à crier, mais le capitaine l'a interrompu d'un geste de la main.

< Aristh, es-tu, à un moment ou un autre de ton séjour sur Terre, entré en contact avec la planète mère ? >

< Oui, capitaine >, ai-je répondu, en défaillant presque de soulagement.

Le capitaine Samilin a compris. Il a tout compris.

< As-tu reçu des ordres à cette occasion ? >

< Oui, capitaine. >

Il a paru sur le point de m'en demander davantage, mais s'est abstenu. Il m'a regardé longuement. Puis, d'une voix beaucoup plus douce, il a dit :

< Qu'est-il arrivé à Elfangor ? >

< Il a été tué. Par Vysserk Trois. Sur la planète. >

Le capitaine a hoché la tête. L'O. T. paraissait en état de choc.

< Le prince Elfangor aurait fait une chose pareille ? a-t-il chuchoté d'une voix troublée. Le prince Elfangor a enfreint la loi de la Bonté de Sierow ? >

< Cette spéculation ne sortira jamais de cette pièce, a ordonné sèchement le capitaine. C'est l'aristh Aximili qui a inconsidérément donné le pouvoir de l'animorphe aux humains. Mais, entre nous, j'ajouterai ceci : j'ai servi sous les ordres du prince Elfangor. J'ai été son O. T. Eh bien, lorsqu'Elfangor faisait quelque chose, il avait toujours une bonne raison de le faire. >

Il m'a regardé droit dans les yeux.

< Elfangor n'était pas seulement mon prince, c'était aussi mon ami. Je veux bien croire qu'il a enfreint les règles. Je ne croirai jamais qu'il a mal agi. >

CHAPITRE
13

– Hé, j'ai une question, a dit Marco en agitant la main dans l'air avec insistance.

< Quelle question ? >

– Où, où, où... Où sommes-nous ?

< Nous sommes dans l'infirmerie du vaisseau d'assaut andalite *Ascalin*. >

J'essayais de ne pas paraître trop heureux. Je savais que mes amis humains seraient catastrophés d'apprendre qu'ils étaient naufragés loin de la Terre.

– *Ascalin* ? s'est étonnée Rachel. Ce n'est pas une nouvelle variété de salade, la scaline ?

< Nous venons de quitter l'Espace-Zéro et nous croisons maintenant à vitesse maximale en direction de la planète Leira. >

– Leira ? La planète des grenouilles télépathes ? a

demandé Cassie. Les créatures que les Yirks voulaient attaquer avec les requins mutants ?

< Oui. >

Comme nous le savions déjà, les Yirks avaient du mal à envahir Leira selon leur méthode habituelle. Les Leirans ont des pouvoirs parapsychiques qui leur permettent de détecter la présence d'un Yirk dans la tête d'un autre Leiran. Les Yirks voulaient donc modifier l'anatomie des requins-marteaux pour pouvoir les infester, puis se servir de ces requins-Contrôleurs comme troupes de choc dans les océans de Leira*.

– Mais nous avons déjoué ce plan sur Terre, m'a interrompu Marco avec impatience. J'y étais, tu te rappelles ? Je me souviens de cette anecdote. Mais je voudrais bien savoir comment nous avons débarqué ici ? J'étais un brave moustique et d'un coup, bing ! je me retrouve en moi-même, le charmant Marco, sauf qu'un Andalite me reluquait en se demandant pourquoi je n'ai pas de queue ! J'ai failli faire sur moi, j'ai cru que c'était Vysserk Trois !

< Il semblerait que notre masse extrudée ait été emportée dans le sillage du vaisseau. Tout le monde

* voir *L'Évasion* (Animorphs n°15)

est surpris et très intrigué. Nous représentons une percée scientifique de grande importance. >

– Ah ! bien... Je me sens tout de suite mieux ! s'est exclamée Rachel sur ce ton que les humains nomment « sarcastique ».

– Comment faisons-nous pour rentrer sur Terre ? a demandé prince Jake.

< Personne ne le sait. Le docteur et les autres savants à bord travaillent sur la question. Il se peut qu'il y ait un effet ressort. Mais ils ne savent pas. Et nous sommes sur le point de nous poser sur Leira. Ceci est un vaisseau d'assaut, ce qui signifie qu'il transporte un grand nombre d'engins d'attaque. L'invasion de Leira par les Yirks n'est plus secrète. C'est devenu une guerre déclarée. Les Yirks ont quatre vaisseaux Bassins et deux vaisseaux Amiraux en orbite. Avec des centaines de Cafards. Nous avons moins du tiers de leurs effectifs. >

– Dis-moi si j'ai bien compris, a repris Rachel. Nous sommes actuellement à des années-lumière de chez nous et nous allons nous retrouver au beau milieu d'une grande bataille où les méchants sont à trois contre un ?

< Exact. >

– Super, a fait Rachel. Et que pouvons-nous faire pour aider ?

– Oh même pour toi, Rachel, c'est un mauvais plan, a estimé Marco.

< Vous ne pouvez rien faire, ai-je expliqué. Je vous ai dit que le *kafit* que Vysserk Trois a morphosé pour m'attaquer était originaire de ma planète. Cela signifie que les Yirks ou leurs alliés ont dû infiltrer ma planète. Nous ne pouvons révéler votre secret à personne. En supposant que vous arriviez à regagner la Terre, vous ne pourrez pas survivre si les Yirks découvrent qui vous êtes. >

Cassie a penché la tête et m'a regardé avec un petit sourire triste.

< En supposant que vous arriviez à regagner la Terre ? Ce qui veut dire que tu ne rentrerais pas avec nous ? >

Pourquoi avais-je employé ces mots-là ? J'avais la tête pleine à craquer de questions, de problèmes et d'émotions de toutes sortes. Je ne voulais pas penser à me séparer de mes amis humains.

Rachel a pris un air mécontent.

– Je vais te dire un truc, Ax. Si on s'attaque aux Yirks aujourd'hui, je serai de la partie.

< Nous devons obéir aux ordres du capitaine >, lui ai-je rétorqué.

– Qui a dit ça ? a fait Marco.

Je commençais à ressentir des émotions encore plus perturbantes. En fait, je frôlais la panique, maintenant. Doublée, curieusement, d'un sentiment de culpabilité.

< Je ne suis qu'un humble aristh. Je dois obéir aux ordres. Comme un soldat humain. >

J'ai regardé prince Jake d'un œil implorant.

< Tu dois me comprendre. Tu n'es plus mon prince, maintenant que j'ai retrouvé les miens. >

Ils m'ont tous regardé. Ce n'était pas un regard agréable.

Prince Jake s'est efforcé de ne pas avoir l'air contrarié. Mais j'ai beau ne pas être un expert en physionomie humaine, je crois que ma déclaration l'avait affecté.

< Tu dois peut-être te demander qui sont vraiment les tiens, maintenant >, m'a murmuré Tobias, sans que personne d'autre n'entende.

< Je ne suis pas comme toi, Tobias. Je ne suis pas un nothlit. Je ne suis pas prisonnier dans un corps d'une autre espèce que la mienne. >

< Non. Mais je crois que tu n'es plus un simple aristh

non plus, maintenant. Et que cela te plaise ou non, tu es l'un des nôtres. >

Je ne lui ai pas répondu. Il avait tort. Alors j'ai dit, aussi délicatement que j'ai pu :

< Le capitaine ordonne que vous restiez tous ici jusqu'à ce que la situation se stabilise. Dans cette pièce. S'il vous plaît, n'essayez pas de circuler dans le vaisseau. >

CHAPITRE
14

L'*Ascalin* fonçait avec toute la puissance de ses moteurs vers la planète Leira. Je me trouvais sur la passerelle de commandement. Pour une raison que j'ignorais, le capitaine m'avait fait venir et semblait vouloir me garder près de lui.

Peut-être craignait-il que la compagnie des humains me soit néfaste. Je ne sais pas. Tout ce que je sais, c'est que, en principe, un aristh n'est pas autorisé à monter à cet endroit. C'était une petite passerelle, comme toujours sur un vaisseau de combat. Rien à voir avec les grands espaces d'un vaisseau Dôme. Il n'empêche, l'herbe était épaisse et serrée sous mes sabots. Et tout autour de cette zone circulaire étaient disposés les détecteurs et les ordinateurs les plus sophistiqués qui soient, commandés par une demi-douzaine de guerriers attentifs et concentrés.

C'était un honneur d'être là. J'étais excité. Alors pourquoi n'arrivais-je pas à chasser de mon esprit l'image de mes amis humains, assis dans la petite pièce adjacente à l'infirmerie ?

Une grande projection holographique scintillait au milieu de la salle. Elle montrait la planète et les vaisseaux présents alentour. Les vaisseaux yirks en rouge, les nôtres en bleu. Il y avait beaucoup plus de rouge que de bleu.

J'ai également repéré un de ces nouveaux écrans de parole mentale : il transmet les données directement au cerveau. « Le top de la technologie », comme aurait dit Marco.

J'ai décidé que je n'avais aucune raison de me sentir coupable. Je m'étais joint aux humains quand nous étions sur Terre. C'était compréhensible. Mais maintenant, j'avais retrouvé mon peuple. Ma véritable place était ici.

J'ai demandé une carte détaillée de la situation au sol sur l'écran de parole mentale.

La planète Leira est à quatre-vingt-douze pour cent couverte d'eau. Restent huit pour cent de terre, répartis en un continent et quelques îles éparses. La bataille terrestre se déroulerait sur le continent. Ni les Yirks ni

nous n'avons de grandes capacités sous l'eau, où les Leirans construisent leurs villes.

J'ai aperçu plusieurs villes leiranes, en général à soixante ou quatre-vingts kilomètres du continent ou d'une des îles.

Quiconque – Yirk ou Andalite – s'emparerait du continent pourrait ensuite prendre le contrôle de toute la planète.

< Que penses-tu de la situation tactique, aristh Aximili ? > m'a demandé l'O. T.

J'étais stupéfait. Il m'avait parlé d'un ton presque cordial.

< Je ne suis pas expert en... >

< Je me doute que non, m'a-t-il interrompu. Je te demandais juste une évaluation. >

< Oui, lieutenant. Les Yirks sont très nombreux en orbite au-dessus de la planète. Je dirais qu'ils ont l'avantage. Mais ils ne veulent pas que la bataille se déroule ici dans l'espace. Même s'ils nous battaient, ils risqueraient d'être trop affaiblis pour envahir le continent et le préserver de la contre-attaque leirane. >

< Je vois. Mais s'ils craignent une bataille terrestre contre les Leirans, pourquoi prendre alors le

risque d'engager le combat sur le continent à la fois contre nous et, éventuellement, contre eux ? >

J'étais à court de réponse. Bien sûr, l'O. T. avait raison ! J'avais dit des sottises.

Il a orienté un tentacule oculaire dans ma direction.

< Parce que, aristh Aximili, les Yirks savent que les différentes espèces ne combattent pas bien ensemble. Nous avons notre façon de faire. Celle des Leirans est très différente. Les Yirks sont unis sous un seul commandement ; ce n'est pas le cas des Leirans et nous. >

J'ai remarqué que le capitaine nous regardait, son O. T. et moi. Il avait l'air pensif et mécontent.

< Il y a une leçon à tirer de tout ça, aristh, a repris l'O. T. Nous autres, Andalites, nous sommes plus forts lorsque nous nous battons seuls. >

< Oui, lieutenant. >

J'avais compris ce qu'il voulait dire. Il parlait des humains. Et je n'avais maintenant qu'à me taire.

< Pourtant, sauf le respect que je vous dois, ce sont mes amis humains et moi qui avons empêché les Yirks de créer une espèce aquatique de troupes de choc destinée aux océans de Leira. Si les Yirks avaient mené ce plan à bien, la situation d'aujourd'hui serait intenable. >

Le visage de l'O. T. exprimait maintenant la colère. Je ne regrettais pas d'avoir parlé, mais je redoutais maintenant sa...

< Déflagrations Dracon ! s'est écrié un guerrier en poste devant un détecteur. Nous avons des déflagrations de rayons Dracon au nord du continent. Et maintenant des tirs d'atomisateur. Le combat a commencé. >

Un instant plus tard, l'hologramme d'un visage andalite est apparu devant nous.

< Prince Galuit-Enilon-Esgarrouth, commandant des forces armées, a annoncé l'O. T. Garde à vous ! >

Personne ne s'est mis au garde-à-vous à part moi. Ils étaient tous occupés. On ne s'y met pas réellement lorsqu'on est en train de faire quelque chose d'important.

Calmement, la tête holographique a déclaré en parole mentale :

< Le combat a commencé sur le continent. Les forces armées yirks sont nombreuses. Appliquez le plan sept-quatre. A nos alliés leirans : que votre grand dieu Cha-Ma-Mib vous soutienne en cette journée. Et à tous les guerriers andalites : le peuple attend de chacun de vous qu'il fasse son devoir. >

L'*Ascalin* a décéléré en entrant dans l'atmosphère épaisse et humide de Leira.

< Lieutenant, quel est mon poste de combat ? > ai-je demandé.

Il a ri, du rire sombre d'un guerrier qui va au combat.

< Pour l'audacieux aristh qui a rendu tout ceci possible ? Tu ferais bien de rester près de moi. >

Le capitaine et lui ont échangé un regard en riant. Je ne savais pas si je devais être fier ou embarrassé. En fait, j'avais surtout peur.

Le continent grossissait à vue d'œil. Il était vert et luxuriant, en grande partie recouvert de végétation. Vert comme les bois et la jungle de la Terre, mais avec aussi de vastes étendues de forêt jaune vif.

L'extrémité nord du continent était moins fertile, plus aride, et sans doute plus froide. C'était dans une des vallées du nord que la bataille faisait rage.

< Visuel, a ordonné le capitaine. Grossissement maximal. >

L'hologramme qui montrait jusqu'alors l'espace s'est changé en une image étonnamment réaliste de la vallée. Je distinguais nettement les troupes yirks, en majorité des Hork-Bajirs, avec une réserve de Taxxons et quelques Gedds, retranchés sur une éminence de

terrain surplombant la vallée. Ils avaient érigé tout un rempart de champs de force sur leurs arrières, ce qui obligeait nos troupes et celles des Leirans à les attaquer de front.

Nos vaisseaux Chasseurs fonçaient entre les rochers et les arbres clairsemés, tirant et essuyant le feu des Yirks. Un bataillon de Leirans escaladait les rochers, presque à découvert, pour attaquer les ennemis.

< Tu vois pourquoi les Yirks ont choisi de livrer combat ici ? m'a demandé le capitaine. Comme te l'expliquait l'O. T., différentes espèces, avec différents commandements, ont du mal à coopérer efficacement. Regarde ! Nous gaspillons nos troupes pour protéger les Leirans et leur éviter de se faire tailler en pièces. Résultat, nous sommes affaiblis. >

< L'*Ascalin* va arranger tout cela ! > a affirmé l'O. T. avec confiance.

< Procédure d'approche >, a annoncé un guerrier. Puis...

< Capitaine ! Il y a une défaillance dans le système de guidage de l'atterrissage ! >

Le capitaine paraissait parfaitement serein. L'O. T. s'est tourné d'un mouvement brusque vers le guerrier qui avait parlé, et il a rugi :

< Quoi ? >

< Lieutenant, toutes les commandes sont bloquées. Et la prise de contrôle manuel m'a été refusée ! >

L'O. T. a bondi vers l'ordinateur. Ses doigts se sont mis à courir fébrilement sur les écrans tactiles et les résonateurs. Je l'ai vu se concentrer pour établir le lien mental avec le système.

Alors, le visage pétrifié d'horreur, il s'est tourné vers le capitaine.

< Capitaine ! L'approche amorcée nous fait atterrir derrière les lignes yirks. Nous n'avons pas l'ombre d'une chance de nous en sortir ! >

Le capitaine s'est avancé calmement vers son O. T. Et puis…

Zacc !

Rapide comme l'éclair, il a fendu l'air avec sa lame caudale qui a touché l'O. T. à la base de la queue.

La queue de l'O. T. Hareli s'est détachée de son corps et a roulé au sol. Tous les guerriers de la passerelle se sont immobilisés, sidérés par cette scène impossible.

Le capitaine a sorti son atomisateur et s'est mis à tirer.

Tsiou ! Tsiou !

Les guerriers tombaient un à un sur la passerelle, inconscients ; l'O. T. saignait abondamment. L'air se transformait en fournaise, et l'électricité statique crépitait en flammes bleutées sur les corps et les machines.

Seul l'O. T. horrifié fut épargné. C'était une insulte délibérée : il ne représentait plus un danger. Le capitaine a ramassé son atomisateur puis il a braqué le sien sur moi.

< Ah, mon bon petit aristh, a-t-il dit. Je ne veux pas prendre le risque de te blesser. Vysserk Quatre serait très fâché si je blessais les créatures qui ont causé tant d'ennuis à Vysserk Trois sur Terre. Vysserk Trois et Vysserk Quatre sont de si bons amis. Reste calme. Tout cela sera bientôt fini. Ensuite vous serez... les invités de l'Empire yirk. >

CHAPITRE 15

Je suis resté là sans bouger, comme si on m'avait cloué les sabots. C'était impossible ! Un traître parmi les capitaines de vaisseau andalites ? Peut-être était-ce un Contrôleur ?

Personne ne bougeait. L'ordinateur guidait l'*Ascalin* dans son approche, le faisait lentement obliquer vers le sol, à quelques centaines de mètres des rochers. Dans quelques secondes, nous nous poserions.

L'O. T. Hareli saignait abondamment, mais je savais qu'il préférerait mourir que vivre privé de sa queue.

Les humains ! Cette pensée m'a frappé avec la force d'un rayon Dracon. Mes amis humains étaient à l'infirmerie. Le capitaine connaissait leur secret. D'ici quelques secondes, l'Empire yirk tout entier le connaîtrait aussi. La nouvelle parviendrait en un éclair à Vysserk Trois. Mes amis ne rentreraient pas chez eux. Jamais.

Et la Terre, comme Leira, tomberait sous l'emprise des Yirks.

< Prince Jake ! Tobias ! Cassie ! Marco ! Rachel ! ai-je crié à leur attention en parole mentale. Si l'un de vous m'entend, sauvez-vous ! Le capitaine est... >

< Le capitaine est une ordure >, a continué la voix mentale de Marco, étonnamment nette et proche.

< Quoi ? Où es-tu ? >

< Eh ouais, Ax ! On a décidé de ne pas rester dans la pièce, les bras croisés comme de gentilles petites filles et de gentils petits garçons, a ajouté Rachel. Désolée ! >

< Ax, nous sommes sur la passerelle, est intervenu prince Jake. Nous avons vu ce qui s'est passé. Du moins, aussi bien qu'on peut voir, dans ces animorphes. >

< Prince Jake, il est absolument vital d'arrêter ce capitaine Samilin ! >

< Nous ne pouvons pas le supprimer, est intervenue Cassie, nous mettrions trop de temps à démorphoser. Mais il se trouve que je suis sur le capitaine, et je peux le distraire très efficacement. >

L'*Ascalin* descendait vers le sol. Par le hublot avant, je voyais des rangs serrés de Hork-Bajirs qui encerclaient la zone d'atterrissage en braquant leurs armes.

< Vas-y, Cassie, ai-je déclaré avec une détermination farouche. Distrais-le et je m'occuperai du reste. Il ne nous reste que quelques secondes ! >

Fasciné, j'ai vu une puce trop petite pour qu'on la remarque se changer en puce trop grosse pour qu'on l'ignore. Elle grossissait à vue d'œil sur le dos du capitaine, avec d'horribles contorsions d'animorphe.

< Qu'est-ce que... >, s'est exclamé le capitaine.

Zacc !

J'ai frappé. Ma lame caudale s'est dressée, visant le cou de Samilin.

D'un bond, il a esquivé. Ma lame a entaillé le haut de sa patte avant droite. Çà et là, des mouches et des cafards que personne n'avait remarqués jusqu'alors commençaient à grossir : mes amis humains démorphosaient.

Le capitaine a dirigé son atomisateur vers moi et j'ai frappé à nouveau.

Zacc !

L'arme a volé loin de sa main et roulé en travers de la passerelle.

Maintenant, nous allions nous battre queue contre

queue, le capitaine et moi. Nous étions face à face, tremblant d'énergie et de concentration, chacun de nous guettant l'occasion qui lui permettrait d'asséner le coup de queue fatal.

En un éclair, j'ai revu la scène avec Vysserk Trois. Pour la seconde fois, j'affrontais un ennemi en combat singulier. Cette fois-ci, mon adversaire n'en réchapperait pas.

Tsiou !

L'O.T. Hareli ! Il avait ramassé l'atomisateur et fait feu. Le capitaine a grésillé, une expression d'horreur sur le visage, puis il a disparu.

< L'ordinateur ! a hurlé l'O.T. Prise de contrôle manuel ! Vite ! >

Boum !

Trop tard. L'*Ascalin* s'est écrasé lourdement. Je suis tombé à la renverse. Mes amis humains, qui avaient tous retrouvé leur corps, ont été projetés en travers de la passerelle. Seul l'O.T. est parvenu à rester debout.

< Ordinateur, décollage d'urgence ! >

< Exécution impossible, a répondu la voix désincarnée. Moteur principal gravement endommagé. >

J'ai vu Hareli vaciller sur ses sabots en entendant cette nouvelle.

< Humains, remorphosez ! a-t-il hurlé. La seule façon de sortir d'ici est d'être invisible. Et toi aussi, aristh. >

< Je ne m'enfuirai pas ! >

< Si, tu vas t'enfuir, aristh Aximili-Esgarrouth-Isthil. Toi et les humains, vous allez vous enfuir et informer le commandant de cet ignoble forfait. C'est un ordre. >

< Mais… >

< Sais-tu obéir à un ordre ? > a-t-il rugi.

< Oui, lieutenant. >

< Morphosez en petits animaux. Je vous lâcherai par l'écoutille de secours. Éloignez-vous le plus possible de l'*Ascalin*. Vous n'aurez pas beaucoup de temps. Tu m'entends ? >

Je savais ce qu'il allait faire. Je savais qu'il n'avait pas le choix. Il ne pouvait pas laisser les Yirks le capturer. Il ne pouvait les laisser capturer aucun des Andalites se trouvant à bord. Et il n'existait aucun moyen d'échapper à ce piège.

< Prince Jake, nous devons morphoser en petits animaux. Euh… en mouches. Morphoser en mouches et voler jusqu'au plafond de la passerelle. Il y a une écoutille de secours. >

Rachel m'a fixé avec un profond mépris. Puis elle s'est tournée vers prince Jake.

113

– Qu'est-ce qu'on fait ?

– On fait ce qu'il a dit, a répondu prince Jake. Allez-y.

Je me suis concentré sur l'animorphe de mouche. Je m'attendais à ce que l'O. T. Hareli paraisse surpris ou horrifié en voyant s'opérer la transformation. Après tout, les mouches sont des créatures assez hideuses, même selon les critères terrestres.

Mais il avait d'autres préoccupations. Il titubait de faiblesse, tant il avait perdu de sang. Et il faisait une annonce qui allait être diffusée dans tout le vaisseau.

< A tous les guerriers et tous les membres d'équipage de l'*Ascalin*. Ici l'officier tacticien. Le capitaine est mort. Nous sommes encerclés. La situation est sans espoir. L'unique chose qu'il nous reste à faire est d'infliger le maximum de dommages aux Yirks. Dans trois minutes, je vais déclencher toutes les armes en notre possession. Il s'ensuivra une réaction en chaîne qui fera exploser le vaisseau. >

Il s'est tu pour laisser l'information se diffuser.

< Accomplissez le rituel de mort, mes amis. Merci pour votre service à bord de ce vaisseau. Vous mourez en servant le peuple et en défendant la liberté. >

Je rapetissais rapidement. Le sol de la passerelle fonçait à ma rencontre. Des pattes et des antennes d'insecte jaillissaient de mon corps. Mais je n'en étais pas moins un Andalite, de tout cœur avec les Andalites à bord.

De tous les coins du vaisseau montait une centaine de voix mentales, qui prononçaient les paroles du rituel. Je ne pouvais faire autrement que de me joindre à elles.

< Je suis le serviteur du peuple >, ai-je dit.

J'aurais dû incliner la tête, mais je n'avais plus de tête à incliner.

< Je suis le serviteur de mon prince. >

Je savais que tous mes frères andalites, à bord, étaient en train de lever leurs tentacules oculaires vers le ciel.

< Je suis le serviteur de l'honneur >, ai-je continué, et l'écho de ces voix fortes m'a répondu.

< Ma vie ne m'appartient pas, quand le peuple en a besoin. Ma vie... est offerte pour le peuple, pour mon prince, et pour mon honneur. >

J'ai poussé sur mes pattes de mouche, agité mes ailes membraneuses et me suis propulsé vers l'écoutille de secours.

< Aristh ? > a appelé l'O. T. d'une voix faible.

< Oui ? >

< Peut-être me suis-je trompé. Peut-être différentes races peuvent-elles être plus fortes en s'unissant. Pars avec tes humains et prouve que j'avais tort. >

L'écoutille s'est ouverte avant que j'aie pu répondre. Un puissant courant d'air m'a aspiré dans le crépuscule leiran.

< Jake... prince Jake, ai-je dit. Nous devons nous éloigner le plus possible. >

Nous sommes partis dans les airs, ballottés par le vent fort qui soufflait et nous emportait vers une destination inconnue. Lorsque l'*Ascalin* a explosé, nous étions déjà suffisamment loin pour échapper aux éclats. Suffisamment loin aussi pour ne pas entendre les cris mentaux d'une centaine de héros agonisants.

CHAPITRE 16

< Bon. Et maintenant ? > a demandé Rachel.

Je n'avais pas de réponse. J'étais incapable de réfléchir. Je n'arrêtais pas de retourner cette idée dans ma tête : un capitaine de vaisseau andalite avait trahi. C'était impossible. Car plus j'y pensais, plus il m'apparaissait avec certitude que le capitaine n'était pas un Contrôleur.

L'*Ascalin* avait séjourné des semaines dans l'espace. S'il y avait eu un Yirk dans le cerveau du capitaine, il aurait eu besoin de rayons du Kandrona pour survivre. Or même le capitaine n'aurait pas pu dissimuler un Kandrona portable à bord.

< J'ai dit... et maintenant ? > a répété Rachel.

< Je ne sais pas >, ai-je répondu.

< Ah bon. Alors si toi tu ne sais pas, qui va savoir ? a-t-elle insisté. Qu'est-ce qu'on va faire ? Partir à la

recherche de la décharge la plus proche pour voir si on ne trouverait pas un bon tas de fruits pourris ? Il nous faut un plan, bon sang. >

< Je... Je... je ne sais pas quoi faire >, ai-je répété.

< Nous devons trouver un moyen de rentrer sur Terre, est intervenu Marco. Visiblement, grâce au sympathique capitaine Samilin, cette guerre tourne très mal pour nous. Je n'aurais pas cru que les Andalites tout-puissants faisaient des trucs pareils. Je pensais que seuls nous autres, pauvres humains primitifs et stupides, étions capables de passer à l'ennemi. >

< Si on le laissait un peu tranquille, maintenant ? > a dit alors Tobias.

< Ouais, le pauvre Ax, a ricané Rachel. Il nous laisse tomber en un quart de seconde pour son grand capitaine, lequel, manque de pot, s'avère être un traître. >

< Rachel, je ne crois pas que ce soit très juste de dire ça >, a protesté Cassie.

< Juste ! Juste ! a explosé Marco. Sans nous, si nous n'avions pas complètement ignoré les conseils d'Ax et de son précieux capitaine, à l'heure qu'il est, il serait mort avec... >

< J'aurais préféré ! me suis-je écrié. J'aurais préféré mourir avec eux. >

Je n'avais pas voulu dire cela. Et je ne le pensais pas vraiment. Je voulais vivre. Cela me donnait horriblement mauvaise conscience, mais je voulais vivre.

< Bon, maintenant, tout le monde la ferme, a ordonné prince Jake, prenant enfin la parole. C'est dur, ce qui s'est passé là-haut. Beaucoup de gens bien sont morts. On est tous choqués. Alors on prend deux minutes pour se calmer. >

Il s'est tu.

< Bien. Voici ce que nous allons faire. Nous volons jusqu'à ce que nous atteignions la limite des deux heures. Nous n'irons pas loin dans ces corps, même avec ce vent, mais nous avons intérêt à nous éloigner le plus possible. >

Nous nous sommes mis à voler en silence. Nos yeux à facettes nous donnaient une vision morcelée de l'étrange planète et nous avancions, presque sourds, en sentant des odeurs que nous ne pouvions pas identifier. Seuls dans le silence de nos pensées. Au bout d'un moment, j'en suis presque venu à regretter les cris et les reproches. C'est terrible de vivre quand tant d'autres ont péri. C'est terrible car vous avez beau faire, une seule pensée vous vient sans cesse à l'esprit : heureusement que ce n'était pas moi.

J'étais heureux que ce ne soit pas moi.

Nous nous sommes posés entre des rochers qui nous offraient une bonne cachette et nous avons démorphosé. D'après ce que j'avais vu sur l'écran de l'*Ascalin*, nous nous trouvions dans une sorte de région déserte entre les troupes yirks et les troupes andalites. La bataille pouvait déferler sur nous d'un instant à l'autre.

– Bien, je suis calme, maintenant, a annoncé Rachel aussitôt après avoir quitté son animorphe de mouche. Donc maintenant que je suis calme, même question : qu'est-ce qu'on fait ?

– Qu'est-ce tu penserais si Tobias allait faire un petit vol de reconnaissance ? m'a demandé prince Jake.

< Je ne sais pas. >

Prince Jake m'a regardé en serrant les lèvres et en plissant légèrement les yeux. Je crois que cette expression signifie « contrariété ».

– Tobias ? Va jeter un rapide coup d'œil, a-t-il ordonné.

Tobias a décollé du sol en battant des ailes. Prince Jake m'a regardé.

– Bon, écoute-moi, Ax. Je sais que tu n'es pas bien en ce moment. Pour plusieurs raisons, sans doute. Mais cela ne te libère pas de tes responsabilités.

< Quelles responsabilités ? >

– Écoute, il y a des Andalites qui tirent sur des Yirks. A part nous, il n'y a pas d'humains dans ce combat. Tu n'es peut-être pas un grand expert, mais tu en sais plus que nous sur ce qui se passe. Alors reprends-toi.

A ce moment-là, Tobias est revenu à toute allure et s'est posé à la hâte sur un piton rocheux, ce qui a dû lui faire un peu mal aux serres.

< Environ un millier de Hork-Bajirs fortement armés arrivent dans notre direction, et ils avancent vite. Ils sont escortés par des espèces de grands vaisseaux ovales et plats qui planent à quatre cents mètres d'altitude en tirant des salves de rayons Dracon. Derrière eux viennent des Taxxons. Et par là-bas, il y a deux douzaines de vaisseaux andalites qui volent eux aussi à basse altitude et, au sol, peut-être une centaine d'Andalites à l'air farouche. Je me trompe peut-être, mais je n'ai pas l'impression que les bons vont gagner cette bataille. >

< Nous devrions essayer de rejoindre les troupes andalites >, ai-je dit.

– Ah ouais, pour nous faire dénoncer par un autre traître andalite ? a lancé Rachel.

Sans même que j'aie eu conscience de bouger, ma lame caudale s'est plaquée contre sa gorge. Elle m'a regardé de ses yeux humains, froids et bleus.

– Qu'est-ce qu'il y a, Ax ? La vérité fait mal ? Tu nous as lâchés pour pouvoir lécher les bottes du capitaine Racaille. Qu'est-ce qui va se passer si nous allons trouver d'autres Andalites ? Tu vas nous dire d'attendre dans un coin pendant que tu feras des courbettes au prochain Andalite que tu rencontreras ?

J'ai replié ma queue, horrifié d'avoir eu une réaction aussi incontrôlée. J'ai senti la colère me quitter. Rachel avait raison.

< J'ai commis une erreur en faisant confiance au capitaine Samilin. J'ai commis une erreur en vous tenant tous à l'écart. C'est… c'est grâce à vous que je suis toujours vivant, et vous m'offrez votre amitié depuis longtemps, maintenant. Tout ce que je peux dire, c'est qu'aucun de vous ne sait quel effet cela fait d'être complètement coupé des siens. >

< Un de nous le sait >, a ajouté doucement Tobias.

< Tout ce que je peux dire, c'est que je regrette. Et je considérerai Jake comme mon unique prince jusqu'à ce qu'il décide le contraire. >

Je me suis tourné vers prince Jake et je l'ai regardé de tous mes yeux.

< Tu es mon unique prince jusqu'à ce que toi, et toi seul, décides le contraire. >

Pour une fois, il n'a pas dit : « Ne m'appelle pas prince. »

Au lieu de quoi, il a répondu :

– D'accord. Maintenant ce que j'aimerais savoir, c'est ceci : y a-t-il quelqu'un, du côté andalite, dont nous puissions être sûrs à cent pour cent ?

C'était une question douloureuse. J'ai senti fondre mes derniers vestiges d'orgueil.

< Le commandant. Si c'était un espion des Yirks, toute cette bataille serait déjà perdue. >

– Oui, ben elle a l'air drôlement mal barrée, a commenté Marco.

< Prince Galuit-Enilon-Esgarrouth, commandant des forces armées, a perdu toute sa famille lors d'un raid yirk sur un avant-poste andalite. Toute sa famille : sa femme et ses trois enfants. Ils ont préféré mourir plutôt que de se laisser capturer. Leurs corps ont été jetés en pâture aux Taxxons. Nous pouvons faire confiance au prince Galuit. >

J'ai soupiré.

< Et nous ne devrions sans doute… faire confiance à personne d'autre. >

CHAPITRE 17

Le plan paraissait simple : entrer en contact avec les forces andalites. Mais il est très dangereux d'avancer à la rencontre d'un grand nombre de guerriers en colère, redoutables, nerveux et fortement armés.

< Le dispositif de défense automatique déclenche des tirs sur tout ce qui se trouve à une certaine hauteur et qui s'approche trop près, ai-je expliqué. Tout. N'importe quelle forme située à plus d'un mètre du sol environ est repérée par les capteurs, visée et criblée de projectiles. >

– Ce terrain est trop irrégulier pour marcher, a dit Cassie, en réfléchissant. Et il commence à faire nuit. Nous pourrions essayer des oiseaux plus petits. Reprendre nos animorphes de mouettes. Non, attendez ! Des chauves-souris ! Moins rapides, mais plus agiles. Et grâce à l'écholocalisation, nous pourrons voler au ras du sol même dans le noir.

– Tous en chauves-souris ! s'est écrié Marco avec une gaieté tout à fait déplacée.

– Nous morphosons, et ensuite nous volons en rasant constamment le sol, a résumé prince Jake. Une fois parvenus derrière les lignes andalites, nous cherchons un moyen de rencontrer ce prince Galuit.

Il m'a regardé.

– Et, quoi qu'il arrive, nous nous tenons à l'écart des combats tant que nous n'aurons pas rencontré Galuit. Compris ?

< Oui, prince Jake. >

Prince Jake m'a fixé, le visage sérieux. Puis il a ajouté :

– Ne m'appelle pas prince.

Et il a esquissé un petit sourire avec sa bouche.

J'avais déjà eu l'occasion de morphoser en chauve-souris et, après les moustiques et les mouches, cette animorphe paraissait presque banale. Tout d'abord, la chauve-souris a de la fourrure. Et je trouve la fourrure très réconfortante, même lorsqu'elle est brun foncé et très différente de la mienne, qui est bleue.

Cependant, les chauves-souris sont vraiment

handicapées au sol. Leurs pattes arrière sont rabougries et balourdes, et leurs pattes avant – ou leurs bras, allez savoir – sont encombrées par des ailes parcheminées. Pour un Andalite, il est perturbant de ne pas pouvoir courir.

Je me suis concentré sur la chauve-souris, cette étrange créature, d'une étrange et si lointaine planète. J'ai rétréci, me rapprochant à toute vitesse du sol. Comme si j'allais tomber dans un des nombreux cratères volcaniques du sol rocailleux.

Mes pattes avant se sont recroquevillées, et je me suis presque retrouvé la figure contre le sol. Ma lame caudale s'est atrophiée en se froissant comme une feuille qui brûle. Ce froissement a remonté jusqu'à la base de ma queue.

Je n'ai pas pu m'empêcher de revoir en esprit l'officier tacticien dans les horribles moments qui ont suivi l'agression du capitaine, quand sa queue gisait, sectionnée, à côté de lui. L'O. T. Hareli ne m'avait pas plu. Il me faisait penser à beaucoup d'autres de ces officiers un peu âgés : arrogants et pleins de préjugés. Il n'empêche qu'il s'était comporté en véritable Andalite. Il était mort en héros.

Maintenant, mes pattes arrière rapetissaient à leur

tour. Elles sont restées parfaitement symétriques jusqu'au moment où elles ont atteint une taille très réduite. Alors, au dernier instant, de minuscules griffes se sont substituées à mes sabots.

Mes bras se sont atrophiés en pivotant de quelques degrés sur l'axe de mon corps. Mes doigts se sont allongés par rapport au reste du bras, qui continuait de rétrécir. Des pans de peau, grise puis noire, ont poussé. Ils me pendaient des bras comme un vêtement humain très large.

Le vêtement est un tissu conçu pour couvrir le corps humain. Parfois, il sert de protection contre le froid. Mais sa principale raison d'être, à ce que je crois comprendre, est que les humains trouvent leur corps en grande partie insupportable à regarder. Ils ont raison, bien sûr, mais ils couvrent les mauvaises parties : rien de plus hideux, par exemple, qu'un nez humain.

La peau s'est tendue et transformée en ailes. Mes oreilles ont pointé. Et, bien sûr, comme presque toutes les créatures terrestres, j'ai acquis une bouche.

J'avais une assez bonne vue. Pas aussi puissante que celle d'un oiseau de proie, mais presque aussi performante que celle d'un homme. Cependant, la vue n'est pas l'atout majeur des chauves-souris. Le pouvoir

spécial dont elles disposent est le suivant : elles peuvent envoyer une série d'ultrasons qui ricochent contre les objets solides et renvoient une image « sonore » à l'émetteur.

Le soleil leiran déclinait rapidement. Les yeux de chauve-souris commençaient à faiblir dans la pénombre. Mais j'avais une image très nette des rochers alentour.

< Bon, allons trouver le grand manitou andalite >, a dit Marco.

J'ai battu des ailes et décollé. Une fois de plus en compagnie de mes amis humains.

Je me sentais étrangement à l'aise. Comme si, malgré la colère de prince Jake, les sarcasmes de Marco, la méfiance affichée de Rachel, j'étais malgré tout à ma place avec eux.

Allez savoir pourquoi, à ce moment-là, malgré les images de la catastrophe de l'*Ascalin*, encore très présentes à mon esprit, je me suis vu loin d'ici, dans un autre corps, en train de manger des beignets à la cannelle avec une bouche.

Je voulais rentrer. Je voulais rentrer sur Terre.

Le capitaine Samilin était passé à l'ennemi yirk. Étais-je en train de passer dans le camp humain ?

CHAPITRE 18

J'ai agité mes ailes parcheminées, lancé quelques salves d'ultrasons, et me suis mis à voler à moins de vingt centimètres du sol. Le sens de l'écholocalisation de la chauve-souris produisait une sorte d'image aux contours nets et aux volumes vaguement esquissés.

Je plongeais entre les rochers, m'élevais dans l'air quelques millimètres à peine avant l'obstacle. Je tournais à gauche, à droite, en volte-face brusques et acrobatiques.

< C'est fou ce truc ! > a hurlé Marco.

Fou, dans la bouche de Marco, peut avoir plusieurs significations. Ça peut signifier « stupide », mais aussi « amusant ». Je crois qu'en ce cas il voulait dire « amusant ». Car même si c'était fou, c'était grisant.

< Yahou ! > a crié Rachel.

Puis elle a rigolé de manière féroce.

Bientôt, le jeu est devenu risqué : jusqu'à quel point pouvais-je raser les arêtes rocheuses sans me déchirer une aile ou fracasser mes os fragiles de chauve-souris contre un obstacle ?

Et cela détournait mon esprit de pensées plus sombres et plus troubles.

Soudain, les oreilles merveilleusement sensibles de la chauve-souris, ces oreilles capables d'entendre le retour de l'écholocalisation, ont enregistré une nouvelle information. Un bourdonnement. Un bourdonnement puissant et syncopé, qui s'accentuait à mesure que nous avancions.

< Prince Jake, je crois que nous entendons les capteurs andalites >, ai-je prévenu.

< Ah, c'est cela ? a commenté Cassie. On dirait presque de la musique. >

Nous avons continué de voler en rasant le sol, frôlant parfois des saillies rocheuses. Soudain…

< Houlà ! Arrêtez-vous ! Arrêtez-vous ! > a crié Cassie, qui volait en tête.

J'ai grimpé à angle droit vers le ciel.

Tsiou !

Les déflagrations des lance-rayons Dracon et des atomisateurs étaient assourdissantes. Et les éclairs aveuglaient nos yeux de chauve-souris. Des Hork-Bajirs, au moins une vingtaine, s'acharnaient contre un groupe formé de trois Andalites et de deux Leirans. Le combat faisait rage. Dans quelques minutes, tout serait fini.

Ce serait un massacre. Mais prince Jake nous avait donné l'ordre de ne pas nous mêler aux combats. Je n'allais pas les décevoir de nouveau, lui et mes amis humains.

Un groupe de Taxxons approchait, prêts à achever les Andalites déjà blessés qui gisaient au sol.

A ma grande surprise, c'est Cassie qui est finalement intervenue :

< Jake, il faut faire quelque chose. >

< N'ai-je pas dit que nous nous tenions à l'écart des combats ? >

< Exact, tu l'as dit, a répondu Tobias. Maintenant, qu'est-ce qu'on fait ? >

Prince Jake a hésité. Puis il a dit :

< D'accord, allons les sauver. On se pose, on démorphose, on remorphose, et vite vite vite ! >

Mais avant que nous ayons pu nous poser, toute la cuvette rocheuse où se tenaient les Andalites et les Leirans a explosé.

Ba boum !

L'onde de choc m'a projeté au loin. J'ai atterri sur le dos, à demi inconscient, assourdi, les yeux inondés de sang. Au-dessus de moi, un vaisseau yirk survolait le terrain ravagé sous les acclamations rauques des Hork-Bajirs.

Une énorme patte griffue s'est abattue à quelques centimètres de moi. Des Hork-Bajirs déferlaient en horde brutale et précipitée, ignorant la minuscule créature ailée que j'étais. Ils tiraient avec leurs lance-rayons Dracon, en poussant des cris de triomphe.

Je n'entendais aucune riposte des atomisateurs andalites. Les troupes yirks avançaient. Le front andalite était percé.

< Prince Jake ! Tobias ! > ai-je appelé.

< Envolez-vous ! nous a tous ordonné prince Jake en criant. Tous ceux qui peuvent encore voler, grimpez dans le ciel ! Grimpez ! >

Pouvais-je encore voler ? Oui. J'ai décollé du sol à l'instant où la première vague de Taxxons déferlait.

Les Taxxons sont d'énormes vers très longs. Comme des mille-pattes terrestres, juste beaucoup beaucoup plus gros. Les Taxxons vivent dans un état de faim perpétuelle. Une faim désespérée. Ils mangeraient n'importe quoi, mort ou vif. Même leurs propres frères, s'ils sont blessés et sans défense.

Je suis passé précipitamment au ras d'une gueule de Taxxon béante, à l'affût de nourriture. J'ai aperçu une camarade chauve-souris, à une cinquantaine de centimètres au-dessus de moi. Je la voyais très nettement. Et puis soudain, en une fraction de seconde, elle a disparu. Bel et bien disparu.

< Où est Tobias ? > s'est exclamée Rachel.

< Tobias ! ai-je crié. Il a… il a disparu ! >

< Comment ça, disparu ? > a demandé prince Jake.

< Je l'ai vu. J'étais en train de le regarder. Et il a disparu sous mes yeux. >

Maintenant, à six mètres d'altitude, j'avais une meilleure vision du champ de bataille. Le rang de Hork-Bajirs était déjà loin devant nous. Les Taxxons ondulaient dans la pénombre.

S'il y avait eu des Andalites dans les parages, ils avaient été décimés. Mentalement, j'ai revu l'écran de l'*Ascalin*, avec la carte tactique. J'ai pu situer notre emplacement actuel ainsi que celui où les troupes avaient été déployées.

< Nous avons perdu, ai-je murmuré, sans savoir si quelqu'un m'entendait. Nous avons perdu. >

Comme pour confirmer ce sombre constat, les flammes des réacteurs d'une douzaine de vaisseaux andalites ont illuminé le ciel, au loin. Ils décollaient de la planète Leira. Ils s'enfuyaient pour sauver leurs vies.

CHAPITRE
19

De retour dans nos corps respectifs, nous étions rassemblés au milieu des restes pestilentiels laissés par les Taxxons. Nous n'avions pas retrouvé Tobias.

Rachel passait sans cesse des cris aux larmes. Marco était assis en silence. Cassie retenait prince Jake, qui n'arrêtait pas de se lever pour faire les cent pas en grommelant à mi-voix, en se demandant ce qu'il aurait dû faire, ce qu'il aurait pu faire.

Je me tenais à l'écart. Je ne pouvais m'empêcher de penser que c'était de ma faute. J'étais humilié. J'avais honte. Je m'étais détourné de mes amis pour faire confiance aux gens de mon peuple. L'un des miens nous avait alors trahis. Et les autres... eh bien les autres s'étaient sans doute battus courageusement. Mais ils avaient perdu.

C'était exactement comme la guerre des Hork-

Bajirs. A nouveau, nous avions perdu, et nous condamnions une autre race à devenir l'esclave des Yirks.

Et quelle race ! Les Leirans sont des amphibiens. Ils peuvent se mouvoir dans l'eau comme sur terre, bien qu'ils construisent leurs villes sous l'eau. Mais ce qu'il y avait de terrifiant, c'est que les Leirans disposent de pouvoirs parapsychiques, limités certes, mais ô combien redoutables.

Des Leirans-Contrôleurs pourraient voir au travers des animorphes, dans l'esprit de la personne. Il serait impossible de les tromper longtemps. Et si jamais des Leirans-Contrôleurs étaient amenés sur Terre, ils auraient vite fait de dévoiler le secret des Animorphs.

Non pas que les Animorphs aient de grandes chances de jamais revoir la Terre.

Cassie m'a tiré de mes sombres pensées. A mi-voix, elle m'a dit :

– Ax, je ne crois pas que Jake ait envie de te le demander une seconde fois, mais à ton avis, que devrions-nous faire ?

< Je ne sais pas. Nous avons perdu. Nous sommes sur une planète étrangère qui tombera bientôt sous la domination yirk. Nous n'avons pas pu

sauver les Leirans comme jadis les Hork-Bajirs. Comme maintenant les humains. >

Derrière Cassie, j'apercevais les vaisseaux yirks qui atterrissaient pour débarquer des troupes de plus en plus nombreuses sur le continent. Bientôt, il serait transformé en une imprenable garnison ennemie.

– Parle-moi des Leirans, a repris Cassie.

J'ai haussé les épaules.

< Je n'en sais pas beaucoup plus que toi. Ce sont des amphibiens. Ils vivent principalement dans les océans. A l'origine, je crois qu'ils venaient sur la terre ferme pour pondre leurs œufs. Maintenant, leur technologie leur permet de le faire sans quitter leurs villes sous-marines. >

– Alors pourquoi s'intéressent-ils à ce qui se passe sur la terre ferme ?

< A priori, ça ne les intéresse pas. Sauf que les Yirks peuvent se servir du continent comme d'une base d'où lancer des attaques contre les villes sous-marines. En dehors de ça, je ne pense pas que les Leirans en auraient... quoi que ce soit à faire... si... >

J'ai retenu mon souffle. Mais oui ! Bien sûr ! Bien sûr, ce devait être cela, le plan de Galuit.

– Quoi ? Qu'est-ce qu'il y a ? m'a demandé Cassie d'un ton brusque.

< Prince Jake ! >

– Ouais ?

< Nous devons gagner l'océan. Si j'ai raison, nous trouverons des Andalites dans les villes leiranes. De toute façon, nous devons rejoindre la mer le plus vite possible ! >

– Pourquoi ?

J'ai hésité.

< Prince Jake... Jake... Tu dois me faire confiance. Nous ne pouvons pas rester sur le continent. Il faut que nous rejoignions l'océan. >

Prince Jake m'a regardé longuement.

– D'accord, a-t-il fini par accepter. Je te fais confiance.

< Autre chose, ai-je ajouté. Si jamais tu vois que les Yirks risquent de nous capturer, si tu vois qu'ils vont m'attraper vivant, ne les laisse pas faire. Tu devras me détruire toi-même plutôt que les laisser me prendre vivant. Promets-le-moi. >

– Quoi ? Pourquoi ?

< Parce que je crois avoir compris ce qui va se passer. Et si j'ai raison, cette défaite deviendra la plus grande victoire de l'histoire andalite. Et cette information ne doit pas tomber dans les mains des Yirks. A aucun prix. Aucun. >

CHAPITRE
20

Le continent était petit, mais cela nous a quand même pris tout le reste de la nuit pour atteindre le rivage. Nous avions morphosé en oiseaux et nous volions. Chaque fois que nous approchions de la limite des deux heures, nous faisions une halte pour nous reposer. Je me demandais sans cesse s'il nous restait assez de temps.

Nous avons survolé des scènes de désolation : des corps calcinés, des vaisseaux de combat yirks et andalites écrasés au sol...

Alors que le soleil se levait sur Leira, j'ai baissé les yeux et aperçu un vaisseau d'attaque air-sol andalite encore fumant, encastré dans un vaisseau yirk. La collision avait été si violente qu'il était impossible de distinguer où commençaient les débris de l'un, et où finissaient ceux de l'autre.

Et puis, enfin, la mer a surgi devant nous. Elle s'étendait à perte de vue, d'un bleu scintillant, infiniment plus brillante et colorée que les océans de la Terre, qui sont en général gris.

J'ai cherché du regard un point de repère. Un relief de la côte qui me paraîtrait familier, en utilisant le souvenir flou que j'avais des cartes holographiques. Mais en bordure de la côte, je ne voyais que des kilomètres et des kilomètres d'eau boueuse, envahie de roseaux, de joncs et d'étranges arbres jaunes, qui s'étalaient à l'horizontale.

< Il est grand, cet océan, a commenté Rachel. Comment allons-nous faire pour... >

< Pour quoi ? > a demandé prince Jake.

Il nous a fallu plusieurs secondes pour comprendre, pour réaliser.

Rachel avait disparu !

< Rachel ! a crié Cassie. Rachel ! >

Nous avons scruté le ciel. Rien. Même nos yeux d'oiseaux de proie ne trouvaient rien. Pas le moindre indice. Aucune trace de Rachel. Rien de rien.

< Que se passe-t-il ? a grogné Marco, qui était en colère car il avait peur. Elle était là ! Elle était en train de parler ! >

< Ax, que se passe-t-il ? a voulu savoir prince Jake. D'abord Tobias, et maintenant Rachel ! >

< Je ne sais pas. Je ne sais pas. >

< Peut-être que quelqu'un lui a tiré dessus depuis le sol, a gémi Cassie. Oh, mon Dieu, Rachel ! Rachel ! >

< Il n'y a eu aucun éclair de rayons Dracon, ai-je répondu. Rien. Elle était là et, tout d'un coup, elle a disparu. >

< C'est peut-être quelqu'un ou quelque chose depuis le sol, a repris prince Jake. Nous devons partir d'ici. Plongez ! >

Nous avons piqué. Je savais que personne ne nous avait tiré dessus, mais je plongeais vers l'océan aussi vite que les humains. J'ignorais ce qui faisait disparaître mes amis, mais j'avais peur. Quelle que soit cette créature, je ne voulais pas être sa prochaine victime.

Ailes repliées, nous tombions en flèche.

Plouf !

Je me suis enfoncé dans l'eau tiède. Aussitôt, j'ai commencé à démorphoser. Je suis remonté à la surface, déjà plus andalite que busard cendré. Mes plumes étaient gorgées d'eau, mais elles disparaissaient. J'ai inspiré par un vilain trou qui était à moitié un bec et à moitié un nez andalite.

Je me suis enfoncé de nouveau dans l'eau et j'ai fini de démorphoser. En remontant à la surface, j'ai vu prince Jake, Cassie et Marco qui pataugeaient en finissant eux aussi leur transformation.

– Animorphes de dauphin ! a ordonné prince Jake. Ax, tu vas devoir prendre ton animorphe de requin-tigre.

– Attends, non ! s'est exclamée Cassie. Nous ne savons pas quels animaux nous allons trouver dans cet océan, mais les Yirks voulaient y semer la terreur en requins-marteaux, n'est-ce pas ? C'est pour cela qu'ils voulaient créer des requins-Contrôleurs, pour combattre dans cet océan. Nous devrions tous morphoser en requins.

– Ouais. Bien vu, a admis prince Jake. C'est d'accord. Tout le monde en requins. Et on se surveille les uns les autres. Nous avons déjà perdu deux personnes. Nous ne voulons pas en perdre une troisième !

« Requin », ai-je pensé, et j'ai commencé à me transformer.

Il faut que je vous explique ce que sont ces créatures que les humains nomment requins. Ce sont des poissons. Ils respirent en puisant l'oxygène dans l'eau, au moyen de membranes qui s'appellent des ouïes.

Certains requins sont d'aimables et pacifiques mangeurs de plancton. D'autres sont petits et ne se nourrissent que de poissons de taille inférieure.

Mais il y a certains types de requins que les humains appellent des « mangeurs d'hommes ». Ces requins-là sont des machines à tuer aquatiques. S'il était possible d'imaginer que le Yirk dispose naturellement d'un corps qui lui serait propre, d'un corps qui corresponde parfaitement à sa nature nocive et impitoyable, eh bien ce serait un corps de requin.

Le requin a d'énormes et puissantes mâchoires, garnies de dents effilées et tranchantes. Sa peau est littéralement couverte de millions de dents minuscules. Une peau dont le contact peut arracher la peau humaine. Et tous les sens du requin sont concentrés sur un objectif unique : trouver la proie. La trouver et la tuer.

Une vision excellente. Un odorat capable de déceler quelques molécules de sang diluées dans un milliard de litres d'eau de mer. Un capteur sensoriel qui perçoit l'énergie des autres créatures vivantes.

Si un savant avait entrepris de concevoir le prédateur marin le plus redoutable, l'arme biologique sous-marine la plus sophistiquée, et qu'il ait abouti au requin-marteau, il aurait de quoi être fier.

Je me suis senti morphoser. J'ai senti la nageoire dorsale jaillir de ma colonne vertébrale, tranchante comme une lame de faux. Senti ma lame caudale se diviser en deux pour constituer la queue en forme de flèche et capable d'entailler la peau. Senti mes tentacules oculaires basculer sur les côtés pour laisser émerger la hideuse tête en forme de marteau. Senti les nouveaux sens s'animer dans mon cerveau. Senti les dents, les rangées de dents triangulaires et pointues, qui déchirent la chair et broient les os.

Et j'ai senti l'esprit clair, froid et brutal du requin s'associer au mien.

D'un coup de queue, je me suis déplacé dans l'eau. Jake, Cassie et Marco nageaient à mes côtés. J'imagine que comme moi, ils se sentaient puissants en ce moment. Et ils se seraient sentis encore plus puissants s'il n'y avait cette terrible réalité : nous aurions dû être six.

Mais seuls quatre requins se sont élancés vers le large, dans l'océan de Leira.

CHAPITRE 21

< Si seulement Rachel et Tobias pouvaient voir ça... a soupiré Cassie, d'une voix où se mêlaient l'amertume et l'émerveillement. Rien de commun avec nos océans. >

Elle avait raison. Le continent était peut-être morne et sans intérêt, mais cet océan était stupéfiant. Les mers terrestres abritent de nombreuses créatures fascinantes et merveilleuses mais, lorsqu'on nage, on voit surtout des eaux troubles et un fond sablonneux.

Dans cet océan, l'eau était aussi claire que l'air. Plus claire, en fait que l'air leiran, qui est tellement chargé d'humidité qu'on a parfois l'impression de respirer des nuages.

L'eau était parfaitement limpide. Nous nagions par une profondeur de douze mètres, et nous pouvions apercevoir le moindre détail du sol marin.

Et quels détails ! D'immenses créatures gonflées comme des voiles, jaune et blanc, triangulaires, avec des propulseurs biologiques. Des vers, ou plutôt des serpents, brillants et bleu électrique, longs d'une vingtaine de mètres chacun, qui nageaient en bancs désordonnés. Une étrange créature qui faisait le yoyo entre l'air et l'eau en soufflant de l'air dans une poche presque transparente. Un merveilleux poisson en forme de vis, qui se déplaçait en pivotant sur lui-même.

Et ces créatures n'étaient pas dispersées çà et là ; il y en avait partout. L'océan leiran était une jungle foisonnante de formes vivantes.

Le fond marin était hérissé de cheminées bouillonnantes, en roche et en terre, couvertes de créatures grouillantes de différentes tailles. Mes sens de requin sentaient l'énergie électrique qui se dégageait de ces cheminées, ainsi que la chaleur intense.

J'ai remarqué soudain un grand banc de vers bleus et brillants qui tournaient autour d'une des cheminées. Tandis qu'ils décrivaient des cercles, mes sens de requin ont senti l'énergie que leur transmettait la cheminée.

< Regardez ça ! s'est écriée Cassie, l'excitation

l'important sur la tristesse. Il y aurait de quoi faire le bonheur d'un millier de spécialistes des océans pendant un siècle, rien qu'en cet endroit. Les animaux, les plantes, les… les je ne sais pas quoi ! Ma mère a une amie qui étudie l'écologie des récifs coralliens, je suis sûre qu'elle donnerait n'importe quoi pour passer une heure ici ! >

< Les créatures se nourrissent de l'énergie géothermique et de la charge électrique de ces cheminées, ai-je expliqué. C'est peut-être un environnement sans prédateurs. >

< Il y a des prédateurs, a répliqué Marco. Les Yirks sont là. Et nous aussi, nous sommes là. Pour le moment. Jusqu'à ce que nous disparaissions, pfuitt ! comme Rachel et Tobias. >

Voilà qui nous a tous ramenés à la réalité. Et pourtant, malgré la peur, malgré la tristesse et même le désespoir, nous ne pouvions pas ignorer le paysage incroyable, fantastique, qui nous entourait.

Nous glissions, sombres et meurtriers, dans les eaux d'une mer pacifique. Les Yirks avaient été malins de penser aux requins pour contrôler cet océan. J'avais beau regarder autour de moi, nulle part je ne voyais de dents effilées ni de mâchoires puissantes.

Marco avait raison. Il y avait des prédateurs, ici. Mais c'étaient nous.

Et puis...

< Hé, ce ne sont pas des Leirans ? a demandé prince Jake. En bas, vers la gauche. >

J'ai regardé. Oui, ils ressemblaient bien au Leiran que nous avions vu sur Terre, en compagnie de Vysserk Un.

Ils étaient presque entièrement jaunâtres. Ils avaient la peau visqueuse, comme si elle était recouverte de vase, mais en même temps d'une texture rugueuse, granuleuse. De grosses pattes arrière palmées. En guise de bras, quatre tentacules disposés autour d'un corps dodu, en forme de barrique.

Ils avaient d'assez grosses têtes, avec une bosse à l'arrière. Posée directement sur les épaules : ils n'avaient pas de cou. Leur visage gonflé semblait se composer uniquement de deux éléments. Une bouche énorme et large, presque ridicule. Et des yeux, grands et protubérants, qui donnaient l'impression d'être éclairés de l'intérieur. Il y avait en tout quatre Leirans. Ils naviguaient sur des jets marins : de longs tubes étroits, évasés à l'avant et en forme d'aile à l'arrière, pour une plus grande maniabilité. Sur toute la bordure de l'aile arrière s'alignaient des grappes de très fins tuyaux qui pointaient vers l'extérieur.

Il était clair qu'ils nous avaient repérés et venaient à notre rencontre.

< Ils se demandent sans doute ce que nous sommes, a supposé Cassie d'un ton prudent. Ils n'ont jamais vu de requins. >

< Ce sont les bons, eux, n'est-ce pas ? a demandé Marco. Je veux dire, ce sont eux, les gars que tout le monde essaie de protéger des Yirks. >

< Oui. Nous devrions peut-être entrer en contact avec eux. Ils pourraient nous indiquer la ville leirane la plus proche. >

< Vas-y >, m'a encouragé prince Jake.

< Leirans ! ai-je crié. Leirans ! Je suis un Andalite en animorphe. >

Pffiitt !

Le harpon a fendu l'eau à peine un peu moins vite qu'une balle de pistolet humain. J'ai fait un écart sur la gauche. Le harpon a transpercé ma queue et poursuivi sa trajectoire.

< Hé ! > a hurlé Marco.

< Je suis un Andalite ! Un Andalite ! ai-je crié de nouveau. Votre ami ! Votre allié ! >

< Aximili-Esgarrouth-Isthil et trois humains de la planète Terre. Pas nos alliés à nous >, a prononcé une voix mentale sur un ton glacial.

Il a ri.

< Vous n'avez aucun secret pour ces esprits leirans. >

Brusquement, l'eau s'est mise à bouillonner, transpercée par une douzaine de harpons.

Pffiitt ! Pffiitt !

Cette fois-ci, nous étions mieux préparés. Mais pas assez rapides, néanmoins. Un harpon s'est planté dans mon flanc. Prince Jake est parvenu à les esquiver tous, mais Cassie s'est fait harponner de part en part. Marco a été touché deux fois. Des filets de sang de requin troublaient l'eau.

Les Leirans-Contrôleurs ricanaient.

< Meurs, Andalite ! Mourez, humains ! Nous porterons vos corps à Vysserk Quatre. >

< Super, cette guerre ! On ne sait pas qui est de quel côté ! a protesté Marco. C'est le Vietnam, ou quoi ? >

Trois d'entre nous avions été touchés, mais personne n'était mort. Les harpons étaient rapides, mais très fins. C'étaient certainement des armes meurtrières pour les Leirans et les autres créatures de cette mer pacifique. Mais nous, ils nous avaient à peine blessés. Rien de grave.

< Je crois que nous ne sommes pas encore morts, voyez-vous >, ai-je annoncé aux Leirans-Contrôleurs.

Ils ont écarquillé leurs grands yeux verts.

< Mais... les harpons haru-chin sont des armes mortelles ! > a bredouillé l'un d'eux.

< Non... Ici, peut-être, est intervenu prince Jake. Mais nous venons d'un monde autrement plus dangereux. >

< Vous croyez que c'est vrai, ce qu'on raconte sur les grenouilles ? a demandé Marco. Vous croyez que c'est vrai qu'elles ont un goût de poulet ? >

CHAPITRE
22

Nous nous sommes élancés vers les Leirans-Contrôleurs. Les requins sont très forts en vitesse de pointe. Trop forts pour que les Yirks en état de choc, à l'intérieur des Leirans, aient le temps de réagir.

Ils ont voulu faire demi-tour. Ils étaient encore en train de manœuvrer leurs jets marins quand ils se sont fait attaquer par quatre personnes en colère, contrariées et effrayées, en animorphes de requins.

Les Andalites connaissent bien le combat au corps à corps. Mais il y a quelque chose de très intime, d'une violence très intime, à attaquer avec une bouche. Cela vous oblige à venir très près de votre ennemi. Vous le sentez et vous le touchez. Nous avons attaqué, la gueule ouverte. Nous avons attaqué et, une fraction de seconde plus tard, les quatre Leirans-Contrôleurs sautaient de leurs jets et tentaient de s'enfuir à la nage.

Ils poussaient sur leurs grosses pattes arrière, mais ils étaient trop lents. Avec leurs pouvoirs psychiques, ils devaient sentir notre colère. Ce devait être terrible, pour eux. Ce devait être terrifiant.

Mais cela m'était égal.

Jusqu'au moment où une très forte vision psychique m'a ébranlé... Une vision qui hurlait avec désespoir, avec douleur et, malgré tout, avec un dernier soupçon d'espérance.

Un des Leirans était arrivé à faire passer cette supplication. Le Yirk dans sa tête était trop occupé à tenter de se maintenir en vie, et il en avait profité pour émettre cette vision.

L'image apparue dans ma tête était horrible. Mais je savais qu'elle était réelle.

< Prince Jake ! Il faut leur mordre la tête ! Arrache-leur le gros lobe à l'arrière ! >

< Quoi ? s'est exclamée Cassie. Ils sont déjà battus, je ne vais pas les tuer. >

Je me suis élancé vers le Leiran-Contrôleur le plus proche de moi. Le Yirk dans sa tête savait ce que je faisais mais, lorsqu'il a effectué un écart sur le côté, j'ai assommé le Leiran d'un coup de queue.

J'ai ouvert grand la gueule et refermé avec force

mes mâchoires sur le lobe qu'il avait à l'arrière de la tête.

Le plus choquant de tout cela, ce fut de voir le Yirk. Délogé du cerveau du Leiran, il se tortillait avec impuissance dans l'eau de mer.

< Les Yirks sont placés dans le lobe arrière de leur cerveau, ai-je expliqué. Arrachez-les ! >

< Ça va tuer les Leirans ! > a protesté Cassie.

– Non, a dit une voix inconnue. Cela nous libérera !

Nous étions quatre contre les trois derniers Leirans-Contrôleurs. Ce fut un travail rapide et brutal. Quatre Yirks gigotaient, condamnés à périr dans l'eau de mer.

– Merci ! ont dit les Leirans.

Ce n'était pas une parole mentale normale, c'était bien davantage. Des images, des idées qui surgissaient dans nos esprits, et que nous traduisions ensuite en mots.

< Vous avez besoin de soins médicaux, est intervenue Cassie. Je pourrais peut-être démorphoser et… >

– Non, ça ira. Nous pouvons régénérer la plupart des parties de notre corps. Cela va nous prendre du temps et nous serons faibles, mais il y a près d'ici des grottes où nous pourrons nous reposer en toute sécurité. Merci ! Merci !

J'ai vécu des événements étranges. Mais quatre Leirans jaunâtres, la moitié du cerveau à l'air, qui nous remerciaient avec chaleur, c'était vraiment l'un des plus étranges.

< Nous avons besoin de gagner la ville leirane la plus proche, a fait prince Jake. Par où se trouve-t-elle ? >

– Cela va être très difficile. Ces derniers mois, les Yirks ont capturé beaucoup d'entre nous et les ont forcés à devenir des Contrôleurs. Entre ici et la cité des Vers, il y en a beaucoup comme nous. Vous êtes puissants, mais il suffirait qu'un Leiran-Contrôleur vous croise et en réchappe pour que votre secret soit dévoilé.

< Alors comment allons-nous y aller ? > s'est demandé prince Jake.

< En morphosant en Leirans >, ai-je suggéré.

– Oui ! se sont-ils exclamés. Oui, morphosez-nous. Et prenez nos jets marins. Du moment que vous évitez les autres Leirans, vous serez à l'abri des sondages psychiques.

< Nous n'aimons pas... >, a commencé Cassie.

– Oui, l'a interrompue un des Leirans, lisant dans ses pensées. Vous n'aimez pas morphoser en créatures douées de conscience. Vous respectez notre liberté. Mais nous vous le proposons de notre plein gré. Nous avons lu dans l'esprit d'Aximili l'Andalite. Nous savons ce qu'il craint, et nous savons que, même parmi les Andalites, il y a des traîtres. Alors, mes amis, prenez notre ADN et aidez à libérer notre peuple des Yirks.

Nous sommes remontés à la surface. J'ai démorphosé. Mes amis humains aussi. Nous nous sommes maintenus la tête hors de l'eau en agitant les jambes, doucement ballottés par les vagues. Le soleil leiran, encore bas à l'horizon, se levait à peine. Tout autour de nous, la mer était dorée.

J'ai tendu le bras et posé la main sur la peau jaune et visqueuse d'un Leiran.

– Là où le ciel rencontre la mer, Andalites, humains et Leirans sont réunis en alliés, a déclaré mon Leiran. Chacun avec ses faiblesses. Chacun avec ses forces.

Cela m'a ému, aussi ridicule que cela ait pu paraître vu de l'extérieur. Des humains et un Andalite pédalant dans l'eau, aux côtés de grosses « grenouilles télépathes », comme les appelait Marco. Trois espèces dans un monde conquis par les Yirks. Si un Yirk avait pu nous voir, il nous aurait sûrement trouvés pitoyables.

< Un officier andalite m'a dit que nous étions faibles parce que nous étions unis, mais que nous ne parlions pas d'une seule et même voix, ai-je dit. Mais cette union ne me paraît pas si faible. >

< Quand des êtres libres s'unissent pour défendre la liberté, ils ne sont jamais faibles. >

C'est Marco qui avait ajouté cela. Peut-être comprenez-vous pourquoi, malgré toute leur bizarrerie, j'aime les humains. Et les Leirans commençaient à bien me plaire, eux aussi.

Nous les avons laissés partir de leur côté, vers les grottes sous-marines où ils allaient se remettre de leurs blessures.

Et nous avons commencé l'animorphe peut-être la plus étrange que nous ayons jamais connue. L'aspect physique était bizarre, certes, mais somme toute pas plus que chez beaucoup de créatures terrestres que j'ai morphosées. Les puissantes pattes palmées, les quatre tentacules sinueux et la tête sans cou étaient presque ordinaires, comparés à un corps de mouche ou de cafard.

C'est le nouveau sens qui était bouleversant : le sens psychique. Non seulement je pouvais lire toutes les pensées qui traversaient l'esprit de prince

Jake, de Cassie et de Marco. Mais en plus, je percevais assez nettement leurs secrets pour en être gêné pour eux. Et, bien sûr, pour moi-même. Car mes propres secrets, mes petites pensées futiles et mes prétentions leur étaient pareillement dévoilés.

Je voyais avec une telle évidence que Marco espérait avoir des nouvelles de sa mère, Vysserk Un. Il se demandait si elle était ici, sur Leira, et si elle avait survécu à notre dernier affrontement.

Je voyais et je sentais le poids de la responsabilité qui écrasait prince Jake. Comment il retournait sans arrêt les derniers événements dans son esprit, s'efforçait de comprendre ce qui avait pu arriver à Tobias et à Rachel. Avec quelle inquiétude il cherchait à protéger le reste d'entre nous.

Et je sentais le chagrin de Cassie, qui pleurait mentalement pour Rachel et Tobias. Qui se demandait si ce que nous faisions était juste. Qui essayait de surmonter le choc des moments violents que nous venions de vivre.

< Bon, a fait Marco, mal à l'aise. Je voudrais juste vous dire que quelles que soient les pensées que vous lisez dans mon esprit, elles sont toutes complètement fabriquées. Complètement irréelles. >

< Pareil pour moi, a vite ajouté prince Jake. Exactement pareil. >

< Hé, a dit Cassie. Ce ne sont que des animorphes, pour nous, n'est-ce pas ? Très souvent, nous avons du mal à contrôler le cerveau de l'animal. Mais en général, nous y arrivons. Alors peut-être... >

< Peut-être que si ce ne sont que des animorphes, nous pourrions débrancher, en quelque sorte, le sens psychique ! > s'est exclamé Marco, qui semblait ravi à cette idée.

C'est ce que j'ai fait, et leurs esprits ne m'ont plus été accessibles. Pareil pour eux.

Je me suis senti bien seul, tout d'un coup, quand nous avons attrapé les jets marins et que nous sommes partis en naviguant sur la mer scintillante. Bien seul, tout d'un coup.

Mais je crois que chaque espèce se sent le plus à l'aise dans ce qui correspond à sa nature. Et pour les humains et les Andalites, les secrets, les mensonges et la solitude de l'intimité sont des choses naturelles.

CHAPITRE 23

Nous sommes passés entre des Leirans assez espacés les uns des autres, qui entouraient les limites extérieures de la cité des Vers. Personne ne nous a interpellés. Nous circulions sur des jets marins de fabrication yirk, et nous nous tenions toujours suffisamment à distance pour que personne ne puisse lire dans nos pensées.

La ville leirane se dressait sur le fond marin comme une tour merveilleuse. Large de peut-être trois cents mètres à sa base, elle rétrécissait pour n'avoir plus que trois mètres de diamètre à son sommet qui effleurait le plafond d'eau scintillante. Il était équipé d'énormes ventilateurs qui aspiraient de l'air et évacuaient les gaz usés de la ville tout entière.

La ville elle-même, dans sa conception, allait à l'encontre de toute logique, du moins d'après les critères andalites ou humains. Les Andalites et les humains ont coutume de se déplacer dans deux dimensions, sur la gauche et la droite, vers l'avant et l'arrière. Mais dans l'eau, la verticale et l'horizontale étaient tout aussi plausibles que la droite et la gauche.

< On dirait un cône géant, avec des millions de trous, a observé Cassie. Regardez ! Il y a des portes partout. Des portes et des portes-fenêtres. >

La couleur dominante était le rose, mais il y avait aussi du bleu, du vert et du violet, de grandes taches de couleurs qui semblaient choisies au hasard. Partout, des ouvertures. Les Leirans allaient et venaient par ces ouvertures, à n'importe quelle hauteur : à trente mètres, à six mètres, partout.

Et, semblables à une tornade au ralenti, les longs vers bleu électrique ondoyaient tout autour de la cité. Ils formaient une auréole troublante.

Même pour les étrangers que nous étions, la tension qui régnait dans la ville était palpable. Des armes pointaient au rebord de nombreuses fenêtres. Et, nichés au pied de la ville, flottaient deux vaisseaux que je n'avais jusqu'alors vus qu'en photo : des sous-marins andalites.

< Ce sont des bons ou des méchants ? > a demandé prince Jake en regardant les sous-marins.

< Un peu des deux, peut-être ? > a lancé sèchement Marco.

< Ce sont des vaisseaux andalites >, ai-je répondu.

< Allons dire bonjour >, a proposé prince Jake.

Nous avons nagé vers les sous-marins. En approchant, nous avons vu qu'un tunnel transparent les reliait à la ville.

Des guerriers andalites le parcouraient au pas de course, la queue dressée, prêts à frapper.

Nous avons plongé vers le fond, absorbant l'oxygène de l'eau par notre peau de Leiran. Nous plongions, redoutant de nous faire interpeller d'une seconde à l'autre, voire tirer dessus. Mais nous avons croisé plusieurs dizaines de Leirans sans qu'aucun ne fasse rien pour nous arrêter.

< C'est le truc télépathique, a expliqué Cassie. Ils savent qui nous sommes et ce que nous venons faire. >

< Alors je suppose qu'ils savent aussi qui nous cherchons >, a ajouté prince Jake.

A ma grande surprise, une réponse nous est alors parvenue. Elle avait la forme d'une vision qui s'est matérialisée dans mon esprit : une sorte de flèche indiquant une porte par laquelle nous devions entrer.

< Booon... a fait Marco. Eh bien, suivons les cailloux du Petit Poucet... >

Nous sommes entrés dans la ville par une des milliers de fenêtres. Je ne sais pas ce que je m'attendais à trouver, mais certainement pas cela. La tour n'était qu'une enveloppe. A l'intérieur flottaient sept ou huit énormes bulles transparentes, peut-être même davantage. Chaque bulle avait plusieurs niveaux, en général une douzaine d'étages. A la base, elles étaient toutes percées d'un grand trou. Certaines semblaient remplies d'eau ; les autres contenaient de l'air. Dans toutes, des Leirans travaillaient, dormaient, vivaient. Et dans une des bulles pleines d'air, une douzaine d'Andalites occupaient un étage.

Nous sommes entrés par le trou du fond, pour déboucher enfin dans une salle dotée d'un sol ferme. Deux guerriers andalites attendaient.

< Démorphosez, nous a ordonné l'un d'eux. Les Leirans nous ont dit qui vous étiez. Le commandant Galuit vous attend. >

< Si j'ai bien compris, l'amabilité, c'est une notion qui ne fait pas partie de l'univers andalite ? > m'a fait remarquer Marco.

Nous avons démorphosé. J'étais soulagé de retrouver mon corps d'Andalite. Mais j'étais inquiet. Tendu. J'avais donné ma parole à prince Jake que lui, et lui seul désormais, déciderait à qui je devais obéir. Cette promesse m'avait semblé facile à faire. Mais maintenant, nous allions rencontrer Galuit ! A l'idée de lui dire non… j'en avais l'estomac noué.

Nous nous sommes précipités vers la pièce où Galuit nous attendait. Sauf qu'il ne nous attendait pas : il accourait à notre rencontre. Il était flanqué de trois gardes andalites à la mine patibulaire et de son aide de camp, un Andalite qui avait perdu un tentacule oculaire et la moitié du visage au combat.

< Aristh Aximili >, a dit Galuit sans se donner la peine de se présenter.

< Oui, commandant, je… >

< Pas le temps. >

Il m'a interrompu avec un geste brusque de la main.

< J'appartiens aux cercles supérieurs, alors je sais tout de tes équipées sur Terre. Les tiennes et celles d'Elfangor. Très déçu par Elfangor. Pourtant, par la galaxie, ton frère savait se battre ! Je ne sais pas comment tu as fait pour te retrouver ici avec tes humains, mais c'est un coup de chance ! J'ai besoin de toi. >

J'étais complètement abasourdi. Déjà, le simple fait que Galuit connaisse mon nom était incroyable. C'était comme si un adolescent humain recevait un coup de téléphone du chef d'état-major des armées nationales.

En plus, Galuit avait besoin de moi. Besoin ? De moi ?

< Commandant, puis-je vous présenter cet humain du nom de Jake ? >

< J'ai dit que j'avais besoin de toi. Maintenant, mets-toi au garde-à-vous et écoute ce que... >

< Commandant, je vous présente Jake. Mon prince. >

Galuit s'est tu tout net. Les gardes ont tous dévisagé prince Jake avec incrédulité. Puis Cassie et Marco, comme s'ils pouvaient fournir une explication.

< Tous les guerriers doivent avoir un prince, et les princes doivent obéir au peuple >, ai-je repris.

Galuit a paru envisager sérieusement de m'asséner un coup de queue. Mais ensuite, il a hoché la tête avec raideur.

< C'est exact, aristh. Nul n'a force de loi pour soi-même. Nous devons tous servir. >

Galuit s'est tourné vers prince Jake.

< J'ai besoin de toi pour sauver cette planète des Yirks. Acceptes-tu de... >

– Oui, a affirmé prince Jake.

< Tu dis oui sans même savoir ce que je vais te demander. >

– Cela sauvera-t-il les Leirans ? Cela préservera-t-il leur liberté ? Et, surtout, cela fera-t-il du tort aux Yirks ?

< Oui aux trois questions. Surtout à la dernière. Si nous sauvons Leira, ce sera un tournant dans la guerre contre les Yirks. >

– Alors nous ferons ce que tu demandes.

Galuit a paru surpris. Peut-être même impressionné. Dans un aparté mental, il m'a dit :

< J'ai connu pire prince que celui-ci. >

CHAPITRE
24

Galuit a expliqué ce dont il avait besoin, et pourquoi.

C'était exactement ce que j'avais soupçonné. La raison pour laquelle nous devions fuir la terre ferme et gagner la mer. La raison pour laquelle je ne pouvais pas courir le risque de me faire capturer par les Yirks : tout cela était un piège.

Un piège pour les Yirks.

< Nous savions que les Yirks allaient déclencher le combat sur le continent, a dit Galuit. Et nous estimions que nous avions de grands risques de perdre cette bataille. Alors nous avons prévu un plan de secours. Nous avons placé une série de bombes à quanta tout autour du continent. Notre plan était d'attendre que les Yirks aient amené toutes leurs troupes sur le continent pour faire exploser les bombes. >

J'ai hoché la tête.

< Oui, je m'en étais douté. >

Prince Jake m'a regardé du coin de l'œil, puis il a haussé un sourcil. Ce n'était pas un regard de colère. Enfin, d'après ce que je peux comprendre des expressions humaines. Mais il contenait néanmoins une pointe de reproche.

Nous étions montés à bord d'un des sous-marins et foncions déjà à vitesse maximale vers un lieu situé au sud du continent.

< Les Leirans n'ont pas besoin du continent. Ils sont très heureux dans leurs villes sous-marines. Mais apparemment, il y a un problème pour le déclenchement des bombes. Nos troupes ont été balayées beaucoup trop vite. Avec les soldats de l'*Ascalin*, nous aurions dû tenir bien plus longtemps. Le détonateur principal n'a jamais été activé. Nous envoyons le signal de destruction depuis des heures, rien. Et les Yirks ne vont pas tarder à découvrir notre piège. C'est maintenant ou jamais. >

J'ai hésité. Devais-je dire à Galuit pourquoi nos troupes avaient été si facilement balayées ? J'ai pris une grande inspiration.

< Commandant, l'*Ascalin* n'a jamais participé à la bataille. >

Galuit a basculé ses deux tentacules oculaires vers moi.

< Que dis-tu ? >

< Le capitaine Samilin était... un traître, ai-je articulé difficilement. Il a programmé l'atterrissage du vaisseau dans une zone située derrière les rangs yirks. Lorsqu'il est devenu évident que l'*Ascalin* était perdu, l'officier tacticien Hareli a pris la décision de déclencher toutes les armes aussitôt le vaisseau posé. Personne n'a survécu. A part nous et deux de nos amis qui ont disparu. >

Galuit a ravalé sa salive. Brusquement, il a paru plus âgé. Plus fragile.

– Pourquoi nous ? lui a demandé Marco. Pourquoi avez-vous besoin que ce soit nous qui allions enclencher ce détonateur ?

< Nous avons peu d'Andalites sur la planète, actuellement. Et aucun qui possède toute la gamme d'animorphes dont vous disposez, a repris Galuit. Tous les guerriers andalites ont le pouvoir de l'animorphe. Mais très peu acquièrent des animorphes ou savent les manier. En général, cette tâche est réservée à nos espions. Aux services secrets. Mais vous quatre saurez peut-être franchir les rangs des Yirks. >

Brusquement, il a paru dérouté. Ses yeux balayaient la pièce.

< J'étais certain que vous étiez quatre. Où est l'autre humain ? >

Un main glacée m'a serré les cœurs. Prince Jake était encore là. Cassie également. Mais Marco...

– Marco ! a crié prince Jake.

– Marco ! Marco !

< Nous disparaissons un par un ! > l'ai-je prévenu.

Galuit a lancé un ordre mental qui a résonné dans tout le sous-marin.

< Officier scientifique, veuillez-vous présenter immédiatement ! >

– C'est de la folie ! s'est écriée Cassie, les yeux fiévreux. Que se passe-t-il ? Nous disparaissons un par un.

Une peur froide me nouait le ventre. J'avais de la peine pour Marco et les autres. Beaucoup de peine. Mais maintenant, j'avais surtout peur. Il ne fallait pas beaucoup d'imagination pour comprendre que nous trois qui restions, nous allions finir par disparaître également.

C'est une chose d'affronter un ennemi. Mais c'en est une tout autre d'attendre avec impuissance qu'une force invisible vous... vous supprime, purement et simplement.

Le sous-marin poursuivait sa course dans le splendide océan leiran. Mais nous n'avions pas le temps d'admirer le paysage aquatique. Prince Jake, Cassie et moi étions entourés d'Andalites. L'officier scientifique nous faisait subir un interrogatoire serré. Et dès qu'il se taisait un quart de seconde, Galuit et un officier du service de contre-espionnage nous bombardaient de questions.

C'était éreintant. Mais au moins cela me distrayait-il de l'horrible suspense... attendre... attendre... attendre qu'un autre d'entre nous disparaisse.

< Combien de temps avez-vous passé dans l'Espace-Zéro ? >

< Êtes-vous certain que le capitaine savait que le vaisseau était programmé pour se poser dans la zone yirk ? >

< Quelle était la masse de la créature que vous avez morphosée sur Terre avant d'être attirés dans l'Espace-Zéro ? >

< Le capitaine Samilin paraissait-il amer, tendu ? >

Enfin, au bout d'une heure, Galuit a mis fin à cet interrogatoire.

< Ça suffit ! Samilin était un traître. Nous devons accepter cette réalité. >

Il s'est tourné vers l'officier scientifique.

< Et vous, vous avez posé les mêmes questions cinquante fois. Avancez une hypothèse. >

< Commandant, je n'ai pas assez de... >, a commencé l'officier scientifique.

< Donnez-moi votre avis ! > a exigé Galuit.

< Je... je crois que ces humains et cet aristh sont pris dans un champ de flux résiduel. Il les attire en arrière pour les ramener vers l'Espace-Zéro. Peut-être va-t-il même les ramener jusqu'à la Terre. Mais, à mon avis, ce qui se passe est un genre d'effet d'extension. Ils ont subi un étirement pour entrer dans l'Espace-Zéro et ressortir dans l'espace normal, mais une petite quantité de leur masse est toujours sur la Terre. Elle pourrait agir comme une ancre. >

– Nous sommes sur une espèce de grand élastique zéro-spatial ? a demandé prince Jake. Il s'est étiré pendant tout ce temps, et maintenant il commence à se rétracter ?

< Oui >, a acquiescé l'officier scientifique, une fois que je lui ai expliqué ce qu'était un élastique.

– Peut-être jusqu'à la Terre... auquel cas Rachel,

Tobias et Marco sont vivants, a réfléchi Cassie. Ou peut-être juste dans l'Espace-Zéro. Dans ce cas...

< D'après les données que vous m'avez fournies, le processus semble s'accélérer, a repris l'officier scientifique. Vous partirez, un par un, et ce de plus en plus vite. Comme vos amis, vous allez tous disparaître. >

Galuit a pris la parole :

< Dans ces conditions, je ne peux pas vous demander de remplir cette mission. >

Prince Jake a haussé les épaules.

< Dans ces conditions, a-t-il répondu, nous n'avons plus rien à perdre. >

CHAPITRE 25

Un des officiers de Galuit nous a donné les détails de l'opération.

< L'unité centrale de déclenchement est bien dissimulée. Elle se trouve dans ce que les Leirans appellent un « trou brillant ». Sur Leira, le passé volcanique a laissé un certain nombre de grandes bulles souterraines dans la roche, et parce cette roche contient de nombreux minéraux et bio-organismes phosphorescents, il y a de la lumière dans ces trous, et donc de la vie. >

– Quel type de vie ? a demandé Cassie.

Même maintenant, elle s'intéressait à la vie sous toutes ses formes.

< Végétale exclusivement, en dehors de certains insectes et animaux microscopiques. Il n'y a que deux moyens d'atteindre le trou brillant que nous avons

choisi : soit depuis la surface, en forant dans la roche sur près de deux mètres. Soit en passant sous l'eau : on remonte un fleuve, puis on pénètre dans une grotte immergée, on traverse un tunnel complètement obscur et, pour finir, on débouche dans le trou brillant. >

Prince Jake a pris une grande inspiration. Cassie a pris une grande inspiration. J'ai pris une grande inspiration. Nous nous sommes regardés.

< Ce n'est pas tout, a ajouté Galuit. Il se peut que le fleuve soit surveillé par des Leirans-Contrôleurs. Par ailleurs, le tunnel sans lumière est habité par une espèce de serpents qui se servent de l'écholocalisation pour mordre tout ce qui passe à leur portée. Ils sont pendus à la voûte du tunnel. Mais, une fois dans le trou brillant, vous serez en sécurité. A moins bien sûr que les Yirks l'aient trouvé avant vous. >

– Est-il trop tard pour changer d'avis ? a dit prince Jake.

Galuit a pris l'air inquiet.

< C'est de l'humour, me suis-je empressé de lui expliquer. L'humour humain consiste souvent à faire semblant de souhaiter quelque chose qu'on ne souhaite pas vraiment. >

– Comment es-tu sûr que je ne suis pas sérieux ? a repris prince Jake.

< Encore une plaisanterie >, ai-je rassuré Galuit.

Le sous-marin nous a emmenés jusqu'à l'embouchure du fleuve. Il ne pouvait nous rapprocher davantage sans courir le risque d'être beaucoup trop visible.

– Je sais que les océans sont salés, ici, comme sur Terre, a dit Cassie, mais qu'en est-il des fleuves ?

< Les fleuves ont une salinité moindre >, a répondu l'officier chargé de notre information.

Cassie a secoué la tête.

– Les requins-marteaux sont des poissons de mer. Je ne sais pas comment ils se comportent en eau douce. Je ne sais vraiment pas. Mais c'est certainement encore la meilleure animorphe pour aller vite et gagner les combats.

< Bonne chance, nous a souhaité Galuit. La liberté de cette planète repose sur vos queues. Ou... ou sur ce que les humains peuvent bien avoir d'équivalent. >

– Les épaules, a fait Cassie.

– Du moment que ce n'est pas trop lourd, a ajouté prince Jake.

< C'est de l'humour humain ? > a demandé Galuit.

– Plus un peu de peur humaine, a avoué prince Jake.

Mais ensuite, il a ri.

Cinq minutes plus tard, nous étions dans le fleuve et nous nagions à contre-courant, fendant la surface de nos nageoires dorsales.

< Voilà qui promet d'être intéressant >, a déclaré prince Jake d'un ton lugubre.

< Je sens des Leirans, ai-je dit. Je reconnais leur odeur. >

< Oui, a acquiescé Cassie. De bons Leirans ou de mauvais ? C'est ça, le problème. >

Nous avons accéléré notre allure. A travers l'eau légèrement trouble, nous les distinguions : deux amphibiens à tentacules, jaunes et grenus.

Des amphibiens télépathes.

Dès que nous sommes parvenus à leur portée psychique, les Leirans ont su qui nous étions. Ils ont fait demi-tour et se sont mis à nager comme si leur vie en dépendait.

< Rattrapons-les ! > a crié prince Jake.

Ils fonçaient vers la berge. Tentaient de se redresser, de sortir de l'eau et de nous échapper. Ils n'avaient pas de jets marins, rien que leurs corps de Leirans.

Nous étions plus rapides qu'eux, mais la berge était

proche, de plus en plus proche ! L'eau était de moins en moins profonde. Pas plus de deux mètres. Un mètre cinquante ! Les Leirans soulevaient de la vase, mais je pouvais sentir leur flux électrique, maintenant, grâce à mes sens de requin.

Aveugle, le ventre rasant la vase, je me suis élancé.

J'ai planté mes dents. Sans lâcher prise, j'ai ramené la créature dans l'eau.

Mais alors, à travers la surface ondulée, j'ai aperçu un immense Hork-Bajir. Deux, non, quatre Hork-Bajirs ! Ils sont entrés bruyamment dans l'eau. J'ai reculé. J'essayais de faire demi-tour malgré le Leiran qui se débattait.

Soudain, je l'ai entendu lancer un cri télépathique aux Hork-Bajirs.

– Des explosifs ! Le continent est bourré d'explosifs ! Il y a une unité de déclenchement. Trou brillant. Il est dans...

J'ai mordu plus fort. La douleur a fait taire le Leiran. Une lame hork-bajir a fendu l'eau. Elle m'a blessé, mais de façon superficielle.

J'ai lâché un instant le Leiran, basculé la tête à la verticale et mordu de toutes mes forces la jambe du Hork-Bajir le plus proche. Son hurlement a résonné dans l'eau.

Le Leiran s'enfuyait. Encore à moitié aveuglé par la boue, je me suis jeté sur lui.

Les Hork-Bajirs avaient battu en retraite. J'ai entraîné le Leiran vers des eaux plus profondes.

< Non ! > a hurlé le Yirk dans sa tête.

< Oh, si >, ai-je dit.

Je suis passé derrière lui et, d'un puissant coup de mâchoires, je lui ai arraché le lobe arrière. Le Yirk est tombé dans l'eau.

< Tu vas t'en sortir, frère Leiran ? > ai-je demandé.

– Maintenant, oui. Merci, ami Andalite ! Dépêche-toi. Dépêche-toi ! Les Yirks connaissent ta mission, maintenant ! Dépêche-toi !

Je suis reparti à contre-courant. Cassie et Jake m'ont rejoint. Ils avaient livré leurs propres combats dans l'eau trouble et peu profonde de la berge.

< Combien de temps faudra-t-il aux Yirks pour trouver ce trou brillant ? > a demandé prince Jake.

< Les capteurs qu'ils ont à bord de leurs vaisseaux en orbite peuvent fournir une carte de toutes les grottes souterraines du continent en moins de cinq minutes. Mais combien de temps leur faudra-t-il pour trouver le bon trou brillant ? Je ne sais pas. Nous devons nous dépêcher. Le sort de cette planète dépend de nous. >

CHAPITRE 26

< Là ! Est-ce l'entrée de la grotte ? > s'est exclamée Cassie.

< Je crois. C'est dans ce secteur. Mais il pourrait y avoir des dizaines d'autres grottes. >

< Pas le temps de se poser des questions ! > a tranché prince Jake.

Nous nous sommes engouffrés dans la grotte. Le sol montait en pente régulière et nous nagions avec acharnement, à l'aveuglette, effrayés et désespérément pressés.

Brusquement, j'ai senti ma gueule pointer hors de l'eau. De l'air !

< Je crois que nous sommes arrivés, a dit prince Jake. Démorphosez ! Cassie, qu'en penses-tu ? On morphose en chauve-souris ? >

Pas de réponse.

< Cassie ! Cassie ! > a crié prince Jake.

< L'effet élastique. Elle est partie. Elle est rentrée sur Terre, ou…>

< Ça arrive de plus en plus vite, a-t-il observé. Les écarts entre les disparitions sont de plus en plus courts. Il n'y a plus que nous deux, maintenant. Et nous risquons d'être happés tous les deux avant d'arriver à ce détonateur. >

A sa voix mentale, j'ai compris qu'il ressentait la même chose que moi. L'impression de ne plus pouvoir respirer. De ne pas pouvoir empêcher son cœur de battre à se rompre. C'en était trop !

< Démorphose. Il ne nous reste plus qu'à nous dépêcher pour essayer de terminer cette mission ! >

< Oui, prince Jake. >

< Tu sais, Ax, nous ne sommes plus que tous les deux, maintenant. On pourrait peut-être laisser tomber cette histoire de prince. >

Il s'est tu un instant.

< Tu pourrais juste m'appeler « Jake anciennement connu sous le nom de prince». >

< Est-ce de l'humour ? >

< Ouais. C'est une plaisanterie. Pas terrible, mais comme Marco n'est pas là… >

A ce moment-là, il a presque achevé sa transformation en humain et perdu sa capacité de parole mentale. Quant à moi, je me suis retrouvé en Andalite, debout dans une grotte froide et plongée dans l'obscurité totale, les sabots pataugeant dans quelques centimètres d'eau.

– Chauve-souris, a dit prince Jake.

Ses sons buccaux ont résonné dans la caverne.

Je me suis concentré sur la chauve-souris. Je me suis senti rétrécir, même si je n'avais aucun point de comparaison visuelle, dans le noir. Mais j'ai presque senti un courant d'air vertical lorsque je suis tombé de ma hauteur à celle du petit corps de la chauve-souris.

< Rien que toi et moi, Ax, maintenant. >

< Oui. >

< Si l'un de nous deux, pour une raison ou pour une autre, est arrêté, l'autre doit continuer. C'est clair ? >

Nous avons lancé des salves d'ultrasons et vu l'image d'un tunnel qui s'enfonçait très loin, plus loin que les plus faibles échos de notre système de repérage.

Nous avons décollé. Agitant nos ailes parcheminées, nous nous sommes élancés au maximum de notre vitesse.

< Il ne faut pas oublier les serpents >, ai-je dit.

< Beurk. Beurk ! Beurk ! Beurk ! > a répondu prince Jake avec un petit frisson.

< Oui >, ai-je acquiescé.

Nous battions des ailes comme si notre vie en dépendait. Zigzaguant entre des rochers en saillie et des stalactites, prenant des virages abrupts, passant brusquement à la verticale pour franchir une cheminée qui se dressait soudain, ou au contraire plongeant tout aussi brusquement dans des puits. Tout cela nous apparaissait en quelques traits sans couleur, en image mentale.

Nous avons pris un coude en épingle à cheveux, et soudain...

Une explosion sonore ! Une véritable cacophonie d'ultrasons.

< Les serpents ! > me suis-je écrié.

Recourant à notre propre écholocalisation, nous les avons vus : ils étaient accrochés à la voûte et aux parois du tunnel et se contorsionnaient pour lancer leurs ondes dans tous les sens. Ils étaient des milliers ! Des millions ! Le feu croisé de leurs salves d'ultrasons perturbaient et brouillaient les nôtres.

Brusquement, dans ce vacarme d'ultrasons, les

images qui me venaient en tête se sont déformées. Je ne voyais plus que des lignes ondulantes et désordonnées. Des objets aux contours instables, qui semblaient avoir perdu leur consistance.

< Qu'est-ce qu'on fait ? > a demandé prince Jake.

< Comme dirait Rachel si elle était là : « on fonce dans le tas ! » >

C'était un cauchemar ! L'air grouillait de serpents venimeux. Désorientés, nous foncions à l'aveuglette, en agitant nos ailes de plus en plus déchiquetées à mesure que les serpents atteignaient leur cible.

Je perdais en maniabilité. Je perdais aussi en vitesse. Je ne savais plus du tout où était prince Jake. Je n'arrivais plus à distinguer le haut du bas. Je tourbillonnais en battant désespérément des ailes. J'étais perdu ! Perdu dans cette obscurité grouillante et hurlante.

Mais alors, hop ! Je me suis senti aspiré loin des serpents. Les murs du tunnel se sont écartés. La voûte du plafond a disparu. Et la lumière ! Une merveilleuse lumière scintillait tout autour de moi.

J'étais arrivé dans le trou brillant.

Je me suis élevé dans l'air confiné en agitant mes pauvres ailes en lambeaux. Les parois du trou étaient couvertes de fleurs et de plantes aux couleurs invraisemblables.

< Prince Jake ! Jake ! > ai-je appelé.

Mais il ne m'a pas répondu.

J'étais seul.

CHAPITRE 27

Je me suis posé sur une touffe de mousse, de lichen... ou de je ne sais quoi d'un orange criant. Et j'ai commencé à démorphoser.

Quelques minutes plus tard, un Andalite se tenait seul, dans un étrange lieu souterrain, complètement coupé du monde extérieur.

Le trou brillant faisait peut-être cent cinquante mètres de long et moitié moins de large. Le toit était à moins de trente mètres au-dessus de ma tête. C'était très grand, pour un trou dans le sous-sol. Mais cela me faisait l'impression d'un tout petit espace.

La pluie n'était jamais tombée ici. Le soleil n'y avait jamais brillé. L'unique lumière était la lueur verdâtre des parois. Une lumière qui n'augmentait jamais en intensité, et qui ne baissait jamais non plus.

C'était un lieu vivant, mais l'atmosphère y était mortifère. Un prodige de la nature, mais un prodige sinistre, qui oppressait l'esprit.

Au centre se trouvait un objet artificiel : un cylindre vertical, haut d'un mètre cinquante et de trente centimètres de diamètre. Sur le côté, un cadran où luisaient des chiffres bleus. Exactement à l'endroit que nous avait indiqué Galuit. Exactement comme l'avaient installé les agents des services secrets andalites.

J'ai regardé prudemment alentour. Pas de Hork-Bajirs, de Taxxons ni de Gedds en vue. Rien que des plantes contre nature dans un lieu contre nature.

J'ai soupiré profondément pour essayer de me détendre.

« Celui qui a eu l'idée de cette cachette a bien choisi son endroit », ai-je pensé.

Je suis parti au petit trot vers le cylindre. Mais le sol était irrégulier, accidenté, envahi de mousses et de lichens, de touffes de fleurs hideuses.

Pour finir, j'ai dû avancer au pas en prenant garde à l'endroit où je posais les sabots. Je ne pouvais presser l'allure que lorsque le terrain me permettait de sauter.

BABOUM !

Une explosion a fait trembler la grotte. La secousse s'est répercutée dans cet espace fermé et m'a fait tomber à la renverse, en m'assourdissant pendant quelques secondes.

Un flot de lumière vive !

Une pluie de cailloux et de gravats.

L'explosion avait ouvert une brèche en haut du trou brillant. Un rayon aveuglant de soleil leiran s'est abattu par l'ouverture.

Et, dans ce faisceau de lumière, j'ai vu des Hork-Bajirs sauter.

Leur chute était ralentie par de petites fusées fixées à leurs pieds et à leur queue. Les fusées dégageaient des flammes rouges. Deux, quatre, douze guerriers hork-bajirs tombaient au ralenti, en armant leurs lance-rayons Dracon. Je les ai vus scruter la grotte du regard tout en tombant. Ils cherchaient le cylindre. Et ils me cherchaient, moi.

Je me suis mis à courir. Tant pis si je me cassais une jambe. Je courais, je bondissais, je tombais et me relevais en toute hâte.

C'était une course entre moi et les Hork-Bajirs qui déferlaient par la brèche.

Tsiou ! Zzzaappp !

Le rayon Dracon a fusé vers moi, m'a manqué de peu et carbonisé un chou bleu vif.

Plus qu'un mètre !

Soudain, j'avais les mains plaquées sur le métal froid. Le code ! Quel était le code ?

Mes doigts ont couru sur les touches.

Tsiou ! Tsiou !

– *Het gafrash nur* ! a hurlé un des Hork-Bajirs.

Tsiou !

< Aaaahhhh ! >

J'ai senti une vive brûlure sur mon dos : j'avais été effleuré par un rayon Dracon.

Le code ! Le code ! Je l'ai composé. Était-ce le bon ? M'en étais-je souvenu correctement ?

Alors…

< Système activé. C'était la voix mentale synthétique et froide de l'ordinateur. Avertissement. Ce système est activé. >

Je me suis effondré contre le cylindre. Galuit nous avait dit qu'après avoir obtenu confirmation de l'activation du système, ils attendraient une demi-heure pour nous laisser le temps de nous enfuir. Une demi-heure, c'était trop long. Dans ce laps de temps, les Yirks parviendraient à désactiver le détonateur. Un énorme Hork-Bajir est tombé par terre juste devant moi.

J'ai enfoncé la touche de communication du cylindre.

< Ici l'aristh Aximili, ai-je annoncé. Allez-y maintenant. Maintenant ! Faites sauter les Yirks, libérez la planète ! >

– *Chaloc* Andalite ! a hurlé le Yirk qui était dans la tête du Hork-Bajir.

J'étais calme. D'un calme effrayant.

< Détonation dans dix secondes >, a averti l'ordinateur.

– Désactive cette arme ! a hurlé le commandant hork-bajir en galard, la langue interstellaire.

< Sept... >

< Non, je ne crois pas, Yirk. Cette fois-ci, tu as perdu. Et tu vas mourir. >

< Cinq... >

Fou de rage, le Hork-Bajir a braqué son lance-rayons Dracon.

– Tu mourras en premier, pourriture andalite !

< Trois... >

Il a appuyé sur la détente. Le rayon Dracon a fusé. A bout portant. A un mètre cinquante de mon visage.

< Un... >

J'ai vu le rayon Dracon s'arrêter, littéralement. Il s'est figé dans l'air comme si le temps s'était suspendu. J'ai entendu un petit bruit sourd : « Pan ! »

Et brusquement, j'ai cessé d'être là.

CHAPITRE 28

J'ai senti la chaleur de la peau humaine sous mes six pattes.

< Quoi ? > me suis-je étonné.

< Qu'est-ce qui...? > a hurlé Rachel.

< Oh, grave, grave ! Non, sérieux, s'est exclamé Marco. C'est bizarre grave, ce truc ! >

J'étais de retour. Sur terre. En animorphe de moustique. Nous étions tous de retour. Tous de retour ! Et tous exactement au même moment. Nous étions dans la chambre d'hôpital, entourés d'humains-Contrôleurs qui s'acharnaient à tirer des balles d'armes humaines par la fenêtre, en visant les buissons d'en bas. Ils essayaient toujours de tuer l'Andalite.

C'est-à-dire moi. Mais ce n'était pas mon principal problème. Car juste à ce moment, alors que j'étais tranquillement posé sur un carré de peau humaine vivante, hérissée de poils géants, un gigantesque objet s'est abattu vers moi, masquant la lumière du jour.

< Il ne manquait plus que ça ! a crié Rachel. Ax, bouge de là ! >

J'ai battu des ailes. L'objet, constitué de cinq doigts gros comme des baobabs, s'abattait violemment.

– Aïe ! a grogné Hewlett Aldershot, en plaquant sa main à l'endroit où je l'avais piqué. Aïe, a-t-il répété.

– Il est réveillé ! s'est exclamé un des Contrôleurs.

– Il ne devait pas se réveiller ! Il est dans le coma !

– Qu'est-ce qu'on fait ?

– Vysserk va nous tuer !

– La police arrive. Fuyons ! a prévenu quelqu'un.

– Sauvons-nous ! Sauvons-nous !

– Qu'est-ce qu'on fait de cet humain ?

– Nous n'avons pas d'ordres.

– Sauvons-nous ! a crié quelqu'un d'autre.

Et cette fois-ci, ils sont tous tombés d'accord avec lui. Ils se sont bousculés pour sortir. Quelques instants plus tard, une infirmière effrayée est entrée.

– Monsieur Aldershot ! Vous êtes conscient.

– Bien sûr que je suis conscient, a-t-il répondu. Mademoiselle, est-ce que vous vous rendez compte que cette chambre est pleine de moustiques ?

CHAPITRE
29

– **A**ttends une seconde, a dit Rachel. Nous avons été aspirés un par un jusqu'ici, à travers l'Espace-Zéro, à des moments différents. Et pourtant, nous arrivons tous ensemble ? Et il ne s'est pas écoulé de temps ?

J'ai hoché ma tête humaine. Nous étions au centre commercial. A l'endroit où se trouvent les excellents établissements d'alimentation. J'étais en animorphe humaine. J'adoptais un comportement humain parfait.

– Exactement, Rachel. Ek-zac-tement. Teu-ment. Nous sommes revenus au moment précis où nous avons été happés. Nous avons tous été happés au même moment donc, logiquement, nous sommes tous revenus au même moment. Happés. Happés est un mot bizarre. Hap-pé. A-P.

– Ouais, est intervenu Marco, c'est surtout ça qui est bizarre : le mot « happé ». Qu'on se soit changés en moustiques pour sucer le sang d'un type qu'on voulait morphoser et, au lieu de ça, qu'on se soit retrouvés au beau milieu d'une guerre pour le contrôle de grenouilles jaunes télépathes, ah, et puis j'oubliais, qu'on ait fait sauter un petit continent plein de Yirks et sauvé une espèce tout entière, puis qu'on soit revenus ici pour voir que monsieur Je-suis-dans-le-coma se réveille quand il se fait piquer par un moustique qui est en fait un extraterrestre-centaure-scorpion-à-quatre-yeux en animorphe, jusque-là rien d'anormal. Une journée comme les autres. Cher journal : encore une journée banale et ennuyeuse, jusqu'au moment où quelqu'un a prononcé le mot « happé ».

J'ai reconnu le ton de sa voix : sarcastique. C'est une forme d'humour. Alors j'ai ri en produisant des sons buccaux.

– Ha. Ha-ha. Ha. Ha.

J'ai réfléchi, et j'ai ajouté :

– Ha.

Prince Jake, Cassie, Marco, Rachel et Tobias, dans sa propre animorphe humaine, m'ont dévisagé.

– Peux-tu nous dire ce que c'était, ça ? m'a demandé Rachel.

– J'ai ri.

– Ne... ne refais pas ça, Ax, a conseillé prince Jake. C'est perturbant.

– Oui, prince Jake.

– Ne m'appelle pas prince.

– Je t'appellerai « Jake anciennement connu sous le nom de prince ».

Marco a paru franchement horrifié.

– Oh, non. Maintenant il fait de l'humour. Grave, son humour.

– En fait, cette plaisanterie était de moi, a avoué prince Jake d'un ton pincé. Enfin, ça va, j'ai pigé, Marco. Tu es incapable de rire de mes plaisanteries. D'accord. Super. Je vais te dire, ça m'est égal.

J'étais un Andalite, tout seul, loin, très loin de chez moi. Loin des miens. Seulement parfois, les vôtres ne sont pas toujours les gens qui vous ressemblent physiquement. Parfois, les gens de votre propre peuple sont très différents de vous.

– Pouvons-nous manger des beignets à la cannelle, maintenant ? ai-je demandé, plein d'espoir. Des beignets ? Gné-gné ?

Loi n° 49-956 du 16 juillet 1949
sur les publications destinées à la jeunesse
ISBN 2-07-052412-4
Dépôt légal : janvier 1999
N° d'impression : 45239
Imprimé sur les presses de l'imprimerie Hérissey

88752